Studien zur
Strafrechtstheorie und Strafrechtsethik

Edited by
der Forschungsstelle für
Strafrechtstheorie und Strafrechtsethik,
Johann Wolfgang Goethe-Universität Frankfurt a. M.

Volume 4

Shin Matsuzawa | Kimmo Nuotio (eds.)

# Methodology of Criminal Law Theory: Art, Politics or Science?

Nomos

**The Deutsche Nationalbibliothek** lists this publication in the Deutsche Nationalbibliografie; detailed bibliographic data are available on the Internet at http://dnb.d-nb.de

ISBN: HB (Nomos) 978-3-8487-6377-1
ePDF (Nomos) 978-3-7489-0475-5

**British Library Cataloguing-in-Publication Data**
A catalogue record for this book is available from the British Library.

ISBN: HB (Hart) 978-1-5099-3683-0

**Library of Congress Cataloging-in-Publication Data**
Matsuzawa, Shin / Nuotio, Kimmo;
Methodology of Criminal Law Theory: Art, Politics or Science?
Shin Matsuzawa / Kimmo Nuotio (eds.)
235 pp.
Includes bibliographic references.

ISBN 978-1-5099-3683-0 (hardcover Hart)

Onlineversion
Nomos eLibrary

1st Edition 2021

# Preface

This book discusses whether criminal law theory, or in more general terms, general law theory or jurisprudence can be regarded as a branch of science. This topic was the center of international debate in the 50's and 60's, but it has never generated a final verdict. However, if we are to claim that the study of the law is a branch of "science," we cannot avoid answering that question. Danish criminal theory has provided a possible answer through Scandinavian legal realism and this answer has been adapted into Japanese criminal law theory by one of the editors, Shin Matsuzawa, a Japanese criminal law theorist. This new theory has come to be one of the leading theories in Japan today.

In 2014, an international symposium titled "Japan/Denmark/Sweden International Symposium 'Methodology of Criminal Law Theory and the Thought Process of Judges from the perspectives of Legal Dogmatics Studies, Legal Policy, and the Scandinavian Experience" was held in Japan. At this symposium, Matsuzawa delivered a keynote lecture on criminal law theory of Scandinavian legal realism. Thomas Elholm from Denmark and Petter Asp from Sweden commented the keynote lecture as Scandinavian experts in the field. After the colloquium, Jorn Jacobsen and Kimmo Nuotio provided additional articles on the subject, and some other international scholars were invited to join. This way the discussion of the subject could be broadened beyond the alternative provided by the Scandinavian legal realism.

The question we wish to address in this book is: Is the criminal law scholarship which obviously informs the legal system remarkably itself a form of science, and in what sense? Can we adopt a disciplined approach to discuss knowledge of criminal law? Can there be systemic developments in criminal law theory? A study on these issues is rather topical since different legal systems interacts with each other more than before, and it would be helpful to understand for instance whether it would be possible to sketch a universally applicable model of criminal liability. Or are we prisoners of our own traditions?

The questions concerning the nature of the knowledge of criminal law in the core areas of the field are of course closely linked with issues concerning what legal science is generally about. A reflective discussion in the field of criminal law on these issues may contribute to the general discussions in legal theory and legal philosophy, but it serves the interest of understanding where criminal law theory stands when legal research is increasingly faced with challenges of interdisciplinarity. How receptive is criminal law scholarship to other branches of science (例 : Law and Economics)? Should it be more receptive, or rather not? By publishing this book, we aim to contribute to the discussion about the methodology of criminal law theory in the 21st century.

This publication was made possible with the support of the Scandinavia Sasakawa Foundation (No. 14-12). We would like to express our gratitude.

Shin Matsuzawa
Kimmo Nuotio

# Table of Contents

# The Methods of Legal Dogmatics of Criminal Law From a Realistic Perspective

*Shin Matsuzawa*

## *I. Foreword*[1]

Can legal dogmatics[2] of criminal law be deemed a science? This question would most likely draw a response that naturally it is a science. And the word "science" is included in "Legal Science" which is the research of law.

How about if I ask does legal dogmatics of criminal law have objectivity? This question would probably prompt divided answers. In one country, legal dogmatics of criminal law is understood to be presentation of systematic dogmatic deemed appropriate by individual scholars of criminal law. In such a country, it would hardly be objective, because the dogmatics of criminal law cannot be established without subjective value judgment by the scholars. Perhaps some people in the same country may argue that there is objectivity. Such argument will be based on understanding that criminal law scholars will select and present objectively correct dogmatic from the legal text. Is such an understanding appropriate?

In another country, legal dogmatics of criminal law is understood to be the description of present status of effective criminal law by the scholars. In such a country, the dogmatics would be considered objective, because the scholars of criminal law only describe the facts. However, can legal dogmatics that only describe facts stand? Moreover, can description of facts always be considered objective? How can we be certain that it does not become presentation of one's opinion disguised as description of facts?

May be some countries fall between the two, by taking a method such as stating the facts and making limited presentation of personal opinions.

---

1 I would like to express my deepest gratitude to Professor Thomas Elholm and Professor Petter Asp for their many discussions in the preparation of this paper.
In this paper, in light of the difficulties in accessing the Scandinavian and Japanese literature, where possible, English or German references have been cited.

2 The "legal dogmatics" here means the German word "die Rechtsdogmatik", which means to interpret the Code in a systematic and consistent manner. In the countries of the continental legal system, the development of D is one of the most important challenges in criminal law.

However, wouldn't such a method ultimately conclude in the first method, in that the dogmatics will evolve based on personal opinions? In addition, how can the difference between descriptions of facts and opinions be established?

Various questions like these may be presented on the characteristics of legal dogmatics of criminal law. In this paper, the author will review these issues by referencing information on the author's native country Japan, as well as Germany, Denmark and Sweden.

## *II. What is Legal Dogmatics of Criminal Law?*

### *1. Characteristics of Legal Dogmatics of Criminal Law in Germany*

The answers to the questions, "what is legal dogmatics of criminal law?" and "what is the academic nature of legal dogmatics of criminal law?" may seem self-evident, but in reality, it is not clear at all. To begin with, the word dogmatics came from dogmatic theology. The characteristics of legal dogmatics of criminal law imagined from this is, just as dogmatic theology seeks to interpret the bible without contradiction, to interpret the criminal code within the scope of its text without contradiction.

Perhaps this approach is most thoroughly pursued in Germany. Nothing can surpass the German criminal law studies in its effort to interpret the criminal code systematically, without contradiction, and normatively through establishment of the central dogma and use of logical deduction to reach conclusion on various dogmatics of criminal law.

For example, there was the doctrine of final conduct (*finale Handlungslehre*) which dominated the German criminal jurisprudence in the mid-twentieth century. According to its proponent Hans Welzel, when human action is captured ontologically, its feature is in its purposiveness (*Finalität*), and he strongly objected to the conventional theory, calling it the causal theory (*kausale Handlungslehre*).[3] Various conceptual results introduced by his teleological theory of human action gave impact to judicial precedence and legislation. However, basically its development was based on the notion that the result produced from the central dogma using logical deduction is duly justified, rather than on the resolution of some problems that arose in society.

3 Hans Welzel, *Das Deutsches Strafrecht* (11th edn. De Gruyter 1969) § 8.

Perhaps the readers may question my reference to the teleological theory of human action which was a theory from the mid-twentieth century. I introduced this theory because it is most typical of the German approach and would be helpful for grasping the framework; however, this style of argument is still the controlling majority in German criminal jurisprudence. For example, more recent debate between the school seeking to construct a system of criminal law based on empirical science led by Claus Roxin[4] and the school advocating a model of functionalism based on the sociological systems theory developed by Niklas Luhmann led by Günter Jakobs[5] show that both sides are utilizing the same methodology whereby the theoretical system is constructed by establishing the central dogma and applying logical deduction. In particular, a student of Jakobs has gone so far as applying logical deduction to the systems theory to assert relativization or resolution of the distinction between illegality (*Rechtswidrigkeit*) and responsibility (*Schuld*).[6]

Perhaps these forms of discussion typically witnessed in German criminal jurisprudence can be described as constructing theoretical system based on the proponent's individual value judgments, and advocating the same under the name of "science." This may be the antithesis to an approach that considers what criminal jurisprudence can do to resolve the practical issues.

## 2. *Characteristics of legal dogmatics of criminal law in Japan*

Above stated approach can be seen in the author's native country, Japan. Under the influence of German criminal theory, Japan has spent considerable energy on structuring the system of criminal theory (*Verbrechenslehre*; a theory discussing the factors constituting the act of crime). There were heated debates between the classic and modern scholars during the first half of the twentieth century. And later happened a debate between the proponents of the "negative value inherent in acts" theory (*Handlungsun-*

---

4 Claus Roxin & Luís Greco, *Strafrecht Allgemeiner Teil, Band I* (5th edn. C.H.Beck 2020); Roxin, *Strafrecht Allgemeiner Teil, Band II* (C.H.Beck 2003).

5 Günther Jakobs, *Strafrecht Allgemeiner Teil* (2nd edn, De Gruyter 1991).

6 Heiko H. Lesch, *Der Verbrechensbegriff. Grundlinie einer funktionalen Revision* (Carl Heymanns Verlag 1999) 2. Kapitel, I; Michael Pawlik, 'Der wichtigste dogmatische Fortschritt der letzten Menschenalter?: Anmerkungen zur Unterscheidung von Unrecht und Schuld im Strafrecht' in *Festschrift für Harro Otto* (Carl Heymanns Verlag 2007).

*wert-Theorie*; a theory that places emphasis on the breach of socio-ethical norms of the "act," and considers that level of illegality differs between willful and negligent acts, so subjective aspects will affect the determination of illegality) and the "negative value inherent in results" theory (*Erfolgsunwert-Theorie*; a theory that places emphasis on the illegal "result," i.e., the occurrence or risk of violation of legal interest, and considers that illegality should be determined objectively)near the end of the century.[7]

However, these debates are also based on the views on human nature in criminal law; or the views of the proponent on the characteristics of criminal law, i.e., whether to emphasize the function of criminal law to maintain social order, or its function to resolve disputes in court. Application of various logic and creative theories will ultimately conclude in determination of philosophical or political value judgment of the proponent.

### 3. *Appropriateness of normative construction of legal dogmatics of criminal law*

Such theory of legal dogmatics mainly evolved as part of discussion on determination of characteristics of norms, based on German criminal jurisprudence. For example, during the first half of the twentieth century, Edmund Mezger's theory argued that by having the evaluation standards (*Bewertungsnorm*: a standard for evaluating an act) precede the determination standards (*Bestimmungsnorm*: a standard for prohibiting or ordering certain acts by citizens), illegality shall be determined objectively, and responsibility should be determined subjectively.[8] In mid-twentieth century Germany, Armin Kaufmann thoroughly implemented the teleological theory of human action, to conclude that standards for determination of illegality and responsibility should be based on the actor.[9] In latter half of the twentieth century Japan, there was a debate on whether to capture illegality under monism or dualism, arising from the perspective of ex ante or ex post determination of the breach of norms.

These debates take the form of "clarification of characteristics of norms," and at first may seem objective and scientific. It leaves the impres-

---

7 Ryuichi Hirano, 'Deutsche Strafrechtsdogmatik aus japanischer Sicht' in Hans Joachim Hirsch and Thomas Weigend (eds) *Strafrecht und Kriminalpolitik in Japan und Deutschland* (Duncker & Humblot 1989).

8 Edmund Mezger, *Strafrecht: Ein Lehrbuch* (3rd edn. Duncker & Humblot 1949) Zweiter Hauptteil, Zweiter Abschnitt.

9 Armin Kaufmann, *Lebendiges und Totes in Bindings Normentheorie* (O. Schwartz 1954) Viertes Kapitel.

sion that by accurately recognizing the characteristics of the norms that exist objectively, truly correct answers can be obtained for various questions presented with respect to dogmatic of criminal law. However, this is not correct. To begin with, anyone who has studied law at all would know that to assume there is a truly correct answer in legal studies is incorrect. A number of conclusions can be reached on one issue. The majority view may converge on one or the other, but this is not because one is "true" or "false"; rather, it is a matter of degree of appropriateness. The difference is purely relative, and the opposite conclusion may be reached at a different time or place. Structuring a theory based on normative logic which may seem objective at a first glance will ultimately have to involve value judgment, and its appropriateness cannot avoid coming under dispute.

### 4. *Orientation towards a more scientific dogmatic of criminal law*

Is it impossible to have a scientific dogmatic of criminal law? Can criminal jurisprudence not stand as a science? Construction of scientific dogmatic of criminal law has been an issue pursued in various countries, with some indication from jurisprudence on the difficult issue of the science of legal studies. Let us review this issue in the next chapter.

## III. *Methodologies for Scientific Dogmatic of Criminal Law*

### 1. *Pre-War: Positivism*

In fact, there was a period when scientific dogmatic of criminal law dominated the academia in Germany. This was the modernist school of criminal theory. It developed the reformatory punishment theory which argued for punishment as a means of improvement and education for the offender, based on the understanding that a crime was a product of the nature of the offender and environment, against the classic criminal theory which argued for retributive punishment as a response to crime, based on the dogmatic that a crime was a product of free will of the offender. The dicta by Franz von Liszt that "Social policy is both the best and most effective crime policy"[10] is very well known, and is founded on positivism, i.e., criminal theory based on scientific research and studies.

Modernist school theory of criminal law was scientific to the extent that it was based on scientific knowledge, but in reality, it could not escape tendencies to consider punishment as "a good thing" for improving and educating the criminal, which resulted in subjective tendencies of criminal theory. Subjectivist criminal theory may become foundation for abuse of power by the State if used arbitrarily. In Japan and Germany where the abuse of power by the State was experienced during WWII, the modernist school declined rapidly after the war.

## 2. *Post-War: Empirical studies of law*

Then, was scientific dogmatic of criminal law totally lost after the war? In reality, orientation towards scientific dogmatic had continued uninterruptedly in Germany and Japan. "*Alternativ-Entwurf eines Strafgesetzbuches, Allgemeiner Teil*" (alternative proposal for the general part of the German criminal law) published in 1966 by a group of West German scholars is very well known. With the slogan "Farewell to Kant and Hegel,"[11] the proposal held "de-metaphysicalizing of criminal law" as one of its aims. It argued that based on the results of criminological research, the purpose of punishment should be focused not only on general prevention, for which the certainty of effect has not been enough proven, but also on special prevention, aimed at education and improvement of the offenders. The proposal argued that to realize the goal of prevention of crimes, criminal law founded on empirical science became necessary. This approach gave significant impact on the revision of criminal law in West Germany, and led to the preventive integration theory (*präventive Vereinigungstheorie*), which aims to integrate the reinforcement of people's trust in the law and the resocialization of offenders, and the comprehensive criminal theory (*gesamte Strafrechtwissenschaft*), which considers criminal law, criminal procedure, and criminal policy in a comprehensive manner, led by scholars such as Claus Roxin.

---

10 Franz v. Liszt, *Strafrechtliche Aufsätze und Vorträge, 2. Band* (I. Guttentag 1905) 246.

11 Ulrich Klug, 'Abschied von Kant und Hegel' in Jürgen Baumann (ed), *Programm für ein neues Strafgesetzbuch: Der Alternativ-Entwurf der Strafrechtslehrer* (Fischer 1968).

In post-WWII Japan, influence from the US legal studies became more prominent, and the so-called empirical legal studies started to influence various areas of positive laws. The "debate on dogmatics" started among the civil code and legal philosophy scholars over the scientific nature of the dogmatics of civil code. Wide ranging topics were discussed in the debate on legal dogmatics, one of which was its objectivity. In legal dogmaticcs, constant blending of facts and values occur, and the issue was how to separate the two to secure objectivity. Legal philosopher Junichi Aomi separated "selection of ends and means," and citing Max Weber, argued that while there is significant room for the value judgments of the interpreter in selection of ends, selection of means can be discussed in a completely scientific and objective manner.[12] He sought the bases of objectivity in selection of means in the recognition of empirical facts. In criminal law studies, Ryuichi Hirano asserted the need for dogmatics of criminal law that emphasize the function of criminal law, in response to the empirical jurisprudence and the debate on legal dogmatics. Hirano, who thoroughly studied Anglo-American jurisprudence, criticized the traditional theory of the functions of criminal law. His reasoning is, in short, that metaphysical concepts should be removed from criminal theory, and that functions of criminal law should be reconstructed from pragmatic aspects. He argues that these functions could be confirmed by empirical facts. The normalizing function and the maintaining function cannot be confirmed by empirical facts. Therefore, he finds that the function of protecting interest and the function of guaranteeing freedom of action are the most important functions of criminal law.

The views of the alternative proposal group in Germany and Hirano in Japan are scientific in that they discuss "what effects arise from which dogmatics," based on knowledge of empirical science. These approaches realized dramatic progress from how the conventional debates in Germany and Japan involved "logical deduction from the central philosophical concept or dogma" or "commingling of personal values under the banner of objectively capturing the structure of the norm." However, how can one ensure that the "end" to which this knowledge of empirical science applied is objectively correct? This is where these theories appear incomplete. Of course, ends such as reducing crimes or securing freedom of citizens are clear and objectively correct. However, determination on what will be considered a crime, or how much of the freedom should be secured in relation

12 Jun'ichi Aomi, 'Gendai Hokaishakugaku niokeru Kyakkansei no Mondai' in Gendaihogaku no Hoho (Iwanami 1966) 3–24.

to other national and social interests (conflict of interests between citizens is also a possibility), ultimately cannot stay free from various values and politics. Rather, it can be deemed to be political. That the West Germany's alternative proposal group and Hirano sought to separate criminal law from ethics was a coincidence, and there is no self-evident relation with having their foundation on empirical science.

This is also evident from the rivalry within the German school of functionalism which emphasize functionality of criminal law caused by the difference in definition of its function, and resulted in the opposing views explained above. That is, Roxin and Jakobs both profess "functionalism," but where the former perceives the purpose of criminal law as protection of legal interests, the latter aims to stabilize the norm through criminal law, resulting in completely different theories.

The situation is the same in Japan. At present, the majority of criminal law scholars agree that the purpose of criminal law is to protect the legal interests that can be recognized with empirical science. That is to say, previously seen proponents of social / national ethics and protection of the spirit of the people as the purpose of criminal law do not exist for most part, and the "infringement of legal interests" doctrine is the overwhelming majority. If this is the case, the doctrine should converge to the negative value theory. However, the debate on whether to choose negative value inherent in acts or results still remains. This is because there are various opinions on when the optimal timing of determination of occurrence and risk of infringement of legal interest is, and intervention with criminal laws is, to achieve the goal. Although they all follow the "infringement of legal interests" doctrine, their theories on criminal law are completely different.

### 3. *Orientation towards science in legal philosophy (science of legal studies): Scandinavian case*

#### (1) Introduction

The scientific approach continues to be pursued in dogmatic of criminal law, but science in legal studies had been debated longer in areas of jurisprudence and legal philosophy. Representative texts include "Pure Theory of Law" by Hans Kelsen[13] in continental Europe, and "legal pragmatism" promoted by Oliver W. Holms, Benjamin N. Cardozo, and Roscoe Pound in the US.[14]

However, strictly in relation to dogmatic of criminal law, these theories do not seem to have had significant direct impact. For example, in Germany, while the pure theory may have had some influence, dogmatic of criminal law that fully implemented the pure theory is almost non-existent, except for some efforts made by Kelsen himself in later years. And in the US, although theories of criminology and criminal procedures that were influenced by legal pragmatism followed by legal realism do exist, they do not appear to have fully developed within the context of theory of dogmatic of criminal law.

In contrast, science in legal studies pursued in jurisprudence had broad impact on regular positive law in Denmark. The methodological theory of Alf Ross[15] is an example. Before we review his theory and how it developed in dogmatic of criminal law, let us take a look at its origin, the Scandinavian legal realism.

### (2) Scandinavian legal realism

#### (i) Uppsala school

Scandinavian legal realism was founded by Axel Hägerström,[16] a Swedish philosopher. As Hägerström was a professor at Uppsala University and the theory was mainly constructed in this university, it is also referred to as the Uppsala school.

According to Hägerström, all concepts must correspond with reality, because concepts that do not have corresponding reality are metaphysical concepts that do not have objective substance. From this perspective, rights and obligations are metaphysical concepts that do not have corresponding reality in the real world. This leads to the argument that "rights and obligations do not exist. They are merely superstitious beliefs." How-

---

13 Hans Kelsen, *Pure theory of law* (Max Knight tr, 2nd edn. University of California Press 1967).

14 Oliver W. Holmes, *The Common Law* (Little Brown 1881); Benjamin N. Cardozo, *The Nature of the Judicial Process* (Yale University Press 1921); Roscoe Pound, *Social Control Through Law* (Yale University Press 1942).

15 Alf Ross, Professor, Univerisity of Copenhagen. 1899–1979.

16 Axel Hägerström, Professor of Philosophy, Uppsala University, 1868–1939.

ever, the concepts of rights and obligations have psychological power in the real world, and produce certain effects. Hägerström argued that this situation is logically contradictory, and is just "magic."[17]

This argument, along with his use of rampant language, brought strong opposition. The theory was developed further by his student, Karl Olivecrona.[18] Olivecrona inherited Hägerström's theory, and constructed a grand theory by incorporating, rather than expelling, the concept of rights and obligations into legal studies. With respect to the situation referred to as "magic" by Hägerström, Olivecrona believes that while rights and obligations certainly do not have semantic reference, the word "right" serves an important function by influencing the human mind and behavior to direct them; therefore, using it as a sign has considerable significance. In general, Scandinavian legal realism is characterized by its analysis on psychological aspects of the binding forces of the law. This is clearly apparent in the way Olivecrona focused on the psychological power that rights and obligations bring to the real society, treated this as a fact, denied the aspects of law that required corresponding reality, and introduced the concept of "law as fact."[19]

Olivecrona's denial of the "ought to be" aspect of the law is crucial. Traditionally, and perhaps still today, most people would have thought the following; the law is to be obeyed because it has legitimacy, and the law is binding because it is legitimized. But, in fact, it's not. The law is binding simply because the vast majority of people feel bound by it (legal discourse or legal something) and follow it. In other words, law is not something to be considered from norms, but from facts. Such a turn in perception is what should be called an "Olivecronic turn", and this paper is based on such a "turn".

### (ii) Alf Ross

Danish legal philosopher Alf Ross was influenced by Scandinavian legal realism, and developed a unique theory based on traditional issues at the center of Danish legal studies. The traditional issues refer to the theory on

---

17 Axel Hägerström, *Inquiries into the nature of law and morals* (Karl Olivecrona ed; C.D. Broad tr, Almqvist & Wiksell 1932).

18 Karl Olivecrona, Professor of Law, Lund University, 1897–1980.

19 Karl Olivecrona, *Law as Fact* (1st edn, OUP 1939).

sources of law. This is a theory on what constitutes source of law, which is supported by interest in where the source of "law with binding force" lies.

The theory presented by Ross[20] starts by attempting to answer this question along the lines of Scandinavian legal realism. The Scandinavian legal realists rejected concepts that did not have corresponding reality in the real world, and structured legal studies purely based on facts. Following this, Ross argued that legal studies must describe objective facts that have corresponding reality in a factual manner. He attempts to distinguish statements on law (legal statements) based on whether it is a statement of facts, or on value judgment and opinions. Ross was interested in a "law with binding force." This means that legal statements are distinguished between statements on law with binding force and statements on value judgments and opinions concerning the law with binding force. Ross classifies the former as dogmatic assertions and the latter as assertions of legal politics, and further divides the latter to proposals to legislators and proposal to judges. He states that only the former is objective and factual, and is befitting to be called science, therefore, its description should be the mission of legal studies. Legal politics which makes proposal to legislators and judges is not denied as activities for legal scholars, but it is deemed to be a supplementary.

In this way, Ross positions the theory of legal dogmatics as a study that provides descriptions of "law with binding force" in an objective and factual manner. The next question would be, what is a "law with binding force"?

## 4. *Ross theory as applied by Waaben*

### (1) Ross theory: The concept of valid law and prediction theory

Ross refers to the "law with binding force" as valid law. This concept is the key to modern Danish legal studies (and broader Scandinavian legal studies). Valid law is referred to as "Gældenderet" in Danish, which corresponds to "Geltendes Recht" in German. German and Japanese scholars would probably assume that it refers to the legal texts themselves. Criminal law scholars in Germany and Japan refer to statements on current criminal laws (Geltendes Strafrecht) as dogmatic of criminal law. This

---

20 Alf Ross, *On Law and Justice* (Jakob v. H. Holtermann ed, Uta Bindreiter tr, OUP 2019).

means that in Germany and Japan, statements on current criminal codes will be part of legal dogmatics on criminal law, whether it be statements of fact or value judgment. As stated above, this is why arguments based on personal opinions and philosophical views are made under the name of legal dogmatic in Germany and Japan.

Ross does not take this approach. He captures valid law from a thoroughly realistic point of view. In sum, valid law is the thought process (ideology) of judges. That is to say, judges make decisions by referring to laws, precedents, practical customs, and opinions of attorneys and prosecutors, but the thought process of the judge that forms the foundation for all of this is the valid law.

The reason why Ross took this approach is self-evident when one considers his position as a realist. Decisions made by the judges have the ultimate authority in real society. Even if certain provisions existed in a legal text, it would not have real authority unless the judges agree so. Ideologies of the judges present themselves to the real society in forms of decisions, and control the real society. Ideologies of judges that are not presented in specific decisions will have controlling functions by predictions of their decisions on hypothetical cases. Describing the thought process of judges is the duty of legal dogmatics.

According to his theory, description of the judges' thought process will enable prediction of future decisions. And if the description made in legal dogmatic is consistent with the future decision, it is proven to be true, and if inconsistent, it is proven to be false. In this way, legal dogmatic can be proven to be true or false in an objective manner, according to Ross. This theory is called the "prediction theory" in Denmark.

### (2) Method of conceptual structure by Waaben: Criticism of German methodology

Ross' theory is the product of his study of jurisprudence, and the conclusion that the thought process of the judges is the valid law was reached as a result of pursuit of science of legal studies and binding authority of laws. As such, it was not created with presumption to apply the theory to dogmatic of actual laws. Therefore, utilization of his theory for dogmatic of actual laws (criminal law in this paper) requires certain adjustments, and the peculiarity of criminal laws must also be taken into consideration. Knud

Waaben[21] tackled this difficult problem, and applied his theory to dogmatic of criminal law.

According to Waaben, "it is wrong to consider the decisions themselves as valid law."[22] And to describe valid law, the reference must be much wider than and include the hidden foundation of, what appears in the decisions. Valid law is the aggregate of thoughts and ideology of judges. The decisions themselves, a judge's thoughts particular to a case, and motivation for the decision, etc., are just part of the aggregate.[23]

Therefore, in describing valid law, studying the judicial precedents becomes important. Studies of judicial precedents in Japan (and perhaps in Germany) would probably emphasize extraction of the basic theory that the decision is founded on from the numerous precedents. Japanese scholars refer to this as the judicial precedents theory.

Judicial precedents theory is based on the general approach of judges, so one might assert it may be referring to the same thing as valid law. Studies of judicial precedents theory are conducted in Germany as well as Japan. What is so new about the approach taken by Ross?

Certainly, they share a lot in common. One key characteristic in common is that they both require objectivity. However, significant differences also exist. The judicial precedents theory is derived from finding shared features among the numerous decisions themselves, and is based on ex post facto inductive reasoning. On the other hand, valid law is not derived from finding shared features among the decisions. It is extracted from analyzing the psyche of the judges, and is determined not based on the decisions themselves, but from the analysis of the motivation behind the decision.

Furthermore, the structure of judicial precedents theory varies according to the theoretical structure adopted by the person performing the analysis. In other words, decisions are categorized based on the personal and philosophical positions of the author, and the objectivity is lost. The situation is probably the same in Japan.

Either way, in Germany and Japan, judicial precedents are grouped into abstract legal propositions. Waaben is also critical of this. He says "German criminal law scholars try to summarize the basic definition in short words to cover all cases presented in positive trial, and often depart from reali-

21 Knud Waaben, Professor in Law, University of Copenhagen, 1921–2008.

22 Knud Waaben, *Det kriminelle forsæt* (Gyldendal 1957) 44.

23 Ross's theory is often referred to as a sub-genre of American behavioristic legal realism, but that seems not to hold true.

ty."[24] In short, according to Waaben, valid law is not something that can be explained completely and uniformly using abstract norm.

Then, can valid law only be described as an accumulation of cases? Should we abandon establishment of abstract normative propositions like the American fact-skeptic Jerome Frank and abandon prediction of decisions?[25] The answer is no. Although Waaben doubts abstract norms, he does not abandon them. His approach is to utilize abstract norms, without considering it to be complete. Valid law is open to future revaluation. As a principle, it expects the abstract norm presented as valid law to be incomplete. Waaben states that "the contents of concept of intent can only get close to full description,"[26] referring to the particular concept he studied.

### (3) Application by the author

I basically agree with Waaben's application of Ross' theory, but with some adjustments, which can be summarized as follows: In sum, valid law is structured by verbalizing, theorizing, and systemizing the thought process of the judges who have the role of creating actual law, including their assumptions. Therefore, it is necessary to apprehend the facts inherent in the judge's thought process by contemplating the depth of the judge's psyche. Valid law can be apprehended from the judge's thought process, so to the extent it can be predicted to exist for real, it is not bound by the wordings in the decision that does not seem to directly reflect the judge's thought process; furthermore, it is not necessarily fully bound by the conclusion of the decision. Accordingly, an dogmatic of criminal law that describes valid law is not an accumulation of analysis of judicial precedents, and highly abstract theoretical structure that cannot be produced by merely analyzing judicial precedents is plausible. Of course, the judges themselves are not processing individual cases based on a perfect theoretical system, so the extracted theoretical system can also be incomplete. There may be cases where consolidation of theories is difficult, but basically, I shall continue to aim to clarify the definition of concepts to enable consistent application (furthermore, to enable the public to act freely with understanding of these concepts). Legal dogmatics of criminal law not only indicates the standard for decision making by judges; it is also a standard that sets forth

24 Waaben (n 22) 363.
25 Jerome Frank, *Law and the modern mind* (Brentano's Inc 1930).
26 Waaben (n 22) 345.

the scope for the public to act freely. In this respect, I will not adopt the method of "listing significant items," such as listing the points for legal determination, or motivation of judges that form the grounds for legal determination.

I have organized a joint research groups based on these methodologies.[27] More specifically, the joint research was conducted among judges and scholars. Scholars presented (what was deemed to be) valid law and sought comments from judges, and also sought critical comments from peers. Through these exercises, we tried to establish a more objective valid law. However, the comments from participating judges were not deemed to be absolute. One may think the judges are best positioned to apprehend the thought process of judges; but in reality, there may be deep psyche or subconscious attitudes that the judge is not aware of, which the scholars can reveal with external observation.

## *IV. Criticism of the Methodology/Issues and Review*

### *1. Introduction*

Against the methodology presented above, various criticisms have been made, against Ross mainly by Danish legal philosophers, and against my opinions that applied Ross' theory, by Japanese criminal law scholars. In addition, there were issues I noticed or got pointed out in discussion with other scholars. Let me summarize and review these issues.

### *2. Is valid law only applicable to thought process of judges?*

Frequent criticism of the methodology is that valid law is not only applicable to thought process of the judges. In particular, in countries that adopt principle of discretionary prosecution (such as the UK and US, of course, and Japan, Denmark, Sweden, etc.), thought process of prosecutors who have the authority to determine whether or not to prosecute actually has significant impact on distinction of acts that will or won't be penalized.

27 The Research Group for Defining Valid Law in Japanese Criminal Justice. http://www.waseda.jp/prj-genkeiken/.

Furthermore, Henrik Zahle,[28] who criticizes Ross' theory from a postmodernist legal perspective, is critical of the one-sidedness of the theory. He argues that the laws that function to regulate real society are not limited to decisions by the court. There are many laws that are effectively functioning outside the courts, such as decisions and orders determined by the administration, and practical decisions made by government offices. They are valid without going through judge's ideologies. Therefore, it should be understood that the source of law has multiple centers, and there are different methods to determine the appropriateness for each.[29]

Certainly, there is some truth in this criticism. In particular, in a country with high conviction rates (Japan), the decision by the prosecutor to prosecute or not has a significant impact. If we are to simply consider what regulates the society, it would be important to consider those points to determine whether the accused is guilty or innocent. However, if we are reviewing whether or not it has the level of substance to be considered a law, decisions by judges and decisions to prosecute by prosecutors do not appear to have the same legal level of substance. In addition, study of the psyche behind the decisions of prosecutors on whether or not to prosecute would have to be conducted with virtually no precedents or evidence available, and would be extremely difficult in practice. If the psyche of the prosecutors cannot be studied, I believe it is beneficial to construct functional dogmatic of criminal law by application to thought process of judges to the extent they can be clarified.

### 3. *Can predictions be proven true or false?*

Ross argues that by reconciling the predictions and facts, dogmatic can be proven to be true or false. This is one approach, as the theory is modeled on conventional natural science. However, it is difficult to reconcile the predictions and facts. Is it sufficient for a prediction to be deemed true if it is consistent with one decision? Is a prediction never deemed to be true unless there is a decision? Many issues remain. These are issues of objectivity in science including natural sciences, and are more of an issue for philosophy of science. If we turn to debates in philosophy of science, presently the

---

28 Henrik Zahle, Professor in Law, University of Copenhagen, 1943–2006.

29 Henrik Zahle, 'Retsdogmatik og retskritik' in E.M.Basse og Vibeke Jensen (eds), *Regulering og Styring I*, (Djøf 1989) 45–52.

debate over distinction between science and pseudoscience is at a stalemate.

In the 1970s Denmark, Preben Stuer Lauridsen,[30] professor of legal philosophy, a successor of Ross, criticized him starting from the point that a solitary statement consistent with the truth does not exist (multiple statements may exist), and ultimately sought to have whether or not debates and criticism among scholars can arrive at an agreement/consistency as the standard for verification. This argument appears to have certain appropriateness. It cannot be denied that whether or not there is an agreement among the peers is one of important indications in evaluation of a theory (so-called coherence theory).[31] With such adjustment, Ross' theory is considered to have appropriateness at present.

However, it would be insufficient if the agreement and consistency referred to only meant that there is a majority agreement, or that it is consistent with the greater majority view of the public. It must be performed as a review by a soundly and reasonably organized group of experts. Then, the next issue would shift to the procedural and methodological point of how to examine whether or not the group of jurists including present scholars (in various countries) is qualified as the expert group. On this issue, we can only assume that the group of jurists in each country is such a group at the moment.

### 4. *Judges subjected to prediction react to the situation: Can there be science in such a relationship?*

This is a frequently presented criticism not just as a question for the science of methodology above, but for social sciences as a whole. On this question, I believe that there is science, at least in the methodology. Judges are most likely to refer to the results of the studies based on dogmatic of criminal law as proposed by this paper; however, they are unlikely to try to outwit the prediction, or intentionally refrain from the predicted opinion due to having read such studies. This is because the results of such studies are not produced for the practical purpose of controlling the judges; rather, they derive from a purely academic interest in clarifying the valid

---

30 Preben Stuer Lauridsen, Professor in Law, University of Copenhagen, 1940–2013.

31 Preben Stuer Lauridsen, 'On a Fundamental Problem in the Legal Theory of Prediction', in *Scandinavian Studies in Law, vol.20* (Stockholm Inst for Scandinavian Law 1976) 203–204.

law. For a judge to try to outwit such result to avoid being controlled is meaningless in reality. If a judge who came across the result of the studies thought "if the present operation is continued, such a decision can be expected in the future; this is not desirable," and changes the present operation, it is a value judgment of the judge rather than influence from the dogmatic, and the judge is controlling his/her own conduct.

Japanese scholar of sociology of law, Takeyoshi Kawashima,[32] promoted predictive legal studies which predict future decisions by courts, based on legal realism's views on trials.[33] He stated that such prediction "is nothing more than a prediction mediated through our practical behavior of controlling future decisions through judicial precedents," and saw it as an issue of "how best to control future decisions with past judicial precedents, and how they should be controlled." This indicates an approach where the judges, who are the subject of observation, try to control decisions by observing the scholars who are conducting the observation. However, considering prediction as such practical activity would bring issues of assessment and value judgment into dogmatic which should be objective. On this point, the view taken by Ross (and this paper) does not aim at such control, and thus would not create such problems.

### *5. Distinction between legal dogmatics and legal politics*

Legal dogmatics and legal politics handle facts and evaluation, and it is often thought that distinction between the two can be made for certain. However, in the area of legal studies where facts and values intersect, these borders may become vague. For example: (i) a judge who read a document shown as a text on legal dogmatics wrote a decision influenced by the text. Should this be considered legal politics?; (ii) or, the author meant the text to be legal politics, but a judge who had not read the piece wrote a similar decision, and it became established as an objective practice. Should this be considered legal dogmatics?

In my view, the answers to both (i) and (ii) are "no." Then, how can legal dogmatics and legal politics be separated? The difficulty is presented due to the fact that the subject of the observation is the thought process of

32 Takeyoshi Kawashima, Professor in Law, Tokyo Univerity, 1901–1992.

33 Takeyoshi Kawashima, *Horitsugaku no gendaiteki Mondaiten: Kawashima Takeyoshi Chosakushu vol.5* (Iwanami 1982) 290–291.

judges, who most certainly will be observing the results from the other side.

I personally have some remaining questions on how to structure the standard for determination, though the conclusion is clear. I would like to present the following provisional statement: Legal dogmatics and legal politics can be distinguished through methodology, i.e., the material that the decision was based on, and the analytical methods that lead to the conclusion. If the materials that the decision was based on were facts of empirical science, and the method used to reach the conclusion was the analysis of empirical facts, it would be legal dogmatics; all others are legal politics. That is to say, legal dogmatics and legal politics may be distinguished by methodology. That is why the methodology for legal dogmatics of criminal law becomes significant.

### 6. *Would it not be an obstacle to nurturing students and jurists capable of external criticism?*

Some point to this, from the perspective of legal education. However, to limit legal dogmatics to description of facts is not to prohibit criticism of the present status. Ross believed that proposals to judges and legislators should be made separately as part of legal politics, as a matter of judgment. The above criticism is out of place.[34]

### 7. *What are the features of judges' thought process?*

Some ask that if legal dogmatics practiced by scholars is description of facts, what is it that the judges do. Judges can be seen as creating laws to resolve specific cases. In other words, application of laws to specific cases is itself a process of creation of law based on certain values. However, individual judges are not free from general thought process of judges. They are not arbitrarily creating laws based on individual values.[35] The decisions are made by paying attention to the shared value judgments accumulated among the judges, and to that extent, they are objective.

34 Those who ask these questions miss the point.

35 The distinction between the two is crucial to understanding the methodology of this paper.

### 8. *Conclusion*

As stated above, although some issues remain to be resolved, certain answers have been obtained to the criticism and inherent problems with respect to the methodology for legal dogmatics of criminal law presented in this paper.

## V. *Method for Dogmatic of Criminal Law: Methodology for extraction and structuring of theories*

### 1. *Methodology for extraction of theory*

Dogmatic of criminal law extracts ideologies of the judges to create a theory. Let me summarize the discussions thus far, and clarify the methodology:

The first point of reference in trying to understand the ideologies of judges is judicial precedents. However, they should not be treated as the golden rule. Because judicial precedents are court decisions on a certain case at the time, and although it will be binding on future decisions, it will not have absolute authority in a country under statutory law system. In particular, the reasoning proposition is likely to be documentation of the judges' thought process, but it does not necessarily reflect all of the judges' thought process, and could be an afterthought in some cases. The reasoning proposition is not deemed to be judicial precedent itself in the study of judicial precedents. Only the conclusive proposition constitutes the judicial precedent. If the judicial precedents are mishandled, it will become case law positivism, which analyses judicial precedents as law. This is inconsistent with the methodology adopted in this paper.

The next point of reference would be literature authored by the judges. They are valuable basic materials that outline the ideologies of judges prepared by the judges themselves. However, they too, do not reflect all of the judges' ideologies. Aside from the fact they are written by the individual, it does not necessarily reflect subconscious thoughts of the writer. Valid law is the entire ideology of judges, so the deep subconscious must be extracted to determine the criteria for the decisions.

The third point of reference is the study of literature that affected the judges. As judges are jurists, they will refer to books and scholarly articles. Books and articles commonly cited can be deemed to have significant influence on the thought process of the judges. By examining such literature, we can infer the theoretical systems and concepts in the thought process of the judges.

The fourth point of reference would be communication with the judges. Communication is essential to seek candid opinion of the judges that do not appear in judicial precedence and literature. For this purpose, as already mentioned, I have organized a research group called "the Research Group for Defining Valid Law in Japanese Criminal Justice" with like-minded scholars, and hold periodic meetings with judges. A judge's positioning varies by country.[36] For example, in Germany, Scandinavia and Japan, Supreme Court justices are neutral and independent of political ideology, but in the US, political agendas are often involved in the appointment process. We must allow for some variables for each country on this point.

### 2. *Method of theoretical structuring*

Creation of theoretical system on judges' ideologies extracted through methods described above will require certain contrivance. That is, to structure a system of criminal theory, the conventional method used in Japan is to follow a system starting from considering the relevance of the general elements of offences (*Tatbestandmässigkeit*), illegality (*Rechtswidrigkeit*), and responsibility (*Schuld*), similar to Germany. However, it appears that a criminal theory system that focuses more on criminal procedure and identification theory needs to be created. The reason being that the criminal theory system created in the judges' ideology would always focus on the resolution of the case, i.e., the procedural law. In Japan, facts that the prosecutors must prove shall be positioned general elements of offences. And in an exceptional case where an issue of law arises, the lack of justifiable cause for noncompliance with law or non-imputability that the prosecutors are liable for proving should be deemed to be justifiable noncompliance or non-imputability. In Anglo-American law, you can call them defence. Thus, as a starting point for dogmatic of criminal law, a system comprising of relevance of general elements of offences, justifiable non-compliance (defence of justification) and non-imputability (defence of excuse) seems to be the most appropriate.

Next, let us turn to the methodology for structure of concepts. I have already explained how abstract concepts may be included as part of valid

36 See, n 27.

law. In particular, the basic approach would be to examine materials centering on judicial precedents without reserve, capture the thought process the judges are applying to resolve the issues, and reflect this on the concept as faithfully as possible. Use of such abstract concept will contribute to mutual understanding and legal discussions among jurists. That is to say, legal concepts are shared codes available for discussion among jurists. To ignore this in dogmatic of criminal law would be unproductive. Note that a perfect concept does not exist, as Waaben has pointed out, and it is unlikely to exist in the thought process of the judges who are the subject of fact finding. However, we shall not give up on creating concepts. It is important to specify and document the concept presented as the terminus of the judges' thought process, using empirical facts as well as conventional normative analysis methods used by the judges in their thought process.

In relation to the above two points, we must consider how best to capture the intricacies of fact finding and legal issues. For example, suppose several seemingly unrelated facts emerge in the process of identification of legal requisites (e.g., in Japanese practice, a party that claimed the largest share of criminal proceeds after the crime is frequently penalized as the principal offender. However, whether or not a person is the principal offender or accomplice should be determined based on their role in the criminal conduct, and should not be related to the situation after the crime.) In addition, not all of the facts need to be revealed, and there are instances when the legal requisites are identified by comprehensive consideration of the facts (e.g., using the above example, if claiming the largest share of criminal proceeds is only one of the reasons the person may be penalized as the principal offender, and such fact is not a legal requisite, but has a significance in the identification process). Such an example is likely to exist in many countries, not only in Japan. Perhaps the common procedure is to create an abstract norm in the study of jurisprudence, and leave the rest to the customary practice in fact finding. However, this does not capture the thought process of the judges. Further, mere existence of abstract norms would not serve much purpose in practice. On the other hand, mere listing of facts would not enable discussions among jurists. Abstract norms are important shared code for the jurists to have discussions and to understand each other.

The question is how to link the facts to be identified and the requisite norms, when they stand separated. I do not have a good answer to resolve this problem. Developing this method will be the key issue.

## *VI. Methods of Criminal Law Policies: Preliminary Observation*

### *1. Foundation of legal politics of criminal law*

According to Ross and Waaben, legal politics of criminal law, i.e., proposal to judges and legislators is a secondary duty for criminal law scholars, unlike legal dogmatics. In Denmark where Ross' theory had a strong influence, this seems to have been the conventional wisdom for a long time. Certainly, when criminal law studies are pursued as science, proposals based on personal value judgments and philosophy would not be considered scientific. But at the same time, it may be necessary to make certain proposals as an expert on valid law, on condition the value judgments are clearly stated as such.

In particular, in recent Denmark, Sweden and Japan, it has been pointed out that there are tendencies to impose unnecessarily strict penalties against the background of a type of populism, and to make legislation that only clarify the value judgments of the government and doesn't have real effects. The latter is referred to as symbolic legislation, and there is a wide debate in Germany about its problems.

Under these circumstances, it seems significant that the criminal law scholars as experts logically develop legal politics of criminal law, and examine the justification for criminalization.

For example, the Danish criminal law scholar Vagn Greve[37] asserted the propriety of practical criminal theory and criminal legislation from the viewpoint of human rights. His book related to criminal legislation regulating freedom of expression[38] are an example of this assertion. In the midst of a myriad of perspectives, Greve says that it is a necessity as a professional to explain how these can be evaluated and analyzed from the viewpoint of criminal theory.

Of course, when there is a situation where basic principles are neglected, such as nulla poena sine lege, the culpability principle, and legal benefit protectionism, it is necessary to object that there are certain questions regarding these topics from a professional viewpoint. When there is also a situation where basic values such as freedom, democracy, basic human rights, and peace are trampled on by the power of the state, it could be said that us scholars are obligated to fight against such power.

---

37 Vagn Greve, Professor in Law, University of Copenhagen, 1938–2014.

38 Vagn Greve, *Bånd på hånd og mund: strafforfølgelse eller ytringsfrihed?* (Djøf 2008).

However, most legislators who are deserving of criticism craft new laws based on advice from legal professionals including jurists. In the case of judges, they are regarded as professionals in the sense that they are practitioners of the law, through amending jurisprudence, specializing in its use, and accumulating experience.

It is very important to voice your opinion, as a specialist of criminal jurisprudence, against those legislators. However, we need to prove and establish on what grounds our opinions are "professional." Are those opinions based on the scholars' self-righteousness? Are they based on political and ideological biases that largely deviate from societal values, norms, and justice? Are they just scholars' own, subjective opinions? Scholars must constantly practice rigid self-discipline and be subject to criticism set upon by the concept of freedom of speech.

Personally, I find nothing wrong with Greve's humane words; I most certainly agree with him. However, that does not mean I can assert with my utmost confidence that his opinion and method of thinking are "objectively correct" as a "professional." A situation where "all" scholars are unanimously in agreement with Greve's dogmatic will and should never exist.

In my opinion I believe that the first responsibility of a criminologist is to utilize Valid Law, and subsequently I believe that Greve's statement is more political than scholarly. If it were so, Greve's statement is not really a study of jurisprudence but an analysis of his own dogmatics from a legal point of view. This is not necessarily said to be aimed to undermine Greve's accomplishments. If anything, the author was deeply impressed by Greve's works. However, the author seems reluctant to label his work as jurisprudence or legal dogmatic studies; mainly because it is almost inevitable to separate objective theory from subjective value judgements, which will render the theory "un-scientific." Rather, it should called something along the lines of "theoretical legal analyses" or "theoretical legal consideration." It is necessary to consider such studies as something independent and completely different from legal dogmatic studies. Such differentiation enables one to clearly see where they stand within the realm of legal studies, and also assert that one's value judgement is derived from which field of study.

## *2. Function of creation of law by judges and legal politics of criminal law*

In this methodology, proposals to judges are considered to be legal politics of criminal law, and part of political activity involving value judgment.

The activity by judges to process cases and prepare decisions is considered to be a function of creation of law, i.e., a type of legislative function. This is where the relationship with the principle of legality becomes an issue. Legalism is a significant corollary of principle of legality. It argues that criminal law must be established in the form of legislation by the parliament. If a judge is involved in the function of creation of law, would that violate the principle of legality?

Karl Larenz of Germany referred to selection of semantics within the scope of statutes as interpretation (*Auslegung*); and where it is outside the scope of statutes, the act becomes creation of law. Under this theory, principle of legality prohibits analogical interpretation in criminal law, requiring interpretation within the scope of statutes, so the judges do not engage in creation of law, and their activities would not violate the principle of legality. Many scholars in Germany and Japan seem to agree. However, if this approach is taken, interpretation within the scope of statutes would mean the act of identifying the objectively correct interpretation among the various possibilities. And notwithstanding that this act is actually based on subjective value judgment. If this is the case, subjective value judgment is being made under the disguise of objectivity, and there will be no means to control this. This is the dark side of legal positivism which assumes that a correct interpretation exists in statues. It is more realistic to think that selecting one semantic from various possibilities in the statutes involves value judgment, and that determination of the meaning of the law, i.e., creation of a law that did not exist, is being conducted.

Against these approaches, one may suggest that it may be less complicated to refer to such acts within the scope of statutes as interpretation rather than creation of law, and this would also avoid violating the principle of legality. However, hiding the activity of creation of law under the name of interpretation would lead to a bigger problem. To clarify that the act involves subjective value judgment, legal interpretation by the judges should be referred to as creation of law. According to this line of thought, principle of legality becomes a standard that indicates the limits of creation of laws in criminal trials, rather than a principle that prohibits creation of laws by judges.

### 3. *On the definition of logic*

There are many people who insist that it is acceptable to label legal analyses as a science, since they are based on meticulous theoretical construction are further based on logic. However, as long as this is based on the speaker's own value judgement, it remains as another criminal policy.

For example, the sentencing theory proposed by Andreas von Hirsch is a theoretical framework that is shared by many scholars. Along with Andrew Ashworth and Andrew Simester, von Hirsch has published collaborative works that do not clearly indicate which portion was done by whom.[39] This is also another theory that is based upon a certain value judgement, and von Hirsch mentions so in various publications. If the pros and cons of a theory analysis are considered by people who shared the same value judgements, the theory does indeed achieve a level of objectivity with the limits of the points in common. However, it is obvious that this type of objectivity is limited to those who share the same value judgements, and consequently the said theory does not resonate to those who do not agree with those judgements.

Additionally if a theory is proven through experimental sciences, it is possible to claim that theory is scientific. However, it is impossible to establish a standard with just facts. It is inevitable to have a certain level of subjectivity to accompany such standards. For these reasons, citing experimental science is simply not enough to call a theory as something totally scientific.

Von Hirsch's sentencing theory[40] happens to cite experimental science. In other words, von Hirsch, through references from criminology, asserts that it is unnecessary to consider preventative effects in sentencing since there are no preventative measures in penalties. There is a certain level of science in this assertion.

However, those who believe that it is important to send a message to regulators of society through announcing to consider positive general prevention (i.e. Jakobs, a supporter of positive general prevention), whether or not there actually are preventative effects, do not think there is any substance in citing experimental science as von Hirsch does. On the other hand, the Luhmann's sociological system theory used by Jakobs has been established as a scientific theory in sociology, but von Hirsch barely holds any interest in it.

There are certain differences in how one normatively evaluates facts, and they are caused by the difference in which value judgement is chosen

---

39 Andrew von Hirsch & Andrew Ashworth, *Proportionate Sentencing: Exploring the Principles* (OUP 2005); Andrew P Simester and Andreas von Hirsch, *Crimes, Harms and Wrongs: On the principle of criminalization* (Hart Publishing, 2011).

40 Andreas von Hirsch, *Deserved Criminal Sentences* (Hart Publishing 2017).

to be emphasized. These value judgements are about which facts are to be chosen to be evaluated, and the theorists' true intentions can be inferred from them. Facts and standards can be separated.

Some theorists say that facts and standards are interactive and are impossible to separate by principle, and therefore dogmatic theories based solely on facts is impossible. Indeed, it is possible for the line drawn between facts and standards to become unclear, and the statement that the definition of a fact can change according to standards. However, those who claim that separating the two are impossible tend to divide de lege lata and de lege feranda. They also do not deny the existence of policy-building activities. The line between facts and standards are indeed ambiguous, but there are clear differences. The same could be said for criminal jurisprudence. The border between subjectivity and objectivity is ambiguous; objectivity is influenced by subjectivity. The gravity of firing a pistol with criminal intent is objectively different from simply firing a pistol by accident, but this does not mean that subjectivity and objectivity should be discussed as a combined, single concept. Concepts that can be separated should be separated where possible. A more objective dogmatic theory should be sought after in order to avoid a Weber-like "war of the gods" situation in the field of criminal dogmatic studies.

## *VII. Conclusion*

I have examined the features of legal dogmatics of criminal law to present answers to the various issues identified at the beginning of this paper.

I believe the most appropriate methodology is one following Ross' methodology, to separate fact finding and value judgment, and limit the duty of legal dogmatics of criminal law to the former, making the presentation of systematic and verbalized thought process of judges as primary duty of criminal law scholars. However, for determination of objectivity of legal dogmatism, rather than the simple reconciliation of theory and facts promoted by Ross, I would adopt the view taken by Stuer Lauridsen that it should be done through coordination and agreement among the peers. I also believe that limiting the subject of fact finding to the thought process of judges is a functional option at the moment.

As to the specific methods, this paper has referred to the methodology of Knud Waaben who specifically applied the view presented by Alf Ross to dogmatic of criminal law, and made certain adjustments. In sum, the code for communication among jurists involves abstract concepts and norms, and this is important to enable legal discussions. Also, as criminal law has the function to secure freedom of activity by the public, it is important to construct and present a theoretical system using abstract norms on condition it is clarified to the point consistent judgment is possible, basically using conventional conceptual structure rather than methods such as "list of important judgment items" which tend to make the determination process vague.

Legal dogmatic studies can be said to be exceedingly academic, in the sense that it involves normative theoretical analysis unique to jurisprudence while keeping experimental science in the picture. I believe there are many legal scholars who will remain skeptical when legal dogmatic studies is deemed unscientific, and my own wish to pursue legal dogmatic studies as a science will remain unchanged. For these reasons, it is vital to remove the unscientific elements and reconstruct legal dogmatic studies that will live up to the name of science.

If, for instance, it is claimed that normative analyses are a science, the inner value judgements will achieve the name of "science" and will consequently become a very powerful influence. Of course, if those value judgements are significant and meaningful for everybody, there should not be a problem; however, needless to say, such common ideas do not exist. Some may refute that value judgements such as democracy, peace, and human rights are meaningful for anybody. Additionally, principles in criminal jurisprudence such as *nulla poena sine lege*, the culpability principle, and legal benefit protectionism may also be regarded as something of universal significance. However, value judgements of this caliber are too general and vague to become a worthy foundation for normative analyses because the value judgements themselves are open to dogmatic and there could be an infinite amount of perspectives. What if one of those perspectives were said to be the one scientific truth? The other existing perspectives will potentially be deemed unscientific and completely obliterated. Establishing just one view as the truth or the correct answer and denying all others should not be allowed in any instance.

Alternatively, what if all perspectives were considered a scientific truth? It seems plausible, but in reality there are many underlying problems. Each theory will assert its correctness and closure will be very hard to achieve. In Japan and Germany, scholars sought after their own criminal jurisprudence theory based on their own value judgements, and because of this, legal dogmatics studies became more subjective, opposition between theories became unstoppable, and discussions stalled. In countries without this sort of history, the repercussions of this stance is less visible. (In Sweden, for example, a textbook on the basic studies of criminal jurisprudence has been successfully published as an allotment-less, complete joint authorship between Jareborg, Asp, and Ulväng, and that publication keeps a solid framework and an undeviating discussion on the system of criminal jurisprudence.[41] This is not possible to achieve in Japan and Germany, because there is always some disagreement between the authors.)

Rather, these problems should be solved by separating legal dogmatic studies from value judgments. Namely, it should be said that the theories of Sweden and Denmark (Scandinavian Legal Realism) are still large influences and retain its significance, even today.

Above attempt is literally just an attempt. I believe it is essential to conduct further examination on the issue through discussion with peers around the world. In this sense, this attempt aims to give objectivity to the dogmatic of criminal law, but it is based on the value judgment I believe to be appropriate. I would like to present these methods of study as a paradigm, but will not say that such approach is objectively and academically justifiable. My main emphasis is that it is important to plainly identify value judgments as such.

---

41 Petter Asp, Magnus Ulväng & Nils Jareborg, *Kriminalrättens Grunder* (2nd ed, Iustus 2018).

# In Defence of a Normative and Non-Scientific Legal Science

*Petter Asp*[*]

*[Introduction]*

1. In his contribution to this book professor Shin Matzuzawa is advocating a non-normative approach to legal science. In professor Matzuzawa's view legal scholars should aim at finding out how judges actually think, *i.e.*, the scholar should not focus on the norms or on the system of norms as such, but rather on the minds and actions of judges. Such an approach gives legal science an essentially empirical character. The fact that legal science gets an empirical character means, *inter alia*, that the yardstick for correctness will be some sort of correspondence between reality (how judges actually think) and the scholar's statements about reality (»this is how judges think«).

2. The aims and the character of the research do, of course, also have methodological implications. If you want to know how judges actually think, the traditional legal method with its focus on the sources of law is, at best, of secondary importance. The traditional legal method tells us what judges ought to do, but not necessarily what they actually do.

3. One of the reasons for choosing this non-normative approach to legal science is that professor Matzuzawa wants to make sure that legal science is »scientific«, which according to Matzuzawa means that the activity is objective and that it is free from value-judgments. His text implies that it would be a good thing if legal scholarship were comparable to activities performed within, *i.e.*, the field of natural sciences.

4. In this short text I am defending a view which comes close to being the opposite to professor Matzuzawas': I am arguing that legal science ought to be essentially normative. I am also arguing that we should perhaps not have objectivity as our main goal and that we should not be too concerned about whether legal science fulfils the criteria for science postulated by others.

---

* I would like to thank Svante O. Johansson for valuable comments on a draft of this text.

5. The thoughts expressed in the text are not, by any standard, original and they are—of course—heavily influenced by the thinking of others. Perhaps one could say that I am defending a mainstream understanding of legal science (at least in the sense that it reflects how most legal scholars act in their scientific practice).

6. Though these paragraphs are written with the purpose of defending a certain approach to legal science, most of them are not devoted to a discussion of different directions in (legal) science. Instead, the lion's share of the text is devoted to a discussion about law and how it works. I think that such a detour is necessary if one wants to explain why a normative approach to legal science is important. Any view on the proper approach in legal science presupposes an understanding of what law is or—if one is averse against the ontological implications of the word »is«—how it works and ought to be looked upon. Our view of legal science is, in this sense, derivative upon our understanding of the law.

*[Law is Janus-faced]*

7. If you would ask people what they think of when they hear the word law, they would probably say that law has something to do with rules, *e.g.*, rules that states what is permitted and what is not, rules on contracts and business *etc.* (but they would not necessarily refer to rules about the applicability of other rules and rules on how to make law, on how reform the law etc.). Asked about the origin of law in this meaning they would probably say that laws (rules) are passed by politicians (by the »legislator«[1]).

8. Most people would, however, probably also refer to the fact that law is something that requires interpretation and argumentation, that it is something that you can tweak or even twist. Perhaps they would add that this is reflected in many movies that include scenes from a courthouse.

9. From such answers it follows that law has a Janus-faced character. On the one hand, law has a factual side. It is about knowing (or finding out) which rules that exist in a certain legal order at a relevant point in time, which cases that exist etc. Thus, we can emphasise the positive rules given by the legislator, the judgments given by the courts, the existing preparatory works etc. On the other hand, law is about dealing with, interpreting, or

1 With this term I mean the rule-making body which in many systems will be the legislature, although other bodies are possible as rule-making power can often be delegated to the government or administrative agencies.

actually making use of, the rules that exist (in a certain state at a relevant point in time) in relation to specific—actual or hypothetical—cases.

Already the simple fact that you may want to consult a lawyer in order to find out how a certain statute should be understood reflects that a distinction can be made between the rule (as such) on the one hand, and the meaning of the rule on the other. It is simply one thing to find the rules (cases etc.) that might be applicable, or otherwise of importance, in a certain case; it is quite another thing to know what they mean in a certain situation.

Thus, we can emphasise the rules, judgments etc. as »things«, or as »materials«, but we can also emphasise the interpretative and the constructive side of the law.

10. There are, of course, standard situations in which the two sides of the law are (more or less) inseparable, *i.e.*, situations in which you may find out what a rule means in the relevant situation simply by reading the wording of the rule (by consulting the preparatory works or by reading a certain case etc.). In such situations the answer to the specific case will follow (more or less) directly from the rules or the cases. As soon as you leave such standard examples, however, things will become more complex and there will—to a lesser or larger extent—be a need for interpretation and for construction work.[2] The law will not be out there, waiting to be found (that applies only in relation to the law as »materials«). It will have to be interpreted and constructed.

11. Law presupposes construction work due to several different factors.

12. One such factor is, of course, that law is built upon language. This means that it will, to a certain extent, be imprecise and that different interpretations of the law will be possible. Another reason for the need for construction work is that a system of rules that reaches a certain level of complexity will inevitably contain rules that conflict with each other. The conflicts may be direct (in the sense that both rules cannot be upheld at the same time) or indirect (both rules can be upheld, but if they are the outcome does not really make sense).

13. On a more fundamental level one could say, however, that one will not fully understand the relative openness of the law—and the need for

---

2 I will use the term construction to denote something that goes beyond the mere interpretation of a certain prerequisite. I should be conceded thought that the two are often hard to separate: in order to interpret a certain statute properly one will often have to construct at least parts of the legal system, *i.e.*, one cannot focus exclusively on the specific rule. Perhaps one could say that construction work includes interpretation and that interpretation often presupposes construction.

construction that follows—unless one comes to term with, and understands, the »weakness« of the idea that rules are binding. In a way it can be said that not even the strictest of rules will be definitive in the sense that it will always tell us—as actors within the legal system—what to do.

*[Rules and principles]*

14. One way of coming to terms with the idea of rules as binding—thereby illustrating the openness of law, the need for construction and thus explaining the need for normative legal science—is by taking a closer look at the relation between rules and principles (and values) and try to display how they contribute to the construction of a legal system.

15. There is a huge amount of literature dealing with the concepts of rules and principles. I will not, in this text, try to make a contribution to the theoretical analysis of rules and principles, but rather try to display how different types of norms and values contribute to the need for »normative legal construction«.[3] This means that I will not go into details as regards the concepts of rules and principles, but rather build on what I would consider as mainstream understandings of these concepts.

16. If one wants to explain what a legal principle is, it might be proper to contrast principles with rules (or other rules, if one is of the opinion that principles are rules of a special type) and note that most analyses of principles include a reference to something that makes principles weaker (in a normative sense) than rules.

For example, reference could be made to Ronald Dworkin's characterisation of principles as norms having a dimension of weight, not being (as rules) all-or-nothing norms, as well as to Robert Alexy's understanding of principles as optimizing commands.[4]

According to an analysis by Nils Jareborg, a principle is basically a rule, but a rule that has »ought« as its deontic operator, in contrast to other rules that have »shall« as their deontic operator. According to Jareborg, this means that a principle does not necessarily have to be followed in each and every case. Rather it says something like: you normally have reasons to

3 Neither will I say anything about the debate concerning legal positivism (though it is closely connected to, or rather often discussed in connection with, the relation between rules and principles). In my view, nothing that I say in this text is not incompatible with a reasonable understanding of legal positivism.

4 See Ronald Dworkin, The Model of Rules, (1967) 35 U Chi. L. Rev. 20 1967–1968 p. 22 ff. and Robert Alexy, A Theory of Constitutional Rights (2009) p. 57.

do x, but if you have strong reasons to do otherwise then you can choose not to do x. In order to emphasise the binding nature of rules Jareborg use the term dogmatic rules for rules that are not principles. The ought-dimension introduced by Jareborg arguably reflects—by and large—the weight dimension as emphasised by others.[5]

17. The all-or-nothing character of rules means that they are either followed or not (and if one makes a new exception it equals to changing the rule), while a principle might be applied or taken into account without being followed.

18. Let us take this as a point of departure: rules are dogmatic all-or-nothing-norms while principles have a dimension of weight and only tell us what we (generally) ought to do (unless there are reasons for doing otherwise).

19. The dichotomy just sketched between principles and rules (or between two types of rules) is helpful in many ways. It may, however, no matter whether you follow Dworkin, Alexy or Jareborg, contribute to an understanding of rules as absolute and binding:[6] principles gives us reason to act in a certain way, but rules provides us with stronger reasons in the sense that they dictate the outcome of a certain case.

There are, however, several factors that make the dichotomy less sharp in practice, from the viewpoint of a person who is supposed to apply the law in a certain situation.

20. One could start by simply noting that principles may have a strong normative force. The prerequisites of a principle might be quite precise and the »ought« contained in the principle (or expressed otherwise, its weight) might be so strong (such) that even though it is formulated as an ought-rule, it comes very close to being a shall-rule.

It could be added that a norm that is referred to as a principle might very well be a rule within a certain legal system. Many constitutional rules are, for example, labelled as principles despite their dogmatic and mandatory character (*cf.*, for example, the status given to the principle of legality in many constitutions).

21. At least equally important, is that there are several factors that make rules weaker than the rule/principle-analysis might seem to suggest.

---

5 See Nils Jareborg, A Lecture on Principles, Festschrift für Heike Jung (2005) p. 363. For my purposes it does not really matter whether principles should be looked upon as a sub-class of rules or as something different than rules.

6 It is, however, evident (as we shall see) that none of the scholars referred to endorse such an understanding of rules.

22. First of all, rules always have to be interpreted. Rules are made up by words, by language, and language is by nature imprecise. This means that a lot of rules in a lot of situations can be read in two (or more) different ways. Thus, rules decide the outcome of a case only after we have construed their meaning, and that is an activity, which is open for many different types of considerations. We may take into account the lexical meaning of the words used, the way a certain interpretation makes sense in the legal context in question, the way the words used are understood in other (legal) contexts, the consequences of construing the words in one way or the other, etc. The basic point to be made is that rules always have to be construed and they must be construed having regard to the legal surrounding in which they are situated.

23. Second, a (shall-)rule might be written in a way that requires the judge to weigh different interests as against each other or provides the judge with the discretion to do otherwise if there are reasons for such. For example, a rule may say that:

*»if a, b and no special reasons for doing otherwise, then x«.*

24. Third, rules—as we find them in the books—are often (or almost always) incomplete. Under all circumstances, rules are always *potentially* incomplete. For example, there might be unwritten exceptions to the rule, which means that preconditions for application must be added before we can say that the rule dictates the outcome. A rule-in-the-book stating *»if a and b then x«* might at the end be applied as meaning *»if a and b and not-c, then x«*. The rule might also be applicable in situations not covered by its wording, *i.e.*, the preconditions for application may have been formulated too narrowly (*»if a and b then x«* might be applied as meaning *»if a and b or if a and c, then x«*). Before we know the full content of the rule we do not know whether it requires us to act in a certain way.

25. If we take a closer look at cases where a rule should not be applied in a situation clearly covered by the wording of the rule, we can see that the reasons behind such a conclusion may be of different kinds.

26. One reason (I will not even try to be complete, but rather provide a few simple examples) for non-application might be that the application of a rule in a certain case would be unreasonable having regard to the reasons for having the rule in the first place.

Let us assume, for example, that a judge is faced with a rule that states that bringing ice cream into fashion stores is prohibited and that such acts shall be punished by a fine. If a person, A, indeed brings ice cream into such a store (and we presume that A has acted with required intent and that there is no justifications or excuses applicable), the outcome may seem given: A should be fined. If we assume, though, that A did bring the ice cream into the store in a sealed Häagen Dazs-container that was placed at the bottom of his or her shopping bag, things might not be that clear. Any reasonable person confronted with such a case would question whether the rule (as written in the books) should be applied in this specific case. This is due to the fact that we all understand the reasons behind the prohibition, *i.e.*, we understand that the prohibition aims at preventing people from going into stores actually eating ice cream, thereby creating a risk for damaging the clothes for sale in the stores.

A similar situation occurs in cases where the application of the rule would have consequences that seems unreasonable having regard to the legal context and the reasons and values that are reflected there. One example might be that the rules within a certain statute generally distributes the risk in a certain way (*e.g.*, a way which provides incentive for the person who can affect the risk to actually do something to prevent the risk from being realized), but that the application of a certain rule in a certain situation leads to a situation where the one and only person who can affect the risk bears no responsibility at all.

27. Another reason for not applying a certain rule (as found in the books) is that application of the rule in a certain situation would conflict with the basic principles of the legal system in question (or even with values anchored in the legal system). In this regard, the classic case used by Dworkin in the Hart/Dworkin-debate—*i.e.*, Riggs v. Palmer—is but one illustrative example. An American court was faced with the question whether an heir named in the will of his grandfather could inherit under that will, even though he had murdered his grandfather for the purpose of inheriting. The court noted that—if the relevant statutes would be applied according to their wording—the answer would be affirmative. However, the court continued by saying the following:

> »all laws as well as all contracts may be controlled in their operation and effect by general, fundamental maxims of the common law. No one shall be permitted to profit by his own fraud, or to take advantage of his own wrong, or to found any claim upon his own iniquity, or to acquire property by his own crime.«

Thus, the heir did not inherit his grandfather.

28. On a general level, this implies that rules do not, despite having a dogmatic character, decide anything on their own. The »rules-in-the-book«, are always binding only conditionally. Strictly speaking, we are not obliged to do as the rule tells us to do, until we have interpreted it and concluded that the rule (as written) should be followed. The presumption

is, of course, that rules should be followed, and even if this presumption is quite strong, it is a rebuttable one.

This is, as trivial as it might seem,[7] one of the main points of this text.

29. What I have said, so far, is not—in anyway—incompatible with an understanding of rules as all-or-nothing norms. On the contrary: as long as an all-or-nothing-theory of rules is based on the idea that a rule—as written in the books—could be incomplete, it is fully compatible what I am saying. My statements about the non-binding character of rules applies to the rules as found in the books (or to rules as found in the books *and* as supplemented by earlier case law etc.); the point being that it is always an open question whether there are yet another adjustment to be made.

In this context one could, *e.g.*, compare with what Dworkin says about the »accurate statement« of a rule in The Model of Rules:

> »If the facts a rule stipulates are given, then either the rule is valid, in which case the answer it supplies must be accepted, or it is not, in which case it contributes nothing to the decision. ... Of course, a rule may have exceptions (the batter who has taken three strikes is not out if the catcher drops the third strike). However, an accurate statement of the rule would take this exception into account, and any that did not would be incomplete.«[8]

What he says is basically that a rule which is not followed[9] is either invalid or incomplete.[10] This do, however, imply that rules might be invalid or incomplete. The all-or-nothing character of the rule is nevertheless saved, since the rule he is speaking about, the accurate statement of the rule, is *the complete and adjusted rule*. For example:

The rule in the book:

> *Anyone who brings ice-cream into a fashion store should be fined.*

The accurate rule (after necessary adjustments):

> *Anyone who brings ice-cream into a fashion store should, unless the ice-cream is kept in sealed container, be fined.*

---

7 In many cases we do not even think of clear-cut reductions as exception, but merely as a natural way of understanding the rule in question.

8 Dworkin, fn 4, p. 25.

9 Dworkins statement do of course also presuppose that any questions as regards the pure interpretation of the rule has been settled. *Cf.* Nils Jareborg, Regler och riktlinjer, in Tidsskrift for Rettsvitenskap (1979) p. 393.

10 *Cf.*, similarly, Jareborg, fn 5, p. 364, in relation to dogmatic rules: »One cannot make exceptions from [dogmatic rules] without changing the rule.«

Thus, there is nothing wrong with the all-or-nothing-characterization of rules, but the point that I am trying to make here is that a judge—or any other person who have the task of applying the law—cannot take for granted that she is confronted with the »accurate statement of the rule« (after necessary adjustments) but rather faces the question *whether* the statement of the rule that she has in front of her is »accurate» (or whether it is incomplete or invalid). Another way of saying the same thing is to say that the prize for characterizing rules as all-or-nothing norms is that one distances one-self from normal position of a judge or any another person who has the task of applying the law (for a person in such a position it is always an open question what the rule in question will actually mean for the outcome).

30. Taken seriously, this means that rules are not necessarily conclusive and that both rules and principles provide us (as actors within the legal system) with reasons to act in a certain way. The starting point, the presumption, is that one should act in accordance with the rules, but as illustrated, this can be nothing but a presumption. And that is true also if one disregards the fact that rules will always have to be interpreted before one know what the rule means. In addition to rules and principles any legal system will contain, embody or express (how you prefer to express this is a question of taste) values that have to be taken into account when constructing the content of the system.

31. I will not even try to provide an account of the proper method for interpreting and constructing the law, but if one accepts what I have said so far, it seems undeniable that it involves making normative (evaluative) judgments, having regard to the existing rules, the existing case law, the existing preparatory works etc., but also to the principles and values of the legal system in question. And as long as normative construction of the legal system is part of the legal reality, legal science must deal with normative questions, should it be able to help us to understand and to deal with the law. Only by researching the system from a normative angle we will find out how different values and interests interplay within the system. And only by doing that we can make sure that like cases are treated alike or even find out what it is to treat like cases alike. A proper slogan for law might be: it is all about reasons!

*[Constructing the law or just working with the materials]*

32. The most obvious way for legal science to contribute is, of course, by using the existing building blocks—the rules, the case law etc.—for the

purpose of constructing the law in a certain area, *i.e.*, by doing the actual construction work. The contribution of the scholars could, however, also take place on a more basic level. The scholar could aim not at constructing the law, but at analyzing the building blocks thereby, *e.g.*, explicating the values and reasons behind or inherent in them.

The value of this type of work could be illustrated by looking at the way principles come to life within a legal system.

33. Principles reflect values and summarize reasons that are present in a legal system. This means that the substance reflected in a principle often (or rather: more or less regularly) precedes the formulation of the principle *qua* principle. As Jareborg says principles are »not promulgated« but rather »invented, created, but they can also be discovered, extracted from a body of rules«.[11]

If we look at things in a chronological perspective we will—typically—see a process in two or three stages. First there is a stage during which a certain pattern of values develops, and then there is a stage during which someone notices this pattern, does the work necessary to anchor the principle in the legal system in question, and formulates it as a principle.

34. A simple example might be the following:

(a) Within a certain legal system, the rules are such that people accused of having committed an offence will not punished unless they are in some sense blameworthy (people are acquitted when they are not even negligent, people are acquitted when they have been involuntarily intoxicated and thereafter have committed offences, people are acquitted in cases where they have committed the offence being very young etc.). The fact that people are acquitted with reference to these factors may be due to specific provisions or due to the development of case law.
(b) Eventually someone notices this pattern and suggests that the pattern reflects certain values generally respected within this legal order and that these values could be summarized in a principle: the principle of guilt (as a precondition for criminal liability).
(c) Others see the same pattern and accept the suggestion made. Actors within the legal system start to refer to the principle of guilt as a reason for legislating in a certain way, as a reason for deciding cases in a certain way etc.

35. One precondition for this type of development—*i.e.*, one precondition for making it possible to »extract«, »invent«, »construct« or »discover« prin-

11 Jareborg fn 3, p. 365.

ciples in this way—is the idea of some sort of basic axiological coherence within the system. If we did not presuppose that »the system« (the legal system) ideally should be at least somewhat coherent in an axiological perspective, the identification of a pattern would not have any general implications. The fact that we, within a certain system, have done things in a certain way (solved situations a, b and c in a certain way), would not have any normative implications for how we should solve other cases (situation d) unless there exist an idea of coherence. Once we accept the idea of axiological coherence, however, no pattern will ever be neutral or indifferent to us: we may argue that the pattern we have found as regards situations a, b and c should not be decisive for the way we solve situation d, but basically this requires justification (and the simplest way of providing such justification is by justifying the conclusion that the cases are not alike).

This is not to say that principles always emerge in this this way. At times principles come to life or are introduced in a certain legal order or a certain legal context simply by way of decision-making. For example, in 1989 a major sentencing reform was made in Sweden. By way of legislation it was decided that the Swedish sentencing law should be based on the principles of proportionality and equivalence. These principles were, of course, known also earlier (proportionality has, arguably, always been of some importance when it comes to sentencing), but their role as primary rationales for the Swedish sentencing law was undoubtedly established by a decision on the part of the legislator.

This all means that principles can come to life in two different ways:

| | |
|---|---|
| (1) Normative pattern | → Principle |
| (2) Statement on the principle | → Normative pattern (which will, eventually, underpin a principle) |

The possibility for the legislator to decide upon principles—i.e., to actually change things by legislation—is normally greater the smaller the relevant area is. For example, the legislator can by way of legislation perhaps change the primary principles (or rationales) for sentencing, but it would much more difficult to do away with the *impossibilium nulla obligatio est*-principle or the general principle of proportionality (means-end proportionality) which has numerous application and permeates most parts of the legal systems. One could say that some principles are so well-anchored in the legal material that a choice to depart from the principle within one area will not actually change the status of the principle in within the legal system in general.

36. The abovementioned way of describing the origin of principles implies that there is not necessarily a great difference between »a principle« and a corresponding pattern. A pattern will—in a legal system based upon an idea of coherence—always have some sort of normative force since it shows that the law attaches value to a certain factor.[12] It is not necessarily misleading to say that patterns in law are, at least if they are clear and consistent, principles that has not been formulated yet.

37. This means that the legal scholar can contribute, not by actually constructing the law in a certain area, but simply by taking part in the development of legal principles, by taking part in the discovery and description of legal patterns, by analyzing the reasons and values implicit in the legal material (e.g., the reasons and values behind, under or above a certain rule or a certain set of rules) etc. etc.

---

12 The late Anna Christensen tried, in an article, to formulate a theory of law as normative patterns in a normative field; see Skydd för etablerad position – ett normativt grundmönster, in Tidsskrift for Rettsvitenskap (1996) pp. 519 ff. Christensen was in a way advocating a way of doing legal research: instead of participating in the construction of a hierarchical system, the researcher should focus on seeing and unveiling basic normative patterns within the law. Despite being written for another purpose I think, however, that Christensen's theory fits neatly in to (also) an idea about normative legal science. The inductive finding of patterns and values is a very important part of the work needed when constructing the law. As we have seen, rules do not, by themselves decide the outcome of cases and one very important factor when deciding whether to follow the rule or not, when deciding whether components have to be added to the rule etc. is the relation between the rule and the system. A rule that is in conflict with basic values of the system will not often be applied in a straight way. One may (and Christensen would certainly) object that her theory was not primarily normative. Her main idea was not that we, by identifying normative patterns, could formulate the normative values and principles of the system, but rather that we, as researchers standing outside the system, could see the (often conflicting) patterns and describe them. That is true. The theory was primarily intended to be descriptive: »this is a pattern in law». The fact that the theory was not intended for such a use, does not, however, mean that it is not apt for such a use. In my view you cannot, within a normative system (that is supposed to be coherent), identify a normative pattern without giving that pattern some normative force. Any pattern identified can be used as an argument within the system. This means that there is little difference between identifying a pattern (calling it a normative pattern) and identifying a pattern as a basis for formulating a principle. In a normative system a strong pattern can always be reformulated as a principle or at least be used for showing that a certain value or certain values are taken into account within the system.

I guess that I do not have to say that such analyses may have a critical potential (*e.g.*, by displaying that the dominating understanding of the law in a certain area conflicts with underlying values or principles).

*[Rules, principles and the actors of the legal system]*

38. It should be observed that the importance of legal principles and value patterns within a legal system affect different kinds of actors of the system in different ways. As indicated above, principles and value patterns provide us with reasons for acting in a certain way. To be provided with reasons for acting in a certain way may, however, have different implications depending on the context.

39. If we look upon principles and value patterns from the viewpoint of the judge, we will see that they are liberating in relation to the written rules of the system, but that they are, nevertheless, confining in the end. This might sound as a contradiction, but it is not.

40. The principles and the value patterns of the system is liberating in relation to the starting point, *i.e.*, that the judge should follow the rules of the system. By invoking the principles and the value patterns of the system, the judge can justify a departure from the rules. Thus, it could be said the principles and the value patterns decreases the stability of the rules. The rules will—due to the fact that there are other relevant standards within the system—not always have to be followed.

This is, however, nothing but a reflection of what has been said above. And it is certainly nothing to be sorry for. When one speaks about formalism in a derogatory way, application without observance of the larger picture is often exactly what one means: a one-sided focus on a specific rule and inability to see the implications of the context and the system as such.

41. The decreased stability of the rules is, however, compensated for in the other end of the process: the principles and values may be deliberating in the sense that they provide reasons for not applying existing rules, but such an effect presupposes that we accept their normative force. Thus, principles and the value patterns bring stability and foreseeability not by increasing the stability of the rules but by increasing the stability of the legal system as such. The judge may be not always be bound by the rules, but he or she is always bound by the system.

Principles and value patterns may, of course, also add to the stability and foreseeability of the system in situations when applying a rule. Imagine a rule without context. The interpretation of such a rule would in the end, and as long as there are two reasonable ways of understanding it, be more or less arbitrary. However, in a legal system which is also filled with principles and value patterns, there will be guidance also »between« or »under« the rules.

42. In relation to the legislator, the principles and the value patterns contained in the legal system have an essentially *freedom-limiting function*. This is due to the fact that the legislator is, as a starting point and within the limits set by constitutional rules, in principle free to construct the rules and the legal system as he or she would like to have them. For example, and as regards sentencing within the criminal law sphere, the legislator could decide upon a rule according to which courts are obliged to add x to any sentence given to someone with a prior record. The legislator is also free to change the rules of the system if she does not like the results produced in the case law of the courts. For an actor that is free (at least in principle and as a starting point), the existence of reasons for acting in a certain way is essentially limiting *even if the reasons are not binding*. If there were no principles and value patterns, the legislator would have more room for maneuver than if there are principles and value patterns which guides the legislator. In a context which is characterized by freedom even reasons that are not conclusive or binding in a strict sense are freedom-limiting.

43. This means that the principles of the system, though they are not binding upon the legislator, delimits his or her freedom. The legislator cannot, at least not without being inconsistent, do whatever the legislator wants, but must make sure that new legislation is keeping within the limits set by the system. The system does not, of course, dictate what the legislator should do, but it does narrow the possible alternatives.

44. In this way the idea of coherence is part of the setting that limits the powers of the legislator. This is one important reason to be skeptical about skepticism about the value of coherence. If we give up the idea of coherence we have also given up one very important feature when it comes to balancing the powers of the state: the state should act coherently and be criticized when not doing so. The idea of coherence is, in this sense, part of a larger idea, that the state does not have the mandate to misuse its power, by acting arbitrary and showing naked power.

*[The system and its ability to determine what judges do]*

45. It is sometimes suggested that the openness and incompleteness of law means that it is misleading to make a distinction between argumentation within the system and argumentation about the system, *i.e.*, misleading to

make a distinction between the law as it is (*de lege lata*) and the law as it should be (*de lege ferenda*). I cannot subscribe to such a view.

46. Admittedly, the need for interpretation and construction and (the openness of law) and the openness of the idea of legal sources do make the borders between de lege lata and de lege ferenda blurry at times.

When deciding upon a really tricky case (or discussing in abstract about a really tricky question concerning the construction of the law)—a case where the sources of law does not provide a clear solution (they may, *e.g.*, be silent or give guidance which is inconclusive and is compatible with two different outcomes)—the reasons relevant for the deciding the case or the question concerning the construction of the law will be very similar to those that would be relevant if the legislator had to decide upon a law dealing with the case in question. Relevant factors could be, *e.g.*, the following:

What solution is most compatible with the interests that we believe is important and which we allow to affect the construction of the law in other situations?

What solution is possible to handle practically within the legal system?

What solution has the best consequences from the perspective of the society (what solution would, e.g., have positive consequences from an economic perspective)?

One example of such a question is the notoriously difficult question of how to deal with *aberratio ictus* -cases within criminal law. When discussing such an issue one will—at least in jurisdictions that has not, by means of legislation or by means of case law settled for a fixed solution—find certain reasons that we consider to be relevant, but these reasons are approximately the same whether we start from »within« the legal system or from the »outside«. This is due to the fact that there is little guidance given in the law. Since the law is open, the judge is pretty much in the same situation as the legislator would be (should the legislator chose to legislate on the matter).[13]

47. One important difference, however, is that while the legislator is, in principle, free to consciously chose a solution which is not supported by reason, the judge is bound not only by the (non-existing rules) but also by the system as such. The judge cannot consciously choose a solution which is second best; he or she must be loyal to the system in a way which the legislator perhaps should be, but does not have to be.

13 The criteria for good reflection and argumentation in such cases are not that different from the criteria for sound moral reasoning. See, e.g., Peter Cane, Responsibility in Law and Morality (2002) p. 19 with further references to Perry.

48. The fact that there are situations in which the sources of law provide little guidance, and in which the judge will have to act as a legislator being loyal to the system, does not, of course, mean that these situations are dominating. In most cases an agent acting within the system will be bound to a (much) larger extent than an agent acting in the position of a legislator. In most cases the written law will exclude, *e.g.*, certain positions that would be possible to take when legislating. This is, of course, a very trivial thing to say, but the fact that it is trivial does not make it less convincing (on the contrary).

49. Thus, though I have great sympathy for a position, which emphasises the openness of law and the need for interpretation and construction, I do not think that the taking of such a position implies that the *de lege lata / de lege ferenda* distinction could or should be abandoned. What that distinction does is simply to say there are certain factors (rules, principles, values, cases etc.) that has to be taken into account by the one who applies the law (within the system), that do not have to be taken into account when arguing about how the law should be.

*[The Meta-Norms on the Sources of Law adds to the Openness]*

50. Within law one often sees references to »the sources of law«. The idea that there are specific sources of law is partly a question of material (what material is relevant when one is trying to find out what the law is?), but it is also (and partly) a question of methodology (how do you find out what the law is?). The reference to certain sources gives basic a sort of basic methodological guidance: when trying to find out what the law is, you should primarily pay attention to certain sources.

51. One way of understanding the idea of sources of law is that the sources of law are exclusive when it comes to providing material relevant for finding out what the law is:

No other sources are relevant in the quest for law. Period.

Such an understanding is, however, problematic due to at least two different reasons. First, it excludes reasons that obviously affects, *e.g.*, court decisions. For example, it seems clear that purely consequentialistic reasons sometimes affect the outcome of a case. A theory according to which the sources of law are exclusive have difficulties in dealing with that. Second, any theory that builds on exclusiveness will have to be clear about which presumptive sources that belongs to the sources of law. Such a theory (I would say) does not exist. Already this simple fact implies that the sources of law are not exclusive.

52. The dismissal of a theory according to which the scources of law are exclusive, do at times lead to the conclusion that there are no rules and that the law can be virtually anything that one can justify. Such a view is, of course, also problematic. It is quite obvious that the sources of law, set boundaries to what one can do as an actor within the legal system.

53. A reasonable view on the sources of law must, I think, combine two elements: (a) that there are certain sources that provide reasons that must be taken into account and which have extra weight in the argumentative process, and (b) that the sources of law are not exclusive. Under such a combination there is nothing contradictory in saying that certain reasons —reasons that are anchored in written rules, in case law, in preparatory works (the accepted sources of law) etc.—have more weight than other reasons, but that does not mean that reasons that are not anchored in this way will lack importance.

54. The importance of »other reasons« will, generally speaking, depend on how open the law is in a certain area. General arguments about positive side effects of A may, *e.g.*, be totally irrelevant if the legislator has taken a stand and—despite these positive effects of A—consciously provided a rule that says B. They may, however, be decisive if the law does not provide clear guidance as regards the choice between A and B. If there is a rule saying that B, reasons about the positive effects of A, once again generally speaking, not be enough to choose A. In a similar way, the importance of non-implemented international agreements will, in a state that have a dualistic theory about the relationship between national law and international law, depend on the openness of the law in the area in question.

55. This adds another layer of openness. Law is open not only in the sense that it has to be constructed. It is (semi)open also in the sense that the sources of law normally referred to are not exclusive.

*[Concluding remarks]*

56. In the text above I have tried to explain why I think that there is need for a legal science with an essentially normative character. The bottom line is that the legal system that is set up by the factual is only a starting point for finding what the law says in a certain situation. The law will not be out there waiting to be found, but will have to be constructed making use of the building blocks provided by the system. The law is characterized by a certain degree of openness. If we are interested in being able to deal with this in a coherent way, where like cases are treated alike etc., we simply need people who work with this normative material in a systematic way.

57. The fact that the law is open in the double sense described above—first by the need for construction, second by the openness of sources—does not, however, mean that there is something wrong with legal dogmatics. On the contrary: it is precisely the openness of law that creates the need for normative legal science. Normative legal dogmatics would be less useful—or not useful at all—should the determination of a legal position be a purely factual enterprise. This implies that the idea of a totally objective legal science, that fulfills the criteria for science used elsewhere, is not very fruitful. Unless legal science allows itself to be normative it will not be able to help us in understanding and help us in coping or dealing with the law; legal science (at least parts of it, see next paragraph) must be normative simply since its object of research is constituted in the way sketched above.[14]

58. This does not imply, of course, that there is no need for other types of legal science. For example, it is obvious that we have an interest in knowing more about:

a. how law is actually applied in practice and about its consequences (→ sociology of law)
b. how we speak about legal questions and how this affects our understanding of the law (→ discourse analysis)
c. how judges think, *i.e.*, how norms are actually made into legal practice by judges (→ Matsuzawaology of law).[15]

59. Thus, the fact that I am defending a normative approach to legal science does not mean that I am arguing for one-sidedness. On the contrary. Law is an important institution in society and we need different forms of knowledge about it. The fact that there is a huge need for qualified normative construction work, does not mean that there is not, for example, a need for critical assessment of the outcome.

---

14 These statements do, of course, build on a certain understanding of the role and value of science. I will refrain from going in to those issues here, but for me it is quite clear that it is more important that legal science is conducted in a way which contributes to the understanding of law, than that it fulfils criteria for science that has been developed mostly with other disciplines in focus.

15 Whether such knowledge (*e.g.*, knowledge about the way the law is actually applied and its consequences) is relevant for the construction of law depends on whether there is room for more general considerations when deciding what the law is (*i.e.*, it depends on how open the legal situation is). *Cf.* paragraph 54 above.

# One Method, Two (Mandatory) Perspectives

*Thomas Elholm*

## *Introduction*

In his contribution to this book, professor Matsuzawa raises the question if legal dogmatics of criminal law can be deemed a science. By the end of his contribution Matsuzawa finds it "vital to remove the unscientific elements and reconstruct legal interpretation studies that will live up to the name of science".

The way the theme is presented here by Matsuzawa implies a number of underlying assumptions. Reading Matsuzawa's contribution, we assume that we know what is meant by notions such as legal dogmatics, science and unscientific. Matsuzawa provides us with a description of these notions, but of course they cannot be exhaustively defined. We still have to imagine what he means by these words and what we mean by them.

Furthermore, in the quotation from Matsuzawa above, he indicates different ways of practicing legal dogmatics. He also indicates that some ways are more "scientific" than others and Matsuzawa prefers a more scientific approach. The quotation above even indicates a kind of "threat" to (or at least incomprehensibility of) present legal dogmatics, because Matsuzawa finds it "vital to remove the unscientific elements".

Matsuzawa offers a way to do this: a non-normative approach, according to which legal scholars should focus – not so much on the norms of the system – but on the minds of the judges; i.e. on the way judges think. Matsuzawa wants to (re)construct a legal science based on the assumption that it is possible for the legal scholars to describe how judges think (the thought processes of judges). Thereby, legal dogmatics becomes descriptive and objective, and the validity can be measured against something "out there", namely the product of the thought processes of judges (and other legal actors if necessary).

Thus, legal dogmatics becomes empirical and descriptive, whereby it resembles other scientific disciplines. Individual and subjective value judgments by the legal scholar can and should be avoided, or rather: it should be called legal politics instead of legal dogmatics.

Another contributor to this book, supreme court judge and professor, Petter Asp, describes his approach to legal science as "close to being the opposite" to Matsuzawa's.[1] Asp advocates for a normative approach to legal dogmatics. He claims that only by including an analysis of the norms and the underlying values and principles of these norms can the legal scholar fulfil her/his task. It is essentially, he says, because a normative character is necessary in order to keep the system rational and coherent. "Only by researching the system from a normative angle we will find out how different values and interests interplay within the system", says Asp and adds: "And only by doing that we can make sure that like cases are treated alike or even find out what it is to treat like cases alike."[2]

Asp's approach implies normative features of legal dogmatics according to which the scholar will prove the "right" or the "sound" application of the law in the light of the fundamental values such as coherence and proportionality.

Both Asp and Matsuzawa are renowned scholars. Looking at the publications by Matsuzawa and Asp, I would describe both of them as legal scholars. There are, of courses, differences in the approach taken in their publications, but until this day I have conceived their publications as primarily being part of what I would call legal dogmatics.

How is it possible, then, that they can disagree fundamentally about the approach of legal dogmatics? How is it possible that they can approach legal dogmatics from two opposite directions and yet both come up with results which are deemed to be legal dogmatics?

In my opinion, the answer is simply: Both Matsuzawa and Asp produce texts which lawyers find useful in order to understand how to interpret and apply the law.

This answer might seem simple and trivial. However, the implications are important. If we assume that both Matsuzawa and Asp produce texts which lawyers find useful, it seems reasonable to claim that: 1) both kinds of approaches are in fact valuable to the functioning of the legal system, and 2) therefore both kinds of approaches must have inherent features which resemble scientific methodology.

In this contribution, I will be taking this view. However, I will also try to show that the two approaches can lead to incompatible positions. Only by merging the two approaches can legal dogmatics be complete. Neither of them should stand alone.

---

1 Asp's contribution, section 4.

2 Asp's contribution, section 31.

### *Highlighting the differences*

What are the differences between the two approaches? Matsuzawa and Asp both describe their approaches in relatively abstract ways. What happens if we apply the approaches on specific cases; do the different approaches lead to different results?

Let me give an example from a Danish context. Although it is not from the field of criminal law, it is still illustrative. The example arrives from a fierce discussion between two professors of constitutional law.

Henrik Palmer Olsen is a professor of law and currently Associate Dean of Research, University of Copenhagen. In September 2005 he defended his doctoral thesis.[3] The thesis is 645 pages long. The topic is division/misuse of power and the focus is an analysis of Section 3 of the Danish Constitutional Act ("*Grundloven*") concerning division of power.[4] According to professor Olsen the thesis is within legal science and based on a legal dogmatic method.[5]

Jens Peter Christensen is today a Supreme Court judge. By the time professor Olsen defended his thesis in 2005, Christensen was professor of public and constitutional law at University of Aarhus, but he became Supreme Court judge soon after. Judge Christensen attended the public defence held by University of Copenhagen and professor Olsen in 2005. Although judge Christensen was not an official opponent, he made an opposition "ex auditorium". His opposition has afterwards been published.[6]

The dispute between professor Olsen and judge Christensen revolves around how "conservative" or "restrained" the legal scholar must be when interpreting the constitution – or at least certain parts of the constitution. The discussion is about Section 3 of the Danish Constitutional Act concerning the division of power.

---

3 *Magtfordrejning. En analyse af magt-fordelingslæren med særligt henblik på den lovgivende magt* (Copenhagen, Jurist og Økonomforbundets Forlag 2005). On the Internet homepage of the university his present research field is described in keywords such as "Jurisprudence, Legal Philosophy, General Legal Theory, Constitutional Law".

4 An unofficial translation reads: "The legislative power shall be vested in the King and the Folketing conjointly. The executive power shall be vested in the King. The judicial power shall be vested in the courts of justice".

5 Cf. the thesis p. 14: "en retsvidenskabelig afhandling, hvori der anvendes en juridisk metode til at belyse spørgsmålet om, hvilket indhold magtfordelingslæren har".

6 [2005] Ugeskrift for Retsvæsen (UfR) B 353. The following remarks are based on that publication.

In his thesis, professor Olsen makes a new interpretation of Section 3, taking a number of sources into account, and he criticises judge Christensen for being too conservative or restrained in his interpretation.

Judge Christensen on the other hand is of the opinion that it is important to be conservative or cautious and restrain oneself by sticking to the traditional legal method.

His main argument is that the constitutional principles are very often a matter of choice between conflicting interests. Many good reasons can be given in favour of each of them. Thus, it is important to restrain oneself otherwise the interpretation could go in every direction depending on the interpreter. Therefore, it is important, judge Christensen says, to restrain oneself by only, or primarily, using the traditional legal sources, which means the wording of the provision, the travaux préparatoires and the case law.

If, on the other hand, the legal scholar resorts to a broad range of considerations by taking ideological assumptions (value judgments) and public interests etc. into consideration, the result of the interpretation becomes unforeseeable and arbitrary.

Judge Christensen argues that some of the results stemming from the method used by professor Olsen are not founded on traditional legal sources. For example, professor Olsen is of the opinion that according to Section 3 of the constitution judges should not be members of Parliament or members of pre-legislative committees. This conclusion is not based on the wording[7] of Section 3 nor on *travaux preparatoires* or case law, says judge Christensen.

Furthermore, the legal practice deemed "unconstitutional" by professor Olsen is not unusual. In fact, many judges are members of pre-legislative committees. Thus, judge Christensen is pointing to the fact that the norm claimed by professor Olsen is not applied by judges in practice and his interpretation will not convince lawyers either.

Thus, according to judge Christensen, the conclusions made by professor Olsen on the basis of a more "modern" or broad legal dogmatic methodology are not only difficult to reconcile with a traditional legal dogmatic method, but also disconnected from reality.

---

7 Section 3 of the Danish constitution (*Grundlov*) reads: "The legislative power shall be vested in the King and the Folketing conjointly. The executive power shall be vested in the King. The judicial power shall be vested in the courts of justice". (Unofficial translation).

If we transfer the discussion between Olsen and Christensen to our present topic, we can see that judge Christensen focuses on the way judges think and behave. He says that judges do the opposite of what professor Olsen says they should. He also claims that judges would never do what professor Olsen says.

Thus, judge Christensen takes an approach to legal dogmatics similar to the one proposed by Matsuzawa. Judge Christensen would probably label professor Olsen research results as "not valid law".

Professor Olsen, on his side, seems to be advocating for the necessity of being normative, using value-judgments to describe how the law is meant to be applied. It seems that according to Olsen, this is also a valid legal method, leading to valid interpretations of the law.

### *Alf Ross and the concept of valid law*

Alf Ross (1899–1979) is one of the few well-known Danish legal scholars and legal philosophers outside of Denmark. He was professor of law at University of Copenhagen from 1935–1969. After graduating from Law School at University of Copenhagen in 1922 he worked for eight years in the state legal department of "*Kammeradvokaten*". However, he abandoned this promising career to devote himself to the scientific study of law. He visited several European capitals, where he met a number of legal scholars, for example Hans Kelsen. He was very inspired by Kelsen, but studies in Uppsala under Axel Hägerström drew him to Scandinavian legal realism.

Ross' theory of "prognosis" or "prediction" says – in essence – that what counts is the behaviour of judges. According to Ross, legal science is a method where the legal scholar must predict the outcome (in court) of a certain legal problem or question.

Thus, legal science is a science resembling other kinds of empirical sciences, but instead of falsifying or verifying a thesis by studying nature or other kinds of objective facts, the legal scholar must study the mind/behaviour/thought processes of judges. The behaviour of judges – meaning the thought processes of judges as they appear through court decisions and judgments – is, so to speak, "the real world" which legal scientific results must be measured against. A good legal dogmatic method is a method which makes it possible to predict the outcome in court. A legal statement corresponding to this reality is a statement about "valid law" and such statements have "binding force".

The theory has been criticised by legal philosophers, for example for being too narrow in the sense that not only judges but also other legal actors like civil servants contribute to the "legal reality" or to legal facts. However, the criticism somehow seems to evaporate, leaving the core of the theory intact. Danish lawyers still seem to be influenced by Ross. Especially the concept of "valid law" (the law as it is applied by judges or other legal actors) seems deeply rooted in Danish lawyers.

The criticism expressed by judge Christensen, mentioned above, can be interpreted in the light of the heritage from Ross. When judge Christensen criticises professor Olsen for not using a method limited to traditional legal dogmatic methodology, the implication of the criticism is the failure of professor Olsen to predict "valid law". What professor Olsen expresses is instead his own personal opinions and value judgments.

Judge Christensen does not necessarily disagree with his opinions – in fact judge Christensen mentions a number of times that he agrees with professor Olsen – but judge Christensen opposes the idea that the statements by professor Olsen are "valid law", that the statements made by professor Olsen can be derived from Section 3 of the Danish constitution and that the statements would say anything about what judges would do. Thus, the statements are not corresponding to legal reality and they have no binding force.

Judge Christensen adds that if a researcher focuses only on the world as it looks from inside the university and thereby fails to understand the legal reality (valid law), the research will not be taken seriously by lawyers in general and practitioners in particular. When carrying out their everyday tasks, lawyers are interested in valid law, not theoretical constructions of a more or less political or ideological nature.

There is one last issue about the dispute between professor Olsen and judge Christensen which deserves attention. According to Ross, statements about valid law are legal dogmatic assertions, while personal opinions based on ideology and value judgments are assertions of legal politics. Ross is not against personal opinions and value judgments as such, but the distinction between legal politics and legal dogmatics is crucial and a good legal scholar must make (or at least try to make!) a clear distinction between valid law and his own personal opinions or value judgments.

According to Ross, legal dogmatic assertions are science and therefore legal dogmatic statements have to correspond to reality (legal practice in court). Personal opinions on the other hand are based on, for example, ideology or political considerations and the legal researcher has to be clear and open about this.

Thus, it is indeed possible that judge Christensen would rest his criticism, if professor Olsen had characterised his statements as being de lege feranda/sententia and not statements about valid law.

*The separation between dogmatics and politics*

If we apply the thoughts mentioned above to the discussion between Matsuzawa and Asp, we might be able to see more clearly what their discussion is about. Matsuzawa wants to separate legal politics from legal dogmatics. His argument seems in line with judge Christensen and Alf Ross. He wants to limit legal dogmatics to the study of (traditional) legal sources of which value judgments are not a part.

Asp, on the other hand, wants a certain element of normative thinking *to be a part of* the legal dogmatic method and he finds it desirable, even necessary, to have a certain "openness of the idea of legal sources" in order to make a valid interpretation and construction of law. He believes this is so even though it makes "the borders between de lege lata and de lege ferenda blurry at times".[8]

As suggested above, the disagreement between judge Christensen and professor Olsen *might* be dissolvable by carefully dividing and labelling dogmatics and politics. Judge Christensen does not disregard the value of being political (de lege ferenda/sententia). It is a good idea, according to Christensen, for legal scholars to propose *new* legislation or new ways of regulating. But we should be clear about the fact that when something is *proposed*, it is eo ipso something new, something which does not exist at the moment, but could *become* (the law).

What Christensen argues against is the tendency to claim that one's subjective believes are "valid law", i.e. something which already exists and is applied in the legal system (in reality). According to judge Christensen (as well as Ross and Matsuzawa), legal dogmatics is about valid law, not politics.

Professor Olsen, on the other hand, claims that he in fact uses a legal dogmatic method, according to which his interpretation of the Danish constitution is the correct interpretation. Hence, his interpretation is already "there", it is "valid law" in the sense that it is the *right* interpretation of the law.

Judge Christensen opposes this view because an interpretation which no judge would comply with is not valid law, it does not exist (only on paper and in the thoughts of Olsen). In turn, professor Olsen would probably say that the behaviour of judges cannot be made decisive for what is valid law. Judges might be wrong. He would probably say that his interpretation *ought* to be applied because it is the *right* interpretation and therefore *valid*.

---

8 Asp's contribution, section 46.

In essence, I believe this is also the core of the discussion between Matsuzawa and Asp. Matsuzawa would say that legal scholars should describe the thought processes of the judges, including the value judgments, but he should carefully separate this from his own value judgments (which is politics, recommendations).

Asp, on the other hand, would claim that the legal scholar should not only describe what is happening in the legal system, but should also give guidelines for the choice between values, especially principles: "Only by researching the system from a normative angle we will find out how different values and interests interplay within the system…".[9] What Asp seems to say (directly or indirectly) is that such guidelines are not only recommendations concerning interpretation of the law, but a *description of the law as it is*. This is due to the fact that it is essential for a society to have a rational and coherent legal system. Therefore, the legal scholar (and the practitioner) *must* choose the interpretation which makes the system more rational and coherent. Such an interpretation – and only that – can be labelled "valid law".

## *Asp vs Matsuzawa – do they agree in the end?*

So far, I have been focusing on the differences between Matsuzawa's and Asp's approach, trying to make clear what the implications are, what it means "in concreto" for the results of the legal method and what the outcome of two research projects might be if you choose one instead of the other. In the following I will try to illustrate that in many regards the two approaches are compatible or at least not so far from each other.

The following subsections will be revolving around 3 hypotheses. They are interdependent, but I will try to separate them in order to make my point clear. In the end, I must admit, the hypotheses are not fully confirmed, they are not irrefutable, but some important arguments (I hope) are displayed. In displaying the arguments, I might make some minor deviations from the correct description of the thoughts by Matsuzawa and Asp. I hope they will have me excused for that.

9 Asp subsection 31.

*Hypothesis 1: A normative approach can be equivalent to a study of the thought processes of judges*

According to Asp: "The aims and the character of the research do, of course, also have methodological implications. If you want to know how judges actually think, the traditional legal method with its focus on the sources of law is, at best, of secondary importance. The traditional legal method tells us what judges ought to do, but not necessarily what they actually do".[10]

Asp might be right, but not entirely. What if the judges are first and foremostly interested in the wording of the provisions? What if they are very conservative in the way they interpret the wording? What if they carefully prioritise the wording of any other source? Could the result of the two approaches – studying the thought processes of the judges and analysing the norms – lead to the same result?

Again, the example from judge Christensen and professor Olsen might be illustrative. What judge Christensen says is that, when it comes to (parts of) constitutional law, judges are conservative. They stick to traditional legal sources and prioritise the wording of the written norm(s) in their interpretations.

Judge Christensen also explains why this is so. He points to the fact that constitutional rules and principles express a compromise between different, opposing interests. There is not one single legitimate way to divide powers between legislative, executive and judicial authority. Rather there are several ways of dividing the powers in a legitimate system.

Thus, although there are solutions which are clearly not legitimate (non-division of power), there is no self-evident way of dividing powers, judge Christensen says. The conflicting interests within the field of constitutional law can be reconciled in a number of ways. Many good reasons can be carried forward supporting one or the other solution.

Therefore, according to judge Christensen, the interpreter has to be conservative when it comes to the choice of legal sources and has to prioritise the wording of the provision. Otherwise, the result of the interpretation is arbitrary and incoherent.

In essence, Asp wants to reach the same result. He wants to avoid arbitrary and incoherent interpretations. However, in his opinion this can be done exactly by taking a normative approach.

10 Asp's contribution, section 2.

The interesting thing is the answer to the following question: What would the normative approach to the interpretation of Section 3 of the Danish Constitution Act be? Very likely, the normative approach would be that a conservative and traditional (restrained) view on legal sources is necessary. Only by taking this approach, can an arbitrary and incoherent interpretation be avoided, just like Asp claims.

In this way, judge Christensen and Asp would reach the same result, coming from two different perspectives.

In fact, this confluence of a normative and judge-mind-based approach is likely to occur in the field of criminal law. In a country based on the rule of law (*Rechtsstaat*), there is strong emphasis on a clear, foreseeable and unambiguous criminal law legislation and a strict basis for criminal liability. Thus, it would be reasonable to claim that within criminal law a restrained and traditional legal dogmatic method is important in order to ensure foreseeability and to avoid arbitrariness.

Therefore, my assertion would be that studying the thought processes of judges, you would come up with the same result as if a normative approach had been taken: judges would adhere to and apply norms of foreseeability, coherence and avoiding arbitrariness.

It should be mentioned, though, that the argument applies mainly to cases where a decision is detrimental to the accused. It is assumed in Danish law that an acquittal can be based on wider considerations (not only the traditional legal sources). This distinction between decisions in favour of or detrimental to the accused is also characteristic of criminal law.

### *Hypothesis 2: Value judgments are necessary for judges*

A key element in the discussion between Matsuzawa and Asp is the notion of "value judgment". Especially for Matsuzawa is this crucial, because he argues strongly against the use of such judgments – or, at least, against calling such judgments legal dogmatics. Neither Matsuzawa nor Asp provide a clear, precise definition of value judgments, but certain features can be inferred from their contributions.

Matsuzawa refers to Ross when he describes value judgments. Ross distinguishes between statements on law (legal statements) based either on facts (legal dogmatics) or on opinions and value judgments (legal politics).

Statements made by the legal scholar are facts if they describe the thought processes of judges in a way which corresponds to the way judges actually think. All other statements on law, which are not based on such facts, are (more or less) subjective opinions and value judgments.

What are the examples, then? Matsuzawa describes value judgments for example like this: "...principles in criminal jurisprudence such as nulla poena sine lege, the culpability principle, and legal benefit protectionism may also be regarded as something of universal significance. However, value judgements of this calibre are too general and vague to become a worthy foundation for normative analyses because the value judgements themselves are open to interpretation and there could be an infinite amount of perspectives".[11]

It is striking how the criticism expressed by Matsuzawa resembles the criticism by judge Christensen against professor Olsen: the "infinite amount of perspectives" which could be *claimed* to be valid gives a certain arbitrariness which is not compatible with the notion of science.

However, as I have argued above, sometimes the value judgments, like *nulla poena sine lege* and the culpability principle, lead to an interpretation of the law which fits perfectly with the thought processes of judges. This is probably so because the judges adhere to and believe in the very same principles which the normative approach claims exist.

According to Asp the legal principles are crucial to both practitioners and legal scholars. Asp says: "As indicated above principles reflect values and summarise reasons that are present in a legal system".

If principles reflect values (which I agree they do) and the judge has to apply principles in judicial practice, which means balancing different (often contrasting values), it seems reasonable to claim that the judge makes a sort of value judgment and that balancing opposing values are inherent in practicing law.

This is especially the case in practicing criminal law. At least some part of criminal law. Criminal law has in many ways a strong element of sentiment. According to the French sociologist Emile Durkheim, criminal law cannot be regarded as merely technical tools to prevent and combat crime. Criminal law provisions and sentences are first and foremostly symbols which express certain *public beliefs and common moral values*.[12]

---

11 Matsuzawa subsection VII. Conclusions.

12 Durkeim's theory of punishment runs through several of his works, including his famous book *De la division du travail social* (Paris, Alcan 1893) (*The Division of Labour* (G. Simpson tr, New York, Macmillan 1933)). It is developed at length in *L'Éducation morale (Cours dispensé en 1902–1903 à la Sorbonne)* (Paris, Alcan 1934) (*Moral Education* (E. K. Wilson tr, New York, Dover Publications 2011)), and in the article "Deux lois de l'évolution pénale" [1899–1900] 4 *Année sociologique* 65–95 (Repr. as chapter 4, "The Evolution of Punishment" in S. Lukes and A. Scull (eds), *Durkheim and the Law* (London, 2nd ed., Palgrave Macmillan 2013).

Or to quote professor Magnus Ulväng from Uppsala: Criminal law is applied moral philosophy.[13] And it is the judge who applies the principles.

Part of Asp's contribution focuses on the fact that judges need to make interpretations. What should the judge do if the wording of a law provision or the traditional legal sources, like travaux préparatoires and case law, does not provide an answer to the present case? Allow me to elaborate on this perspective in order to underpin the idea that from time to time legal practice must necessarily entail interpretations based on value judgments.

Asp has described how the judge must be aware of certain fundamental values within the criminal law system in order to be able to make a valid interpretation. I would even say that modern criminal law provisions in many European countries make it necessary for judges to make value judgments more and more often.

As claimed by Durkheim, many criminal law provisions are meant to convey a common belief or common moral value. In some cases, the judge is forced to clarify what this common moral value means in general and for the specific case. This interpretation implies or necessitates value judgments.

One example:

For many years it was unclear according to Danish criminal law, including case law, how intentional spitting in the face of another person should be punished.[14] In the mid-20th century spitting would *not* be regarded as assault (i.e. not punishable with a maximum of 3 years imprisonment according to the Danish Criminal Code Section 244 on assault).

However, in the nineties and the beginning of the new century, the courts found in some cases that intentional spitting *was* in fact an assault according to Section 244. You can see from the case law that there was widespread disagreement between the judges involved in these cases. In 2006 the Supreme Court clarified the situation by determining that intentional spitting in the face of another person is assault and punishable according to Section 244.

To summarise, without changing the criminal provision, the courts changed the law. Valid law today differs from valid law anno 1950. Most people will probably find the change reasonable. Society has changed and

---

13 Magnus Ulväng, "Förord", in Nils Jareborg, *Prolog till straffrätten* (Uppsala, Lustus Förlag 2011) 6.

14 See G. Toftegaard Nielsen, T. Elholm og M. Niels Jakobsen, *Kommenteret Straffelov. Speciel del* (Copenhagen, 11th edition, DJØF forlag 2018) 105.

the general sentiment regarding physical integrity has changed. This is most likely the reason why valid law is different today. The present situation – valid law of today – is consistent with common moral values.

Second example:

Let me give another example where the value judgment is more specifically related to fundamental principles of law.

There has been a discussion in Denmark about the possibility of expulsion of criminals. The majority of the members of Parliament want to expel as many criminal persons as possible. Therefore, there has been a clear tendency to try – via new legislative measures – to have more and more criminals expelled, even for less aggravating crimes and even though the convicted person has a strong connection to Denmark (has lived here for a long time, family and children etc.).

However, international obligations, mainly stemming from the ECHR, set certain limits to expulsion of criminals. The Danish courts have been struggling to find the right balance between the requirement from the Danish legislation and the international obligations. The court practice has been criticised in the public debate for not being "challenging" enough towards the ECHR. Courts were criticised for being too reluctant to expel criminals. The director of the Danish Institute for Human Rights said publicly that it would be possible for the courts – within the limits of the international obligations – to expel to a larger extent than what has been the case.[15]

The culmination of the discussion came recently, when the Danish Supreme Court overruled decisions by the city court and High Court by expelling a gang leader for a minor crime.[16]

It is my contention that in a case like this, the Supreme Court can hardly avoid bringing value judgments into consideration. Otherwise, they would not be able to reach a different result from the city court and High Court. However, the specific arguments of the Supreme Court in the present case are not so important for discussion here.[17] Rather, it is inter-

---

15 <https://www.altinget.dk/christiansborg/artikel/jonas-christoffersen-danmark-kan-udvise-flere-for-grov-kriminalitet> accessed 10 January 2019.

16 Supreme Court, decision of 24th of May 2018, case 42/2018 (1. *afdeling*).

17 After an "overall assessment", Supreme Court found (very much in line with the argumentation of Asp regarding the role of fundamental principles in court cases?) that unconditional expulsion was not a disproportionate infringement of art. 8 of the European Convention on Human Rights, see decision of *Højesteret* of 24th of May 2018, case 42/2018 (1. *afdeling*).

esting from a general point of view to try to imagine the kind of value judgments which would easily occur in situations like this.

Possible value judgments in cases like these could very well be: Whether the Danish courts were to follow the intention of the Danish legislator or the international obligations stemming from the European Court of Human Rights. It could also be value judgment in the sense of weighing opposite fundamental values stemming from the ECHR-system. Or value judgments of the range of the principle of legality.

The judges will often have to assess what the intention of the legislator is. In doing so, you could say that they have to make value judgements. The judge will often have to find out which values are at stake, which of the conflicting values should have priority and how general fundamental principles should be applied in the present case. Quite often, the Danish judges will call this process "an overall assessment" (en samlet vurdering), like they did in the present Supreme Court case.

### *Hypothesis 3 – Both approaches are beneficial to society*

If we accept the idea that it is necessary for practitioners to make value judgments, what are, then, the implications for legal scholars? Should they also make value judgments, or should they only describe how the judges make value judgments?

One of the underlying questions of the entire discussion between Matsuzawa and Asp is this: What is the purpose of the legal dogmatic method?

My contention is this: The purpose of having laws is to regulate society. The purpose of having legal scholars is to contribute to the regulation of society. Thus, the aim of legal dogmatics is not to find the objective truth, as it is for natural science, but to contribute to the functioning of the regulation of society.

The legal scholar makes his/her contribution by describing how the system functions. This makes the functioning of the system transparent to legal actors and to society in general. Being transparent, the system is equipped with an important tool which can prevent arbitrary and incoherent decisions.

However, the legal scholars can also contribute to the functioning of the system by providing convincing (rational and coherent) interpretations of the norms, simply because the legal system from time to time needs such interpretations, especially when judges have to deal with complicated cases involving value judgments.

What does that mean in practice for the legal scholar? Let us try to investigate some (fictive) examples.

A legal scholar influenced by Matsuzawa wants to describe the thought processes of judges. She studies a lot of judges and case law and finds out that the judges, when confronted with certain value judgments, tend to choose a rational and coherent solution. This leads to a certain interpretation of a specific law provision. She describes all of this.

Another legal scholar, influenced by Asp, wants to make a normative interpretation of the same law provision, based on the normative idea of a rational and coherent legal system. After having discussed all the relevant provisions, principles and values and weighing them against each other, he comes up with the same interpretation of the law as presented by the first scholar.

Both of the scholars publish their works. The judges agree that the description made by the first scholar is accurate and they (of course) also adhere to the result of the interpretation of the second scholar (may be even for the same reasons!).

In a case like this, how important is it to label the work of the second scholar as politics, as *not* scientific, *not* legal dogmatics?

Let us change the example. The second scholar, influenced by Asp, makes again a normative interpretation of the law provision, but he comes up with a *different* interpretation of the law, showing that the interpretation made by the judges (and described by the first scholar) is not the most coherent and rational.

His research is published and the judges agree that the interpretation they have made so far is arbitrary and incoherent. They immediately change their interpretation, because they believe that a legal system must strive to become rational and coherent.

In a case like this, how important is it to label the work of the second scholar as politics, as *not* scientific, *not* legal dogmatics?

Let us change the example once again. The second scholar, influenced by Asp, makes a normative interpretation of the same law provision. He comes up with an interpretation showing that the interpretation made by the judges is not the most coherent and rational.

His research is published, but the judges *disagree* that the interpretation they have made is arbitrary and less coherent. They find that the argumentation of the second scholar is inconsistent and based on values which they do not adhere to. They are not going to apply the interpretation presented by the second scholar.

In a case like this, how important is it to label the work of the second scholar as politics, as *not* scientific, *not* legal dogmatics?

The reason why I present the three situations above is the following:

A) The two kinds of approaches are both valuable in order to fulfil the task of legal scholars, namely to make the functioning of the legal system transparent and coherent. This is the core of the assumption made by Asp: "...the idea of a totally objective legal science, that fulfills the criteria for science used elsewhere, is not fruitful."[18]
B) However, not every kind of descriptive and normative approach seems valuable for the regulation of society.

First of all, it is necessary to distinguish clearly between the two kinds of approaches. This is the assumption made by Matsuzawa. Furthermore, in order to make a valid description of the thought processes of judges, it would be crucial to be strictly objective and apply the scientific standards presented by Matsuzawa. If the normative and descriptive approach is mixed with unscientific elements, e.g. political and mora beliefs or sentiments, the result of the descriptive approach would be flawed.

Secondly, not every normative approach is valuable, but it seems more difficult to pinpoint the relevant criteria in order to distinguish between the good and the bad normative approach.

It seems important to measure the results of the research against something outside the method itself; a kind of yardstick, something "in reality". This is also the reason why Matsuzawa requires the result of the legal dogmatic method to be measured against something "outside", namely the thought processes of judges.

However, what can the yardstick be? One of the reasons why Asp has become Supreme Court judge is most likely that the normative approach in his research was sought by the judges in order to provide an answer to difficult questions (involving value judgments) *and* because his (normative) answers fitted well with the way judges think; they were directly applicable.

Therefore, my contention is this: If the purpose of having legal dogmatic research is to contribute to the well-functioning of the regulation of society, then the validity of the normative approach depends on the applicability of the result. If the results are widely rejected by the actors of the legal system, then the results are not applicable and something probably went wrong during the research.

Thus, even a scholar with a normative approach has to know how the legal system functions and what the judges are thinking. In this way, the

---

18 Asp subsection 57.

descriptive approach of the thought processes of judges, proposed by Matsuzawa, can even help to make the normative approach fruitful.

In this sense, the two kinds of approaches must (to some degree) be interdependent *in order* to be valuable. If the normative approach provides interpretations which are widely rejected by the actors of the legal system, it is not of much use. We are inclined to call it subjective, unscientific, even fantasy. On the other hand, if the descriptive approach consolidates an irrational and incoherent practice – by calling irrational and incoherent thought processes of judges for valid law with binding force – the functioning of the legal system is impaired. Therefore, we are inclined not only to criticise this from a normative point of view, but also to claim that the practice is invalid and the normative approach must have "binding force".

### *There is Nothing New under the Sun?*[19]

Actually, it seems like we (the legal scholars) are discussing the same problems and proposing – more or less – the same solutions as always. Lawyers have been struggling for decades to explain and legitimise the legal method as science. The two positions, the normative and the descriptive, have been opponents for a long time.

Having found my own position in the discussion, I discovered that my thoughts were not new at all. Anders Vinding Kruse (1921–1995), a Danish professor of legal science, started his carrier as a barrister, then became professor at University of Aarhus and later at University of Copenhagen. His research mainly concerns legal dogmatics in private law, but he has nevertheless expressed his view on legal dogmatic science in a way which reflects my own.

In the following, I will summarise his main points[20] and comment on some of them by adding a few words (*in italics*).

1) Lawyers tend to think that legal dogmatics can be made into a purely descriptive business, but in fact, this is only possible within a rather limited framework. (*However, the legal scholar must still try to conduct the research in an objective way*).
2) If legal dogmatics have to comply with traditional scientific requirements, the presentation of valid law would be so template-like, vague

---

19 Quote from The Old Testament, Eccleciastes 1:9.

20 Anders Vinding Kruse, *Erstatningsretten* (v/Jens Møller, Copenhagen, 4th edn, Jurist- og Økonomforbundets Forlag 1986) 18 ff.

and indefinite that it could not fulfil the needs of practical legal life. (*However, the Ross-approach to legal dogmatics seems to have been quite successful among Danish legal practitioners*).

3) Once the legal scholar systematises case law, not to mention makes contributions to the resolution of unlawful cases, based on the "nature of the case" ("*sagens natur*"), one must necessarily make use of ideal ideas represented by fundamental principles and fundamental values of society. (*When no clear answer occurs from the traditional legal sources, this is where the normative approach becomes necessary*).
4) Indeed, the legal scholar must seek to leave out his own personal and subjective beliefs. Instead, he should choose his assessment criteria among the more widely accepted moral and legal principles of the society in which he is working. (*This is the "yardstick" I have mentioned above. Only, my suggestion is more focused on the assessment criteria of the actors of the legal system. Thus, my proposal leans more towards the thought processes of judges*).
5) The legal scholar (and practitioner) must try to empathise with society's fundamental values and let her/his assessments, as far as possible, reflect this. In a sense, this approach can be described as "objective". (*At least the judges must from time to time make value judgments based on common moral beliefs*).
6) Keeping "private" or "subjective" assessments completely out of legal science is quite a difficult task. Not least because the legal rules cannot be interpreted as an expression of a uniform assessment pattern since they rely on diverse historical, cultural and social assessments, having been created at different times and under changing circumstances. (*The fact that the system is not coherent does not mean that we have to stop striving for a system which is as coherent as possible*).
7) The legal scholar (and practitioner) is therefore often faced with a choice between several options. But where doubts can arise as to which legal starting points for the assessment he or she has used, the legal starting points should be formulated (*and made transparent to the reader*).
8) These considerations require a normative source of law, the content of which must be expressed in categories of duty such as: a judge must or should judge by the words and intentions of the law in accordance with generally accepted legal principles, etc. (*As Asp claims, even though such fundamental principles might be vague and subjective, they still contribute to making the system coherent*).
9) In doing so, the legal researcher approaches legislative considerations; the research lays between de lege lata and de lege ferenda. There is

nothing wrong with this, as long as the research clearly states when it is in one or the other category. (*Which can be very difficult from time to time*).

10) The dogmatic research must therefore always try to uncover on which legal assessment the rules are based, because this is the most important guideline when interpreting legal provisions and case law. (*This seems in line with Asp's idea that the normative approach enhances the understanding of the entire system*).

*Conclusion*

Both Matsuzawa and Asp produce texts which lawyers find useful in order to understand how to interpret and apply the law. In my opinion, this is (good) legal dogmatics, fulfilling the aim of legal dogmatics.

By revealing the thought processes of judges, legal scholars contribute to the transparency of the legal system. Thereby, they contribute to the functioning of the legal system. Likewise, legal scholars contribute to the functioning of the system by providing convincing (rational and coherent) interpretations of the norms, because the legal system needs such interpretations, especially when dealing with complicated cases involving value judgments.

Therefore, it seems evident to me that the legal scholar should not only describe the necessary value judgments by describing the thought processes of judges. Legal scholars should also take value judgments into account and provide normative interpretations of the norms.

Thus, both kinds of approaches are in fact valuable for the functioning of the legal system. However, both approaches can be flawed and they can lead to incompatible positions.

In describing the system, the legal scholar must strive to be objective, leaving private beliefs and sympathies out. Otherwise, they will become sources of errors. This applies to a descriptive as well as to a normative approach.

When applying a normative approach, the analysis must be based on widely accepted moral and fundamental legal principles. I would even say that it should be based on – as far as possible – those moral and fundamental legal principles which are normally applied by the actors of the legal system (whereby the thought processes of judges could become important). Thus, a yardstick is introduced, which indicates the level of "correspondence" between the results and "reality" and therefore also how valuable the approach is to society. This implies that 1) the legal scholar must try to avoid private beliefs and sympathies, and 2) the normative approach has to be adapted to the specific field of legal research, because the legal actors do not necessarily apply the same moral and fundamental legal principles in every discipline (as indicated by judge Christensen), and 3) the normative scholar must carefully display the fundamental principles and values involved in the analysis.

Finally, all legal scholars should thoroughly dissect his/her own method, being conscious of which approach she/he has taken and what the basic requirements for doing such research are. Thus, by merging the two approaches, legal dogmatics becomes most fruitful, fulfilling the task of legal dogmatics in society.

# Criminal Law Scholarship – Should It Be Able to Present Itself as Science?

*Kimmo Nuotio*

## 1. *The Finnish entrance point*

It makes indeed sense to try to figure out if criminal law scholarship could or should be regarded as science. It would help defend criminal law in the eyes of other sciences if we could show that it rests on the solid footing of science. Unfortunately this exercise will not be easy. The topic is not new since at least after the rise of the natural sciences, social sciences and humanities have generally been set under the pressure to define themselves as sciences. Law is no exception to that.

In fact, if we look at text-books for criminal law, we rather rarely find any deeper considerations as regards to the scientific character of criminal law scholarship. In most cases, the text-books run simply from the basic concepts and principles, discuss the legal sources and how to interpret them, etc. It seems that the criminal law scholarship has outsourced some of its foundational questions to philosophy of law and legal theory. Criminal law theory may have been mainstreamed in the sense that a doctrinal approach to penal liability simply moves in internal circles, as a fight between different theoretical positions, and without any need to refer to deeper sources of the doctrines. Doctrines may thus work as stop rules for legal reasoning.

First, we need to differentiate between criminal law and criminal law scholarship. It makes sense to see a difference here. We would talk about practices of criminal law, and even about norms of criminal law, even if we had no particular science looking at it. The practices we have had for centuries, much before we started theorizing about them.

Science produces knowledge, and criminal law as an object of science emerges as a separate body of knowledge. In the German scholarly tradition, the $19^{th}$ century saw first a wave of Hegelian idealism, followed by a von Lisztian sociological realism. The birth of the Finnish criminal law science connects directly with a Hegel-inspired scholarship[1] which, for that matter, consolidated itself in the Finnish Penal Code of 1889/1894. From those years onwards we can see that the Finnish criminal law scholarship has grown and matured under this tension between classical (and later neo-classical) ideas and a conscious sociological, social policy oriented view about crime and criminal law.[2]

During the heyday of Scandinavian legal realism in the 1940's and 1950's the Finnish criminal law theory was not very strong and receptive. We could rather see that there were different strands of conservative thought, some of it more liberal, some more conservative. But in those debates theories of knowledge were not present. It was probably only in the 1960's that the criminal lawyers' monopoly to discuss crime was challenged and the practices of crime control were challenged by many experts representing a variety of other academic areas. The famous Nordic critical criminology started getting criminal law professors involved, and it all led to critical reformist criminal policy ideas.

Thus, in Finland we actually never entered a serious debate about whether what we do is scientific. The critique of criminal law by the reformers was a *justice critique*, and the old school had to give room to new thought since the belief in special prevention and treatment of the offenders had simply lost credibility.[3] The academic critique was not the only reason for reform, since the entire society was receptive to reformist ideas, and the reforms carried out were many. A project was started to reform the entire body of criminal law. First, a committee worked on the leading principles that would have to be followed, and later the project was carried through.

In the 1970's neo-classical thought took the lead since this was sort of a common denominator that many could agree on. Act-proportionality and similar values of justice were being stressed. This justice thinking was,

1 Markus Wahlberg, Den finska straffrättsvetenskapens födelse I. Forum iuris 2003.

2 Cf. Kimmo Nuotio, "The Reform Story of the Finnish Penal Code: Ideological turns and waves of modernization," in Goodall, K., Malloch, M. and Munro, B. (eds.), *Building Justice in Post-Transition Europe? Processes of Criminalisation within Central and Eastern European countries*, Abingdon and Oxon: Routledge, 2013, pp. 78–93; Kimmo Nuotio, "The transformation of criminal law and criminal law theory in Finland and China, Peking University Law Journal, 5:1, pp. 1–23, DOI: 10.1080/20517483.2017.1330807.

3 See, generally, on the debate within Nordic criminal law as well as concerning the Finnish situation, Juhana Mikael Salojärvi, A Menace to Society. Radicalism and Legal Scholarship in the United States, Scandinavia and Finland, 1965–1980. Faculty of Law, University of Helsinki, 2013, p. 195–214, 300–314.

however, rather socially informed, and the idea was to redefine the role criminal law should play in a modernizing society. For that purpose one needed criminal policy insights. The aim was to tailor criminal law to serve rational and humane criminal policy interests and to avoid excesses of use of criminal law. Traditional criminal law was suspected even to have been a tool for suppressing people with a lower social status. Theory and practice of criminal policy were a primary interest, and 1970's or 1980's were decades of updating and real reform, and there was less effort yet to theorize how a modern doctrine of criminal liability should look like. We should also note that in the philosophical debates analytical philosophy of action became one source of inspiration, as can be seen in the dissertation on criminal intent of Nils Jareborg from 1969, to give just bone example.[4] The former rigid positivism gave way to the idea that *language* should be the main target of our interest since we only can reach truths by means of language. In Finland the interest in analytical philosophy could also be observed, but it became important mainly in other areas of legal scholarship, rather than in criminal law.

Only after the reforms of the special part of criminal law had already started, began the thinking of how structures of penal liability should be construed in a modernized society. In the 1990's the need for a rethinking was already pressing, since in 1995 areas such as safety at work crimes and environmental crimes had been revised, and it was obvious that new doctrines were needed concerning how to allocate penal liability in organisations. Even a corporate penal liability had been introduced.

To cut the long story short, we could say that once again the Finnish criminal law scholars had to try to make the best out of what was available. There was the own Finnish legal and scholarly tradition, but you also wanted to understand the legal models that were being discussed in other Nordic countries, especially in Sweden, as well as the in the German scholarship. The Finnish perspective was pragmatist, and the idea was to adopt what works but to avoid too complex and irrelevant theorizing. Some of the scholars studied German sources, and for instance Claus Roxin and the doctrine of objective imputation received some attention,[5] but still, in practice, such theorizing never really hit the everyday life of criminal law doctrine.

4 Nils Jareborg, Handling och uppsåt. Norstedts 1969.
5 Cf. the dissertation on criminal negligence: Ari-Matti Nuutila, Rikosoikeudellinen huolimattomuus, Lakimiesliiton kustannus 1996.

In the 1990's there was also a growing concern that the text-books were badly outdated. Then a few came out, and since then you may find somewhat different presentations of the concept of crime. Anyway, the differences between them are relevant rather pedagogically than theoretically or as regards the legal applications. None of those textbooks goes beyond a legal doctrinal level to any serious philosophical discussion.

In 1990 an international colloquium was organized in Helsinki to celebrate the first centenary of Finnish Penal Code. Tens of significant foreign scholars were invited to comment the first drafts for the revised general part of the Penal Code, namely the draft articles about elements of penal liability. The academic articles were published and they were taken into account in the preparatory work that followed.[6] The revision was completed in 2004 when the new provisions entered into force. Even though some of the criticism was weighty, I would dare to say that already at this point the German scholarship had lost some of its authority. The Finnish law drafters were most likely also reluctant to adopt theories which were not very well known to them. We see here that the connection to the German legal culture had become thinner, and the law drafters were mostly concerned about the clarity of the rules to be proposed and that they would have a good grounding in the previous law and legal practice. It had also become clear that the Supreme Court was an important player. The Supreme Court had never been engaged in theoretical debates, at least openly, even though there were renowned criminal law scholars amongst the judges: Olavi Heinonen, a former associate professor of criminal law, later served as the president of the Court, to give an example.

Finnish criminal law scholarship was finally standing on its own feet as it was taking its first baby steps. And it had to learn to cope with a variety of new issues. There was not enough time engage with all possible theoretical and philosophical debates. A serious modernization of the special part was underway and new issues were raised as a result. The so-called general doctrines was only one of such areas. There were other bigger issues. The system of punishment had to be reformed and the sentencing options broadened, membership in the Council of Europe and its ECHR triggered new issues as well as the fact that the European Union began to develop its approach to give framework rules on criminal law cooperation.

In the Finnish criminal law debate the relationship between criminal law and constitutional law became important, since also the constitutional

6 Raimo Lahti – Kimmo Nuotio (Ed. by/Hrsg.), Criminal Law Theory in Transition. Strafrechtstheorie im Umbruch. Finnish Lawyers Publishing Company 1992.

law provisions had been revised in 1995, and the new doctrines on how fundamental rights may be limited were also applied in the criminal law area. This was not just plain theory since the Constitutional law committee of the Parliament started screening *ex ante* the compatibility of the proposed criminal legislation against the background of the fundamental rights as well and as the human rights standards. The *Zeitgeist* was not favorable to any philosophical critique of the valid law, but rather the question was how to adjust interpretations of different normative legal materials to each other. A pragmatist attitude prevailed. I will back to some of these issues later, towards the end of my presentation. We need to engage first with some discussions and debates that have been taking place rather on the level of legal theory.

## 2. *Criminal law as a science*

Empirical sciences would look at the practices of applying criminal law, but this is not typically what we do in law. If we accept that criminal law science can have norms as its objects, such a science will produce knowledge about criminal law norms.

These days the practical and the theoretical are intertwined. In contemporary societies we could not even think of a criminal law had we not been instructing the drafting and development of our laws with the help of legal research. Professional legal education means precisely this: knowing law is an academic enterprise, and the legal practice builds on theoretical knowledge. In the Nordic setting we could say that from 1960's onwards criminal law professors had to understand at least the basics of criminology and criminal policy and thus also, the phenomena of crime. There was no way back to a purely positivist legalistic approach.

Sometimes a difference is being made between a *legal order* and a *legal system* to make precisely the point that legal science is able to present law differently, as an interpreted and systematic unity, which is more than just a set of norms. This may be an oversimplification, and certainly legal science can do more than that. In any case, the law itself and the legal science are today intertwined in a manner which makes it difficult to draw any clear distinction. Criminal law is the object of scholarly criminal science as a field of knowledge, but the science itself is also needed in order to construct criminal law (as part of the legal system, say, Finnish criminal law).

Criminal law scholarship or science is a practice, an activity which focuses on criminal law. It seeks to analyze, explain, present, construct, interpret, even criticize criminal law. Scholars use different methods in their scholarly work, and we have more than just one way of doing it. In sociological terms we might even define this scholarly activity as being what the criminal law scholars do. It is a joint enterprise of the scholarly community, and the community itself defines the necessary borderlines; it states what merits to be called legal science and what not. We do not even always have to be conscious of the limits of what counts as legal scholarship. Rather, we simply adopt views and definitions in our everyday practices, for instance, when assessing doctoral dissertations or when carrying out academic assessments in the context of professor recruitments. Certain types of studies count as merits as concerns recruitments, whereas some might not. I would claim that these days many more methods and approaches are being accepted in legal studies than the case was maybe a century ago. Research traditions such as law and society, law and literature etc may be marginal, but do exist.

In the field of criminal law also the link between research and teaching deserves mention: knowledge about criminal law is a requirement of a law degree. This, in turn, reflects the fact that lawyers may have to apply criminal law or serve clients that face criminal proceedings. We should avoid any too narrow definition of what counts as legal science. Criminal law scholars contribute to the knowledge of a system of criminal law, and therefore they should be aware of that impact and have a sense of responsibility. This expectation of a sense of responsibility is a plain fact which does not presuppose the ability to answer the deepest questions of ontological truths about criminal law normativity. Sending people to prison is a brute fact which shows that there is always a link to reality.

In fact I would prefer speaking about criminal law scholarship rather than about criminal law science. This has to do with the fact that the methods used in criminal law research are not necessarily such that would satisfy strictest requirements of natural sciences. Law is not a thing you usually study in laboratories. You do not test hypotheses empirically. Legal scholarship may draw on knowledge from such kind of sciences, but most of what we do is something different.

Description of criminal law science as scholarly work tells to my mind better what this is all about. Scholarship aims at learned, informed, grounded views. Often we say that the aim of legal research is interpretation and systematization of law. Even though this does not tell much without further qualifications and explanations, there are at least some hints.

One important element there is that criminal law scholarship is meant to engage with legal practice, that is, the work of the legislatures and the work of courts when they deal with criminal law. Due to the fact that law itself can no longer hardly be understood without a legal education and the results of criminal law scholarship, we might even wish to include in legal practice legal scholars' work, at least in the broad sense, since the real life of law is always embedded in a scholarly setting. The law drafters, to give an example, need to understand the system of law; otherwise it would not make sense to adopt specific changes in that system.

Judges apply the law on the cases brought before them. Judges decide individual cases. The scholarly activities reflect on the legal issues on a higher level of abstraction. The judges are themselves engaged in a similar activity than what the scholars do, but they are more or less bound by the legal constraints of the case since the legal order itself imposes them restrictions as regards how law should be understood and applied. A judge is expected to follow some canons, conventions which are experienced as binding, concerning how legal sources should be organized, how conflicts of norms should be solved, and the like. Also certain conventions on style matter. We find in the world examples of very "scholarly" legal decisions with lots of references to sources, including legal literature, but in most cases the courts avoid such references and focus on reasoning directly serving the decision-making.

The judge is however, without further qualifications, not a member of the academic scholarly community by the sole characteristic of sitting in court. When writing commentaries of law the judges jump into a new role; as scholars they have no privileged position to interpret the law.

Much of the canons on how to organize the legal sources and how to interpret the laws, and the rules and principles inscribed in them are in fact at least to some extent a product of legal scholarship. In order to perform his or her duties, a judge needs to know legal scholarship. Legal education is under the modern conditions the gate to legal professions.

Legal scholars working at the universities or research institutes in turn do not have the burden or privilege of having to decide cases. But, in order to produce knowledge that is relevant also for the legal profession, the legal scholar needs to share some of the core understandings of law the judge has. This is very central if the scholar wishes to contribute by his or her analyses to what the legal profession in more narrow sense are doing. This is a rather important feature concerning especially doctrinal work in the field of criminal law. It reaches out to the legal practice and it develops an understanding of it by building contexts in a way which a court could not do.

Of course criminal law scholarship may depart from this close link to the legal practice and choose to take other avenues. It can for instance reach out only to the community of scholars, or it might even mainly seek to address scholars of other disciplines. Most often, in any case, some link to the interpretation and systematization is being preserved. Comparative criminal law, for instance, looks at two or more systems of criminal law without giving a priority to any one of them. A work on restorative justice, to give an example, may present and discuss models of dealing with crime which are other than the ones we have now. Such knowledge may be important in reforming the procedural arrangements which we have.

The question of whether criminal law scholarship is or could be made a science most obviously leads to questions of how we understand law more generally. A Kelsenian theory would reduce the relevant questions to questions of validity of certain norms as part of a legal order. Questions of legitimacy or justice would not be permitted since a pure theory of law would not allow for that. A realistic theory of law would again seek to reduce law to facts as it would not allow for a normative perspective beyond that.

Courts are indeed interpreting law, but systematisation is something which falls mainly only the scholarly practice. This is due to the limitations that the courts face in carrying out their job. Systematisation could for instance be taken to mean all efforts aiming at maintaining the coherence of the legal system. The legal system is in constant change and there is always the risk of inner inconsistency. One of the traditional goals of legal science is to try to avoid inconsistency.

Why is it then in fact a problem? Why should we strive at consistency, and even coherence? The answer is simply that our normative commitments tell us so. We read our legal materials with the aim of being able to serve some core principles of justice. Equal treatment, legal certainty, principles of justice require that we should try to organize the legal materials accordingly. If two rules collide, one of them has to give way. Coherence of the legal system cannot of course always be granted, but it is a helpful ideal.

Coherence could be taken to mean coherence in terms of values and principles. If we regard criminal law materials in terms of weighing and balancing of legal principles, we see that interpretative activity almost by necessity has to strive to at least some sort of systematic coherence. These days criminal law has obvious links with constitutional law and the doctrines of fundamental rights, as well as the human rights law. The values and principles that criminal law is presupposed to cherish may have a backup in normative realms outside of criminal law in a narrow sense. Criminal law is part of larger normative settings.

In the scholarly activity of today we see rather much efforts in critical analysis. Criminal law is being criticized for being too formal. Women and their specific needs have been neglected. Rights of the animals play a limited role only. Criminal law promises too much and delivers too little.

Criminal law is being used politically, as a means to an end, often excessively.[7] Criminological critique has stated that the state is stealing the conflict from the parties. What a strong metaphor! Criminal law is itself a crime!

Fragmentation of criminal law is one important topic. Do we any longer have a coherent legal order? Do the same general doctrines of penal liability apply across all the special part of criminal law (that is, the provisions on specific crimes)? I believe we are witnessing a certain fragmentation, and in fact the necessity to develop general doctrines that only apply for certain parts of criminal law tell precisely about this. International criminal law, to give an example, has developed new doctrines of its own, and as even domestic legal systems include provisions about these offences, it has been necessary to include provisions on specific doctrines of liability in the domestic legal orders.

We should now, after this brief setting of the scene, return to the question of the nature of legal science. First, to really be able to formulate requirements for the criminal law as a science, we would have to define what we mean by science. This is certainly not too simple, but if we would adopt a definition in line of scientific realism, we could say that science needs to tell about real world, and the claims of scientific knowledge would have to possess a truth value that can be tested.

As has been presented by Shin Matsuzawa elsewhere in this volume, Scandinavian realism á la Alf Ross could provide an example of theorizing which would satisfy rather high criteria of scientificity. This is indeed one option. We need to be mindful of the premises of the so-called Uppsala school and the Scandinavian realism that followed. It all started with the philosopher Axel Hägerström and his criticism of metaphysical thought. Hägerström criticized especially idealistic views about morals. For him, moral statements were only expressions of emotions.[8]

Vilhelm Lundstedt was the legal scholar who took the initiative to clean legal science from metaphysical thought. Lundstedt attacked the principle of guilt, for instance. Criminal law was seen in its social function only. For Lundstedt, the most important was to elaborate on the mechanism criminal law operates in the society. Even if the approach could be called social engineering, it was not a sociological approach. Criminal law played a role

7 See, for example, the powerful discussion in Husak, Douglas, Overcriminalization. The Limits of The Criminal Law. OUP 2008.

8 I have dealt with Alf Ross and Scandinavian Realism in my article Alf Ross som straffrättsfilosof. Nordisk Tidsskrift for Kriminalvidenskab *86* (3), 1999, p. 151–173.

as it could be used to steer human behavior. It is crucial how this was thought to take place.[9]

Whereas von Liszt and the sociological school had emphasized the special preventive function of criminal law, the Uppsala school and the Scandinavian realists emphasized the general prevention. The general prevention was, however, not understood as being based on the fear of punishment, as it had been presented by P.J.A. Feuerbach, for instance. Criminal law was understood to perform its function in that it was supporting and creating morals in the society.

How was it now possible to assign criminal law such a function, taking into consideration that talk about moral principles was non-sensical, only expression of emotions? For the Scandinavian realists the feelings and attitudes of the people were real, and these were now being used in steering people away from wrongful and harmful behavior. The function of criminal law was seen in the necessary moral education of the people. This, in turn, required that the emphasis should be given to the level of acts, not that of the actors. The level of action was seen as the mediating social level.

The idea of moral education as the aim of system of punishment was not a new one. It had been presented already by Ludwig von Bar in Germany and, as usual, most likely the traces could even be followed beyond that.[10] As regards the Swedish scholars, Per-Olof Ekelöf was particularly interested in how criminal law performs its function in moral education.[11]

In this sense, the Scandinavian realism was different from American realism. The former was critical and reductionist, but it did not change completely how law was being seen. One sign of this was that in the work of Alf Ross, doctrines of legal sources continued to play a role. The prediction theory was being applied, but it did not completely do away with legal reasoning. For Ross, law operates through the mind of the judge. The judge feels being socially bound to law and thus attaches it a normative meaning. A purely behaviorist analysis could never reach this mental link which accounts of the validity of legal norms.[12]

A prediction theory (or: a prognosis theory) leads to problems if the validity of law is being denied completely. The most obvious problem is that

---

9 Lundstedt, Anders Vilhelm, Die Unwissenschaftlichkeit der Rechtswissenschaft. Zweiter Band. Erster Teil. Berlin 1936, p. 25 pp.

10 Von Bar, Ludwig, A History of Continental Criminal Law. Little etc, Boston 1916, pp. 497–547.

11 Ekelöf, Per Olof, Straffet, skadeståndet och vitet. En studie över de rättsliga sanktionernas verkningssätt. Uppsala 1942, pp. 12–74.

12 Cf. Alf Ross, On Law and Justice, University of California Press, 1959, Ch. 2.

if we adopt the position of a judge who is sitting a difficult case and faces a problem concerning how to interpret the law, it does not help the judge further to ask the question about his own future behavior. He (or she, for that matter) is not in need of a prediction of his own future actions, but instead he needs help in reasoning for a good judgment.[13] So we fall back on the issue of normative reasoning. In easy questions it may indeed be possible to do this transforming operation, but dealing with easy cases is not the core function of what the courts do. And routine cases are not too interesting from the point of legal scholarship either. Easy cases are easy precisely because we know how they should be solved. It is not a surprise that much of the legal thought focuses on reasoning in so-called hard cases. The work of Ronald Dworkin provides the well-known example. For him legal reasoning is an effort in constructive interpretation.[14]

Kaarlo Tuori has pointed out that Hart's critique of Scandinavian legal realism misses the point. The aim of the realists was to reformulate the basic legal concepts so that legal dogmatics could pass the test of scientificity rather than to change the character of all legal research. One obvious merit of the work of Ross, for instance, was to elaborate a more fine-grained conceptual framework of the concept of property; one which contained a set of relationships and one which made it possible to see that various rights could the transferred at different times during a process of change of ownership. The realist redefinition was thus in fact better equipped to matching with the needs of a dynamic market economy than a classical concept formation á la *Begriffsjurisprudenz*.[15]

Ross was famous for his criticism of use of concepts that do not have a reference in reality. He used the word '*Tû-Tû*' to describe such concepts. For him, 'guilt' was one of such metaphysical concepts. When Ross wrote about criminal law, he had already moved more towards analytical philosophy. He reinterpreted the principle of guilt in terms of the opportunity to act otherwise. This has been called the principle of conformity. Together with this move, the significance of language and linguistic analyses grew. It was no longer that important to follow the program of Scandinavian Re-

---

13 This critique was presented by H.L.A. Hart when he wrote the review of the book by Alf Ross. H.L.A.Hart, Scandinavian realism. Cambridge Law Journal, 17(2), pp. 233–240, at p. 237.

14 Cf. Ronald Dworkin, Law's Empire, 1986.

15 Tuori, Kaarlo, Ratio and Voluntas. The Tension Between Reason and Will in Law. Ashgate, 2011, pp. 124–129.

alism and accordingly, even moral and legal expressions could be studied by using the tools of language.[16]

It is rather interesting that even though the Scandinavian Realism faded away, some of its core views have continued living. The idea that criminal law serves the interest of moral education entails a rather different look at how prevention works compared to hard general deterrence. This so-called positive general prevention sees the people as basically law-abiding, and the point of criminal law is to strengthen this attitude. In terms of criminal policy, this approach avoids the risks that failed prevention always motivates harsher criminal punishments. It is no wonder that in the Nordic countries as well as in Germany, for instance, the crime policies have been more moderate than U.K. or U.S. which have witnessed the punitive turn. Even the crime policy approach of the European Union seems to have adopted a somewhat harsher deterrence view than the one based on positive general prevention. [17]

This brings us to the other obvious option for a realist and scientific legal thought, namely, law and economics. In fact most of law and economics studies should rather be placed on the level of legislature than on the level of adjudication. Law and economics scholarships is based on a utilitarian theory that legal rules should contribute to the good of the society. Law and economics also includes some presuppositions concerning how people choose and behave. Individuals are seen as maximizers of their interests, especially economical interests. Behavior of such individuals can again be steered by adding the cost of harmful behavior in order to steer the behavior of individuals towards acting within the limits of what is lawful.

Even this conceptual framework is rather reductionist since it grasps human action only from the point of view of economic interest, and it also presupposes a certain model of rational action which the individuals are suggested to be following in their decision-making. Richard Posner has observed that if only Jeremy Bentham's 'pain and pleasure' -principle be interpreted to mean cost and benefit, Bentham could be seen as having intro-

---

16 Ross, Alf, On Guilt, Responsibility and Punishment. Berkeley and Los Angeles 1975.

17 Cf. Nuotio, Kimmo, A Legitimacy-based Approach to EU Criminal Law: Maybe We Are Getting There, After All. *New Journal of European Criminal Law*, 2020, *11*(1), 20-39. https://doi.org/10.1177/2032284420903386

duced an economical analysis of non-market behavior. This made law and economics possible.[18]

Reductionist approaches seem to lead to over-simplified models of human action. From the point of view of reductionist theories it may not be helpful to try to formulate subtle and fine-grained theories of culpability, for instance, since why would this be needed, if such normative principles do not have any real standing of their own? The entire legal doctrinal work of scholars seems rather redundant and unnecessary, if the law is being regarded in its regulatory function only.

During the last years, interestingly, law and economics has been challenged from the inside. The behavioural sciences have progressed which has led to an important critique of the rational action model which is so central for law and economics. Namely, empirical research has shown that human beings reason very differently from what has been suggested. Human mind reasons mostly rather intuitively and it tends to make systematic errors in exercising its capacities in the actual world. This has led to efforts to rescue the law and economics by adding new insights to it, which merits the name behavioral law and economics.[19] Such corrections may be necessary from a theory-internal point of view, but still, as concerns a full theory of criminal law as we know it, the problem of being far too reductionist stays. Behavioral sciences could and should feed into the legal realism as well since maybe what the courts do is not so rational after all. The various biases that the behavioral sciences have found in human decision-making may be present in the actions of the courts as well. Anyway, this is of course precisely what the argumentation theory seeks to counteract in making sure that the reasoning of the courts would pass a test of intersubjectivity.

This is all the more important if we take into account the so-called linguistic turn. The point is that there is actually no direct entry to the world as facts without involving the means of language. And the way language relates to world as an external point of reference cannot be grasped as if we would produce in the language a model of the real world, a kind of a picture of this real world. There is no way we could check that we have the

---

18 Richard A. Posner, Frontiers of Legal Theory. Harvard University Press, Cambridge 2001, p. 54–55.

19 See, e.g., Russell B. Korobkin, Thomas S. Ulen, Law and Behavioral Science: Removing the Rationality Assumption from Law and Economics, 88 Clif. L. Rev., s. 1051–1144 (2000); Richard H. McAdams, Thomas S. Ulen, Behavioral Criminal Law and Economics, (John M. Olin Program in Law and Economics Working Paper No. 440, 2008).

things right. Therefore a correspondence theory of truth cannot give us definite answers; there is no way we could reach beyond language.

We could also add here a brief note regarding the use of artificial intelligence in (criminal) law. If we look at recent trends in applying artificial intelligence and similar technological tools in reasoning, we face a problem. It might indeed be possible, at least in theory, to replace the courts by machines which could deliver the same quality of end products. But that would presuppose that we were able to formalize all necessary legal reasoning in the form of algorithms. There is a long way to go before we could trust such predictions. It is precisely the quality of legal reasoning which creates trust and accounts for the legitimacy of the entire legal system. The principles of justice themselves need to be articulated.

The legal system is a product of two levels of legal reasoning; we have the levels of law-making and legal adjudication, and we have the level of legal scholarship. Legal scholarship aims at presenting the legal materials in a coherent manner, also explicating the inherent values and principles. This holistic feature renders formalization of what courts do extremely difficult. The task is actually very difficult even for human beings, and that is part of the attraction. The courts need to work to achieve high quality, even if there cannot be any final guarantee that a court ever could reach the best possible solution. The more we understand that the legal system is a construct and that by changing some of the presuppositions within this construction the entire game may change, the more we appreciate legal reasoning. And legal reasoning is also the stepping stone for a critical analysis of law. A critical analysis aims at challenging, either in a particular context, or even more generally, the objectivity of legal knowledge.[20]

Theories of law which would satisfy the requirements of scientific realism would in fact have to be of reductionist nature. As regards criminal law, such an effort seems to risk losing much of the achievements that the elaboration of concepts and principles of penal liability has delivered in terms of coherence and also in terms of a justice perspective. Are we really willing to sacrifice all this just for the sake of meeting criteria set by such sciences which emphasize controllability and empirical nature of legal knowledge? We also need to ask why an empirical approach would be needed. It is only for scientific reasons? We should, namely, be aware of that the Scandinavian Realism was also connected to a social engineering

20 Cf., for instance, the famous work of Martti Koskenniemi, From Apology to Utopia. The Structure of International Legal Argument. Cambridge University Press, Cambridge 2005.

perspective. Knowlegde about practices of law was instrumental – in the true sense oft he word – in running the society. If we believe that criminal law should rather concern something else, if we take it to be a way of organising freedoms in a society and not only suppressing harmful behavior, I believe that we will have to avoid purely instrumental theorising of law and social life.

If we can say that the reductionist theories of law cannot handle criminal law in a way which would account for its inherent values and principles, we need to be searching for other avenues. Could we justify criminal law and criminal law scholarship any other way, as some kind of reconstructed normativity?

This is maybe as good as it gets. Reducing criminal law contents to meet the standards of empirical sciences seems not to work. But maybe we could look at the legal doctrinal work as a practice of explaining and justifying the contents of law in the normative realm? It seems to me that such an effort would not be waste of time since it may be that what we really expect criminal law theorizing to provide is an account of the central principles that stand for its coherence and fairness. If we wish to say, for instance, that the principle of guilt excludes introducing of strict liability as a form of liability in criminal law (according to the criminal law of England and Wales, in fact strict liability applies for so-called regulatory offences), this is a matter of principle. We may wish to discuss and debate what we mean by guilt and culpability in criminal law and what consequences the various concepts and understandings may have, but nevertheless there is no external final point of reference we can point at. All this is a matter of normative reconstruction. Many discussions today are difficult and we just have to work out best possible solutions. In Finland there is some law-drafting underway to scrutiny whether a process for medically assisted suicide should be introduced by issuing new legislation. Not having a regulated procedure causes not only the risk that some people have to suffer more than necessary, and also a possible contributor may face harsh punishment. But again, having a procedure would risk overuse and would bring matters of life and death on the table of human decision-making.

One of the characteristics of science is that it is able to establish at least some sort of controllability of its results. A normative reconstruction of the contents of law is a paradigm which fulfils at least some of such conditions. Accordingly, it will be possible to organize the body of knowledge and present it in a systematic fashion. There will be a point of view of critical assessment and critical insights. In social sciences and humanities much of scholarly activity deals with conceptualizing phenomena. This is what we do. Our conceptual tools and our work with principles enables us to search justice by way of pointing out deficiencies and injustices.

Criminal law scholarship according to continental or Nordic understandings is rather obviously characterized by this systematic nature of the enterprise. One of such features is the aim to present the concept of a crime as an umbrella concept. Accordingly, all general prerequisites of criminal liability could be presented as occupying a place in the structure of crime understood in this meaning of a systematic and coherent totality.

### *3. One step back towards a normative understanding of criminal law*

If we take a look at the case of Finnish criminal law and the scholarly activities in that field, we could see a certain return of the normative approaches. As we mentioned above, 1970's was a time of starting the comprehensive reform of the Penal Code, an effort which was a product of an in-depth critique of the then prevailing views and of the outdated legislation. The ideological premises which the law had been built upon simple had lost much of their credibility. Belief in punishment as treatment had proved illusionary. The new way of thinking about criminal justice built on much more cautious presumptions concerning what criminal law can deliver. The entire area of criminal law had to be reassessed.

The point was, in fact, not so much to criticize criminal law on the basis of the lack of a scientific basis. It was much more the case that the values informing the legislation were outdated. The special part did not represent a modern view of what role criminal law should be given in various fields of life. The views concerning the purposes of punishment were outdated, and the penal sanctions were being used way too easily, without a real consideration of the costs and consequences of running such a system.

1970's saw interesting new phenomena, such as the rise of Marxist critique of criminal justice. That was, in any case, in Finland a rather marginal phenomenon. The legal reforms were in fact supported broadly by the academic community. For the first time not only lawyers but also experts in sociology and legal policy participated in drafting the principles that should guide the work towards the reformed Penal Code.

The reform meant that criminal law was being looked at from new perspectives, especially that of criminal policy. An overall theory of the legitimate aims of criminal policy was created. The biggest difference vis-á-vis the previous thinking was that crime should not be combatted at any cost, but rather criminal policy should be based on realistic expectations. Crime cannot be made disappear. The policy of reacting to criminality needed to be based on sound values and rational principles. We could say that elaboration of such principles was also a scientific effort. Not only was this part of general policy making affecting and informing legal studies, but it could draw on also empirical knowledge from other fields, mainly criminological studies.

If we look at this new contextualization of criminal law scholarship, it certainly changed the landscape. The situation is maybe not all that different than was the case of (West-)Germany, when the local criminal law reform started and the *Alternativentwurf* drafted by the leading professors was presented. For Finland the broader context of criminal policy was even more significant. We should, however, note that for instance in the work of Claus Roxin the role of criminal policy was very significant since he tried to build his doctrinal views on penal liability on the broader criminal policy goals.[21]

If we think about the impact of the big reforms on the so-called general part of the criminal law, and especially on the doctrines of penal liability, the new insights did not change the landscape completely. It seems that even tradition plays a role. These are doctrines that have developed over the years, and there is a constant interplay between the scholarly interpretations and the application in practice. During the 1970's, when the legal policy approach grew important, in Finnish criminal law scholarship rather little interest was addressed to the details of the general doctrines. One could say that the general doctrines remained traditional longer than some other parts of criminal law.

As regards the case of Finnish criminal law scholarship, the textbooks by Brynolf Honkasalo need to be mentioned. He was a scholar who knew very well the German scholarship of the 1920's, and he produced a set of textbooks and commentaries, which remained significant up until 1990's, when new textbooks started to be published. The doctrines presented by Honkasalo continued playing a role since every educated lawyer knew that body of work which therefore influenced heavily the scholarly thinking of all relevant actors in the field. Honkasalo could be characterized as a professor who defended legalistic values during a time when also less legalistic views were present – to put it mildly. Honkasalo was a classical legal scholar who was not much worried about whether what he was presenting was scientific or not. The level of reflection did not reach that deep.

---

21 Roxin, Claus, Kriminalpolitik und Strafrechtssystem. 2. Auflage. Berlin, New York 1973.

A legal tradition has a strange feature that it may grow deeper. As concerns Honkasalo's views, his way of thinking filled in many of the gaps that the legal provisions did not have answers to. The Penal Code of 1889/1894 was rather scarce on rules regarding the general part. Kaarlo Tuori has in his theory of critical legal positivism maintained that the legal phenomena can be looked at on three different levels of law.[22] On the surface level we have the turbulent flow of cases and individual legal decisions as well as the fragments of legal norms. Underneath this level, in turn, we see law as a legal culture, law in the light of legal concepts and general doctrines of law. On the deepest level of law we have the most fundamental constituents of our legal thinking, that is concepts such as legal subjectivity. They are presuppositions of legal thinking and they characterize a certain legal form. Changes on this level are rare, since such shifts might lead us to a completely new epoque.

Tuori's theory of the symbolical-normative levels of law helps us see how tradition works in defining the legal culture. Honkasalo's views were important in the development of this particular aspect of legal culture simple because they represented the dominant way of thinking and theorizing, and in this way, over the years, they grew in importance.

The general part of Finnish Penal Code was reformed in 2004. On that occasion, however, it was not just about codifying existing practice but on some points Honkasalo's views had already lost dominance. We could take the definition of criminal intent as an example. Honkasalo was a proponent of so-called will-theories. The direction of the will of the perpetrator was decisive as far as the intent was concerned. During the 1970's a concurrent model which was called the probability model of intent gained a foothold. Such doctrines were known in other Nordic countries, especially in Denmark and Norway. Since the doctrine of intent is so central when determining penal liability, it was regarded important for reasons of legality principle to formulate the doctrine in written text of law, even though it was known that in most penal codes oft he world one would not have a provision on that.

The new model had been identified by the law reformers, and it had also already some influence on the case law of the Supreme Court of Finland especially in cases in which a drunken person had killed another by stabbing with a knife. Often the perpetrator could not give clear reasons why he had stabbed since maybe the entire group of persons involved had been drinking heavily. From the point of view of bringing evidence on the

22 Tuori, Kaarlo, Critical Legal Positivism. Ashgate, Aldershot 2002.

circumstances it was easier to prove that the perpetrator had regarded the deadly outcome as probable compared to defining the precise direction of the will. In the law reform, a probability concept of intent was finally codified. It only applies, however, with regards intent vis-á-vis the consequences of the action. Later the Supreme Court of Finland has broadened the probability concept to be applied also for intent which refers to a circumstance at hands during the committing of the action.[23]

The legislature was in a way a bit unsure how to handle the situation since it was understood that defining legally the doctrine of intent without a will element might produce strange consequences in some areas other than drunk killings. But the legislature trusted that the Supreme Court will find ways solve the necessary problems. It has been working on these issues quite a lot during the recent years, testing the doctrine and fixing some slight modifications to it. It seems that ultimately the choice of doctrinal lead concepts and principles have to be based on justice considerations, even though other considerations may be relevant as well. As regards criminal intent, even the psychological contents need to be credible.

Thus it seems clear that albeit the forces of tradition play a role, even on the level of legal culture changes may occur and, as in this case, be purposefully introduced. It is no wonder that some of the views held by Honkasalo had to be abandoned since they had been created for a completely different situation. The will-based construction was being regarded too broad in terms of criminal policy reasoning whereas the probability model of intent was better adjusted to the criminal policy reasoning. Anyway, there are some slight indications that even the new model might be need another look.

The Supreme Court dealt with one case in which the accused had twice pulled the trigger of a roller revolver that he had pointed from close distance to the face of another person.[24] There was one bullet in the roller, and the roller had been rolled in between the two events. It was all random so that the gunman did not know whether pulling the trigger would result in a shooting or not. Luckily nothing happened. The Supreme Court dropped the charges concerning an attempted killing since it had been, from the point of view of the gunman, more likely that the shooting would not take place than that it would.

23 Kimmo Nuotio, Todennäköisyystahallisuuden tilasta ja tarinasta, Lakimies 7–8/2017, 970.

24 Supreme Court of Finland, Judgement 2013: 82.

In fact, the probability of a deadly outcome would after two random trials would be roughly 30,6 %; after three random trials 42,1 %, and first after four trials would we cross the line of 50 %, namely it would now be 51,8 %. The probability of a single event is 1 : 6, and the events are not related. Most likely the judgment of the Supreme Court went almost without a notice, since it was a logical application of a settled doctrine. But, we should ask, would the Supreme Court have followed the same line of thought even if the victim had been less lucky and if he or she had been killed in this strange game. This was the question that I raised in the article referred to above. Our intuition becomes much more unsure. Modern psychology even teaches that human minds are not very accurate in assessing probabities. The law-drafters in a way anticipated this when stating that crucial should be an everyday view on probability instead of a mathematical or statistical calculation. This is clearly a wise note, but then we could add another one: do we know then how to apply that probability intent principle? How much progress have we made by adopting the new theory?

In the 1970's the neo-classical school of thought, if we wish to use this name which is only partially fitting, formulated the lead values of criminal justice system very differently from its predecessors. Individual prevention as well as blind retribution or hard general deterrence were abandoned, and a more modest view of what criminal law can deliver was adopted: criminal law should be about communicating blame and blameworthiness. This communication should be understood rather as a symbolical enterprise than a strict way of enforcing these values in a society. Rule of law should prevail, which meant that values of act-proportionality as well as the principles of legality and guilt should be recognized as lead stars.

As for Finland, something very interesting has followed. The constitutional law framework has grown in significance with relation to criminal law. In the 1980's the principle of legality with its four sub-rules or subprinciples mainly only existed as a construction of criminal scholars, a decade later it had the support also on the level of human rights law as well as constitutional law. In 1995, the new bill of rights of the Finnish Constitution entailed a provision on this matter. The wording of it was, as can be expected, rather close to what the European Convention of Human Rights equally provided.

In terms of Tuori's critical legal positivism we should state that the principle of legality gained increasingly institutional support from norms of a constitutional nature, which of course strengthened this principle strongly. From now on the legal doctrinal work had a new task: to explain how the various provisions about the principle of legality in criminal law should be interpreted when applying domestic law in individual cases. Criminal law and constitutional law became closer to another. A normativist reading of these legal materials was needed as the doctrines of legal sources had to be enriched. It would have been a very difficult effort to try to reduce all the relevant normative materials to some predictions á la Scandinavian realism. The heyday of Scandinavian realism had already passed. The weak ambitions of neo-classical ideals became stronger as the novel principles now could be embedded in a constitutional framework.

It may deserve a mention, however, that the same period of time not only meant a sedimentation and victory of neo-classical values, but there were also signs of disruption. Neo-classical thinking had proclaimed a simple system of criminal sanctions which would increase the legal certainty and make the system more transparent. The search for alternatives to punishment together with new models that had been tested in other Nordic countries, the system of punishment was enriched by elements unforeseen in the 1970's. Community service, for instance, was introduced in order to promote the reintegration of the society of the convicted. Anyway, it was not quite simple to find the right place for it in the existing system of punishments. It obviously was a sanction which only could be applied in case where there was a good chance that the convict would be able to serve the sentence in this form. Victim-offender mediation was also a novelty which originally was meant to take place completely in the shadows of law. Later, it was being formalized, however. Victim-offender mediation was a new out-of-court practice which grew out of insights drawing on critical criminology. The system of punishments grew more complex, but this could be regarded as a positive development since it allowed for a more reasonable choice of punishment and determining of the criminal sentence, albeit to some extent at the cost of the values of simplicity and legal certainty.

Constitutionalisation of criminal law is a feature which certainly changes the normative framework somewhat. Norms other than criminal law have to be taken into account. In fact the constitutional provisions usually do not control legal adjudication by giving strict rules, but it is rather a matter of giving normative guidelines. Another even more important feature is that the constitutionalisation of criminal law not only brings constitutional law to the criminal law field, but it also creates a common ground for criminal law scholars and constitutional law scholars. Scholars need to start getting interested in each other's fields, since neither of them can restrict themselves to the relevant provisions only; instead, it is a matter of interpreted provisions, and partly the interpretation is again a product of scholarly work.

Is there any sign here that the science of legal scholarship has progressed? Is the new model of criminal intent scientifically more sound than the old one?

It is not that easy to answer such questions. In some sense the probability model is more realistic than ist predecessor since certainly theorizing about the direction of the will was more strongly founded on metaphysics. One of the targets of the Scandinavian realists was precisely the metaphysical concept building which had a long time been an important part in the German criminal law theorizing.[25] This, of course, is no wonder, since during the 19th century Hegelian thinking was, to give an example, strongly present. There may have been an effort to avoid unnecessary use of metaphysical concepts. Talk about probability could also be more easily be linked with criminal procedure and especially the ways intent could be proven in a concrete case. You might thus interpret this as a step towards more enlightened and scientifically minded theorizing. But, one could almost quite as well just name it an example of a general Nordic pragmatism. The thinkers and actors who were engaged with this issue maybe simply were interested in developing a formula which would be good enough to serve in the daily life of courts and legal practitioners. The concept-formation was being looked at from the point of view of rationality in terms of criminal policy.

If we look at the big picture of the development of Finnish criminal law, we might really see some rather punctual points in which the scientific progress or scientific knowledge have had an influence. But in fact no ground-braking revolutionary reform of the entire body of criminal law knowledge at the same time. Scandinavian realism never really hit the market in Finnish criminal law. This may have been a matter of timing. The Finnish law reforms started far too late. Certainly, Scandinavian legal realism may have inspired some criminal law scholars especially in the 1970's or before that, and maybe this was one of the reasons they were so willing engage with new ideas. But we should not say that what they did was just an application of Scandinavian legal realism. This would be a clear exaggeration.

The question about scientific ideals and how they have been received among circles of criminal law scholars is, however, an interesting point of even more generally. We might think of phenomena such as an almost Darwinist emphasis on biological roots of criminality in the beginning of

25 See, e.g., Kaarlo Tuori, Ratio and Voluntas. The Tension between Reason and Will in Law. Ashgate, Farnham 2011, p. 124–129.

20th century. The sociological school headed by Franz von Liszt gained the support of biologically informed scholars. Von Liszt and Karl Binding were the leading proponents in the *Schulenstreit*, in which von Liszt was arguing for a positivist and utilitarian model of criminal sciences. It looked progressive to seek to protect the society against the threat posed by dangerous criminals, especially the habitual criminals. Special treatment of dangerous recidivists was introduced in Nordic countries; in Finland the legislation entered into force in 1932. Such features which at their own time seemed rational and which in fact really also were based on science of the time, would later look like outdated and in many ways inefficient and harmful ways to react socially on crime. The new social policy -based approach in the 1970's aimed especially at replacing the remains of such old doctrines.

Thus, we should maybe not even seek to purify all criminal law scholarship from materials which cannot be based on science. Instead, we could say that criminal law scholarship has often at least in some ways reflected the general trends of scientific thinking, especially when thinking about the models and ideals adopted.

Finnish criminal law scholarship has maybe not been very strong in reflecting on its own development. Only few sources could be cited which aim at presenting the traditions and storylines of Finnish criminal law scholarship. The criminal law professors have been too busy in doing their daily job.

We could finish by commenting with few words the German criminal law scholarship. German scholarship was especially in the late 19th century an important source for Scandinavian and Finnish criminal law knowledge. The significance of it in fact grew weaker mainly after the world war II, when the anglo-american influence became visible together also with the rise of the social sciences including criminology.

The German criminal law scholarship has, however, continued its work domestically. In the globalized world of today, German criminal law scholarship has found new niches of influence and export. Especially Latin America and Asia have been important regions of academic influence. It has been interesting to note that for instance Japanese scholars often have been trained in German criminal law scholarship so well that they can reproduce even the finest doctrinal achievements of the German elite scholars. Markus Dirk Dubber has claimed that this is a result of longterm conscious effort to export German criminal law thinking by inviting foreign scholars to Germany, to provide language education of them and to support their work to carry the torch further. Textbooks, such as the one by Claus Roxin, have been translated to foreign languages and are being used in teaching lawyers locally.

This phenomenon is interesting in itself since it tells about the power of developed criminal law theorizing. Importing or exporting criminal law doctrine is, however, not quite unproblematic. We might read this as a way of colonizing academic communities by bringing in completely new doctrines, maybe as adjusted to fit the local needs. This is what scholars have always been good at. But what is special about this movement is the sheer volume of the German scholarship. Hundreds of professors have for two hundred years researched criminal law and have over the years worked out a certain conceptual system, the main contours of which they are able to share. This has made it possible to create the "general doctrines" of penal liability.

There is nothing wrong with such an effort. I would, anyway, make an observation concerning the situation now, compared with the one which existed in the $19^{th}$ century. In the Nordic countries quite clearly very few scholars would any longer recognize this sort of superiority of German legal scholarly work. This results from the fact that the Nordic legal orders have created their own traditions. They have continued discussing some of the findings of German criminal law scholarship, but German scholarship operates rather as a point of reference than as a source to be copied and introduced. This fact that a legal culture develops on its own right, on its own terms, could be seen as a sign of maturity. The Nordic criminal law and the Nordic criminal law scholarship are standing on their own feet, finally.

If you wish as a scholar to develop your own doctrinal system of criminal law, how should this happen? Is it best to borrow from more developed legal cultures, or should you work rather towards building something own? This is a very central question. Maybe we should start by stating that borrowing might be a good solution if you can trust that either the doctrinal solutions are universally valid or that they are expressing values and principles which can be shared in both societies. Probably a modern (or post-modern) understanding rather sees doctrinal efforts as not universal, but precisely work in progress.

If we see doctrinal work as work in progress, then we should ask about the drivers of that progress. If I'm right, critique of a doctrine always or almost always in some sense presents itself in terms of academic validity and credibility. Justice problems have always been the drivers when former doctrines have been attacked and new doctrines proposed. I would claim that probably this link to justice considerations is what ties doctrines to the own society and to the perceptions of justice involved. For that reason a mixture of borrowing and developing the own, internalizing the results, may be a way forward. In some articles included in this volume we find interesting remarks concerning how to handle the dilemma.

Accordingly, we could say that the criminal law scholarship seems to be able to contribute to the development of a legal culture which may be national or regional, but most obviously we are not witnessing any strong movement towards a unitary world criminal law doctrine and scholarship. Too many forces are pointing to the other direction. The power of the quality of dogmatic work is not enough in order to lower the borderlines between various legal orders. Criminal law scholarship continues thus to be somehow relativist: it is relative to the needs and challenges of the particular legal and political communities in which the law lives. Harari has written in his *Homo Sapies* about the trend towards unified thought models in the modern societies. Criminal law seems to be one of the areas where we could see increased communication in the scholarly world. It would, however, be premature, to take this to mean that we are moving towards a more universal and unified criminal law doctrine.

### *4. Where to go next?*

In his book on "The Dual Penal State" (2018) Markus Dubber has suggested that we could analyse the criminal law from the point of view of two different modes of government; law and police. The first one takes the liberal legal-political project into account and could be called citizens' criminal law whereas the police mode of governance locates the issues to be dealt with by a prerogative state, as managing objects rather than persons. This second mode comes close to the enemy criminal law, a term coined by Günther Jakobs in Germany.

Dubber's proposal for criminal science is to start with a critical comparative-historical analysis in other to win insights of what the liberal legal-political project has achieved, and even more so, of its failures. What is important in the suggested task for legal science is to dig deeper than just interpretation and systematization; instead, we should reach the level of mode of governance. The idea of using such a critical analyse hangs together with the second part: that we should work towards solving – if possible – this fundamental penal paradox by bringing in the normative expectations created by the liberal legal-political project. This project was started by the Enlightenment and it still is a unifying factor in Western societies. Our problem is, however, that we have never really lived according to the expectations. The point is that we would need a new type of dialogical, transnational science of criminal law, which would focus on these premises and conditions which stands for the legitimacy of state penal police qua law, as law.[26]

Dubber's work is an anti-thesis of a thesis which would seek to reduce criminal law and the scholarship around it to any science in the strict sense. According to his analysis the involvement of a scientific approach has rather often derailed the project of criminal law from its liberal legal-political premises. The fundamental questions concerning the legitimacy of law, and in fact, use of penal power, cannot be easily met by strictly scientific tools. Not even the criminal law doctrines would always be enough to grant this legitimacy to the use of penal power, since even scholars have contributed to the emergence of enemy criminal law by proposing norms and systematizing them.

The question of what really counts as science is thus worth asking. Maybe we should not be too strict in limiting ourselves since otherwise the obvious risk is that we lose something important, or even the most important content. The choice of methods also depends rather obviously on what we are aiming at doing. Are we the critics, and with reconstructing, what do we do, actually? I would be especially cautious in adopting reductionist methodologies which measure the law from the point of view of another rationality. It seems that certain questions are especially inviting new scientific approaches, namely questions for which you do not have answers in law. Think about the release on parole from a life sentence. Or other similar instances in which the legal rules require assessment of risk of reoffending. How can we tell that?

We can use medical understandings, or we could play with statistical data, we can fill in the gap with any relevant knowledge. But predicting human behavior is a very different task than judging acts already committed. A citizen's criminal law seeks to reduce precisely those points in which the law has very little to say and human action is being regarded from another angle, that of taking the person as an object, as a risk factor, and not as a citizen, a person with a capability to commit to law, should he or she so wish. Sometimes the shift of perspective is only a small one. But this shift means a lot in terms of what kind of law we are talking about.

26 Dubber, Markus Dirk, The Dual Penal State. The Crisis of Criminal Law in Comparative-Historical Perspective. Oxford University Press, Oxford 2018. Cf. Nuotio, Kimmo, The Dual Penal State á la Markus Dirk Dubber. Bergen Journal of Criminal Law and Criminal Justice, vol. 6, no. 2 (2018) , pp. 178-187. https://doi.org/10.15845/bjclcj.v6i2.2723.

Thus, the way we define the limits of science in criminal law scholarship has an impact on what we are studying, in fact. And even more: we may mean different matters with criminal law. I believe we should try to be clear about what we believe we should be doing when engaging in criminal law scholarship or criminal law science. There may be situations in which a more critical approach is being called for, and situations and times where and when more reconstruction is needed. Criminal law scholars have the advantage that they can make use of all the various methods and approaches that are generally available in legal studies. Criminal law is also the field where there is a long tradition of interdisciplinary and multi-disciplinary approaches. Thinking in alternatives and learning from others always remains an option.

# How Can Legal Doctrine be a Scientific Discipline? Methodological Groundworks for the Norwegian Criminal Law Doctrine

*Jørn Jacobsen*[*]

## 1 *Introduction*

Can legal doctrine, i.e. the exposition of rules, principles, and concepts of positive law, be a science, and if so, how?[1] This *justification challenge*, despite the many advanced attempts at dealing with it, has haunted the discipline for a long time.[2] It affects, given legal doctrine's central place within it, the entire idea of a legal science. Furthermore, even if the justification challenge applies to doctrinal studies of all legal fields, it is, as we will see, a particular challenge for the criminal law doctrine. Still, legal doctrine can be defended as a scientific discipline, but only if it deals with positive law from a specific knowledge perspective.

To explain how, we must (logically) work our way through three issues. First, as any specie must conform to its genus in order to be a specie of the

---

* Jørn Jacobsen, Professor, Faculty of Law, University of Bergen, Norway. I have benefited from many discussions with colleagues on the subject, all of whom I am grateful to, not least to prof. Alex Sarch (Surrey) for his very thorough reading and commenting on the article.

1 This preliminary definition is inspired by, but simplified compared to the one found in Jan M. Smits, 'What is legal doctrine? On The Aims and Methods in Legal-Dogmatic Research', in Rob van Gestel, Hans-W Micklitz, and Edward L. Rubin (eds.), *Rethinking Legal Scholarship – A Transnational Dialogue* (CUP 2017) pp. 207–228, p. 210. The expression 'legal doctrine' is not too common in English, where 'jurisprudence' or 'legal doctrinal scholarship' are more familiar. At least the latter well reflects the subject of this article. I have still opted for the bit simpler 'legal doctrine', which also is more in line with Continental phrasing (see e.g. Mark van Hoecke and François Ost, 'Legal doctrine in crisis: towards a European legal science' (1998) 18 Legal studies 197). Another alternative is 'legal dogmatics', corresponding to the well-used Norwegian *rettsdogmatikk*, German *Rechtsdogmatik* and so forth. The term 'dogma' has however too strong references to the opposite of scientific reasoning (see below), so this is not preferred.

2 See also e.g. Jan C. Schuhr, *Rechtsdogmatik als Wissenschaft: Rechtliche Theorien und Modelle* (Duncker & Humblot, 2006), p. 19.

relevant kind, we must clarify the *concept of science.*[3] Second, to understand the character of law as a candidate for a scientific study, we must look into the *concept of law*. Here, in line with the aim of legal doctrine, we will focus on the (meaning of the) *rules* of law, and not for instance legal practices from a sociological point of view. And finally, we must apply the general standards of science to the specific character of law to be able to justify legal doctrine as a scientific discipline.[4]

The aim of this article is first and foremost to outline a viable alternative to the traditional style of Norwegian criminal law doctrine, which thereby provides the entrance point for the article (sect. 2). The article proceeds to the concept of science (sect. 3) and the concept of law (sect. 4), which together will lead us to a more detailed examination of the specific character of legal doctrine's justification challenge (sect. 5). Thereafter a response is offered, one which emphasises the *dual citizenship* of legal doctrine, as it engages intimately *with* law *as* a science (sect 6).[5] A response to the justification issue does not give answers to all issues relating to legal doctrine, its role, character, and functions, today. At the end, however, the question will be raised whether the development of law and society call on us to turn our attention to other forms of research in law (sect. 7).

## 2 *Aim and Actuality*

Norwegian criminal law scholarship has been dominated by a pragmatic, anti-intellectual style of reasoning. It's founder, Anton M. Schweigaard, turned against the Kantian and Hegelian German philosophy and legal science in the mid 1800's, favouring a pragmatic, utilitarian, and positivistic style of reasoning.[6] His successor, Francis Hagerup, criticised this ap-

---

3 As we will return to, the term 'science' is not considered as limited to the natural sciences, see also e.g. Paul Hoyningen-Huene, 'Systematicity: The Nature of Science' (2008) Vol 36 Philosophia <DOI 10.1007/s11406–007–9100-x> accessed 19.05.2020 p. 168.

4 See also e.g. Arthur Kaufmann, 'Über die Wissenschaftlichkeit der Rechtswissenschaft: Ansätze zu einer Konvergenztheorie der Wahrheit' (1986) Vol. 72 Archiv für Rechts- und Sozialphilosophie 425, p. 427.

5 Emphasised also by Kaarlo Tuori, *Ratio and Voluntas: The Tension between Reason and Will in Law* (Routledge, 2011) p. xiii.

6 For an historical outline, see Jørn Jacobsen, 'The Methodology of the Norwegian Criminal Law Doctrine', in Thomas Elholm *et.al.* (eds.), *Liber amicarum et amicorum Karin Cornils – Glimt af nordisk straffrätt og straffeprosessrett* (DJØF, 2010), pp. 243–266.

proach, most importantly because of its lack of basis in a proper theory of science, and emphasised the importance of theoretical perspectives as found for instance in the works of German scholars such as Savigny, Ihering and Liszt.[7] Still, Schweigaard's approach, in the style of Johs. Andenæs, came to dominate the 20th century, not least through his influential outline of the general part of criminal law.[8] His approach implied a firm rejection of theory, a strong focus on (the reasoning of) court practice as the preferred mode also of legal science, and a fluid selection and balancing of arguments, unclear blends of value considerations and instrumental reasoning included. The opportunity to grow into a mature scientific discipline offered by Hagerup's engagement with the justification challenge, was not picked up on.

Rightly so, to bring legal science in line with the concept of science was a central ambition to Alf Ross and his legal realism and prognosis theory.[9] Legal realism cannot however be seen as a theoretically more clear-cut explanation or founding of the traditional Norwegian criminal law doctrine. Despite overlap in time with Andenæs and his sweeping recognition of Ross' ideas, the differences are clear. Ross' legal realism seems for Andenæs most of all as a 'buffer' with two 'benefits': as a convenient response to the justification challenge and, given Ross' non-cognitivism, an excuse for omitting further investigations into the normative principles of criminal law. Beyond this, Ross' legal realism seems not to have had much impact on Andenæs.[10] His enterprise is rather a kind of pure pragmatism, which does not see any need to theoretically justify itself in the way philosophical pragmatists often do.[11]

---

7 Cfr. Francis Hagerup, 'Nogle Ord om den nyere Retsvidenskabs Karakter', *Tidsskrift for Retsvidenskab* (1888) pp. 1–55, p. 3 ff. See further Jørn Jacobsen, *Hagerup og den strafferettslege ansvarslæra* (Fagbokforlaget 2017).

8 Johs. Andenæs, *Alminnelig strafferett* (Universitetsforlaget, six eds. 1956–2016 of which two after his death in 2003). See further Jørn Jacobsen, 'Zur gegenwärtigen norwegischen Strafrechtsdogmatik: Andenæs und die Folgen' (2011) Zeitschrift für die gesamte Strafrechtswissenschaft 609.

9 See Alf Ross, *Om ret og retfærdighed – En indførelse i den analytiske retsfilosofi* (Nyt Nordisk Forlag – Arnold Busck 1966) pp. 53 ff, and further, e.g. Henrik Zahle, 'Legal Doctrine between Empirical and Rhetorical Truth. A Critical Analysis of Alf Ross' Conception of Legal Doctrine' (2003) Vol 14 (4) EJIL 801.

10 So also in Nordic legal science more generally, cfr. Zahle (n 9) p. 814.

11 Andenæs's approach may thereby have more in common with American realism, but also here differences apply, such as Andenæs' rejection of a clear-cut instrumentalist approach to law. See also Tuori (n 5) p. 111.

Anyway, as we will return to, legal realism is not a proper solution to the justification issue, so the justification challenge is still a task for contemporary legal doctrine.[12] It is also particularly pressing today. As we will return to, the contemporary development of law challenges the relation between law and legal science. Legal doctrine is also challenged from within legal science. As gradually becoming less hegemonic within legal science it 'seems inevitable that legal doctrine must search for new foundations if it wants to compete with newer types of research in law'.[13]

### *3 Starting Point: The Concept of Science*

The nature of science is the subject for the philosophy (or theory) of science, which seeks to discuss and justify science as a distinct and reliable form of knowledge production.[14] Additionally, the history and sociology of science, which describes and explains how science historically has evolved and explores it as being a distinct social field, contribute to our understanding.[15] A comprehensive theory of science should engage all of these. However, to get started, elaborating some essential characteristics of science is helpful.

a) It is a crucial premise for the following line of reasoning that science is a *distinct form of knowledge production*.[16] Science is the systematic and comprehensive study of what we (can) know about a subject, whether this

---

12 Contemporary Norwegian legal theory offers however alternatives, see e.g. Hans Petter Graver, 'Rettsforskningens oppgaver og rettsvitenskapens autonomi' (2011) 124 Tidsskrift for Rettsvitenskap 230, see also e.g. Synne Sæther Mæhle, 'Gjelder det andre regler for rettslig argumentasjon i rettsdogmatikken enn for domstolene?' (2004) 34 Jussens venner 329. Differences from the approach in this article seem to relate first and foremost to (implications of) different underlying conceptions of rationality.

13 Smits (n 1), pp. 227–228.

14 See e.g. Gerhard Schurz, *Einführung in die Wissenschaftstheorie*, 4. Aufgabe (WBG 2014) and Søren Harnov Klausen, *Hvad er videnskabsteori?* (Akademisk Forlag, 2005).

15 See e.g. Peter Weingart, *Wissenschaftssoziologie* (Transcript, 2003).

16 This also provides the starting point for e.g. Hoyningen-Huene (n 3) p. 168. As we will return to, the theory of science is for this reason intimately connected to epistemology. This reflects itself in theories of science often being one aspect of comprehensive philosophical projects, with epistemology at its apex. See for instance for Kant's part, e.g. Thomas Sturm, *Kant und die Wissenschaften vom Menschen* (Mentis 2009) p. 129, here with a particular view to his empirical science of humanity.

is the planets, biology, human behaviour or other subjects. Scientific knowledge differs from both unsecure *beliefs and opinions* of the kind that we all have about a series of subjects and from other types of *knowledge* that we have without having a profound, general, and systematic explanation of the relevant subject. Whereas I have certain beliefs and opinions about national politics, based on information from the media and so on, I have (unless I am a political scientist) no comprehensive understanding of politics, i.e. a theoretical basis and a broader set of empirical data, to analyse national politics. And whereas I know (intuitively) *that* I write this article on my laptop, I have no comprehensive understanding of *how* this is possible, i.e. of how a computer works and so forth. Science starts out from the recognition that many issues are quite complex and hence difficult to grasp. So, opposed to rash judgement of the kind that we all, partly for functional reasons, partly for laziness, have a strong tendency to make in everyday life, science is supposed to give us *a better and broader picture*, as we presuppose that the more effort and dedication we put into understanding a certain object, the better we will understand it. The latter point reminds us of how we as individuals, through our ability to reason (theoretically or practically), can *understand* something that we put effort in inquiring. In line with this, we can usefully describe science, being a public project (organised in publicly regulated and funded institutions, accessible by merit etc.), as the way we have *socially institutionalised* the capacity for reason that each of us possess. We will return to science being a collective project below.

b) Science is *critical* in the sense of scrutinizing opinions, dogmas, and power. A general feature of human thinking and beliefs is that we often are wrong.[17] Due not least to our mentioned inclination to rash judgements, our understanding of the world is limited and opinions we hold often prove to be erroneous, or at least in need for revisions, nuances, etc. To a large extent, our beliefs and our practical decisions are results of tradition, cultures, dogmas, limited (group or individual) perspectives and interests, power, lack of investigation, and so forth. Science for its part aims to avoid the inherent limitations of such opinions, to subject them to scrutiny, to look for alternative ways at looking at them, and so on, with the view of deciding which opinions are valid and which are not.[18] This

17 See on the following also Hoyningen-Huene (n 3) p. 174.

18 In this way, we apply the term 'critical' in a Kantian, not radical *Critical Legal Studies*-style. On critique, see Christoffer C. Eriksen, *Kritikk – Konfrontasjoner med rett og makt* (Universitetsforlaget, 2016).

requires a *critical* and *impartial* approach. The political scientist who wants to study national politics, for instance, will take care not only to read left- or right-wing media's reports and will be reluctant to be (too) engaged in the discussions of the kind that he or she is supposed to study, as this easily will have a negative impact on how the same individual will describe the debates.

This critical aspect of science is intimately related to science's commitment to *reason* as its authority. Viewpoints and opinions, no matter whose, can always be subject to critique and judged upon by their ability to *convince* the scientific community by their reasons, not by their stamina. One way to express science's critical commitment to reason, which will be helpful when we approach law, is to say that science is committed to *an open rationality*: By 'open', as opposed to a 'bounded' rationality, I imply that it is reason alone that ultimately decides on the validity of a certain claim, no other (more limited) standard. However, human reason is not 'free' in a relativistic sense. That would dissolve the very notion of reason. Reason is subject to, justified, and limited, (only) by its own principles.[19] From a *sociological* point of view, science may not be this kind of institutionalised open rationality.[20] However, even if power structures, incompetence, gender discrimination, and more, appear also within science, such features never work as justifications and legitimate arguments within the field.

c) To develop and apply reliable *methods* are essential for science. When we, as fallible adjudicators, seek to understand the complexity of a subject, for instance whether regular use of hashish significantly damages the brain, we cannot easily decide on the matter. Given the critical approach, the set of premises required and the many pitfalls that should be avoided, it is essential to have a reliable way to go about. This has two dimensions: (the use of) methods are required to achieve the *optimal understanding* of the given subject at stake and to allow for *controlling the validity* of the study and its results. These aims are intimately intertwined. Controlling

---

19 A Kantian conception of rationality is thereby indicated. For an elaboration and demonstration of the contemporary relevance of Kantian philosophy in this regard, see Otfried Höffe, *Kant's Critique of Pure Reason – The Foundation of Modern Philosophy* (Springer, 2009). In line with this, the interplay between *Verstand* and *Vernunft* is essential, see e.g. Kaufmann (n 4) p. 428 flg. Building on Kant, Kaufmann emphasises the importance of the latter, conceived as 'Begriff freier Argumentation' (p. 429).

20 See Jørn Jacobsen, 'Rettsvitskapssosiologi – ei spire', in Karl Harald Søvig *et al.* (eds.), *Undring og erkjennelse: Festskrift til Jan Fridthjof Bernt 70 år* (Fagbokforlaget, 2013) pp. 267–278.

the results gives us (additional) reason to hold the outcome of the study as valid.

In regard to the first aim of the method, the optimal understanding, different scientific subjects require different methods, (basically) either *analytical*, as in at least certain essential dimensions of conceptual investigations; *empirical*, as in studies of the nature of the corona virus; or *normative*, as in whether it is right to shoot down an aircraft hijacked by terrorists. It is therefore not possible to speak, at least not in a specific sense, of *the* scientific method.[21] Rather, it is a basic task (one that this article is engaged) for each scientific discipline to develop valid methodological approaches to their respective subjects that both satisfies general scientific standards and are sufficiently adapted to the relevant subject.[22] This need for specialised methods is not only due to the differences between analytical, empirical, and normative investigations. Moral philosophy and legal doctrine may, as we will return to, both work with normative issues, but to study the principles of morals and positive law easily face different challenges, which their methods also must respond to.[23] It follows that the approach advocated here does not limit science to empirical knowledge. Even if the abilities and successes of the empirical sciences are well-worth cherishing, for reasons described below, this is an unwarranted limitation on the project of science.

In regard to control of the results, the second aim of the scientific method, this is another outcome of the critical approach in science: Even if one scientist applies an acknowledged method, this is still no guarantee for the correctness of the outcome. This can be erroneous for several reasons, such as not representative data or misinterpretation of the data by the scientist. Scientists are humans too, and hence prone to make mistakes. For that reason, it is essential that the study can be documented, is transparent, can be reproduced, and critically scrutinized by others. We will return to this when we address science's collective dimension.

---

21 See also e.g. Hoyningen-Huene (n 3) pp. 170–171 on 'the unity of science'.

22 It follows that I am skeptical towards to claiming that the scientific founding of a discipline must be justified *either* by reference to its subject or to the methods applied, see e.g. Christoph-Eric Mecke, 'Objektivität in Recht und Rechtswissenschaft bei G. F. Puchta und R. v. Jhering' (2008) Vol 94 Archiv für Rechts- und Sozialphilosophie 147, p. 148. These are too intertwined to be presented as alternative routes to go about.

23 The challenges to studies of positive law will be further elaborated in sect. 5 in particular.

Furthermore, even if correctly applied, it may be that the scientific method itself, even if generally acknowledged within the scientific community, proves to be flawed. For that reason, a continuous debate on the methods of science, *i.e.* a meta-discussion where methodologically deficiencies in contemporary knowledge production are identified and sought dealt with, is essential. Science should in other words be *methodologically self-reflexive*.

d) A general aspect of science (as in all other human knowledge production) is that we cannot gain knowledge without engaging concepts. Kant's philosophy makes it clear to us how we are actively involved in the construction of the reality we experience.[24] Appearances must be fused with (our own) concepts and systematically arranged by means of the latter, including higher-order concepts. Reason ordains a *unified and systematic* structure on how we may grasp the world.[25] The further elaboration of this system is essential to arrive at a comprehensive understanding of a subject, which typically requires theoretical work to be done. All scientific disciplines, the empirical ones included, depend on conceptual and hence theoretical starting points that we are the authors of. Ultimately, science depends on philosophy.[26] Furthermore, reason does not allow us (normatively) to hold conflicting opinions on the same subject in different regions of our thinking. As several intellectual fields are intertwined, in the way for instance psychology relates to (conceptions of) the biological construction of the brain, consistency and coherence becomes essential.[27] In this sense, science can be considered as a *web of (well-founded) beliefs*, where one premise relates closely to another in a large system.[28]

---

24 A central idea in Immanuel Kant, *Kritik der reinen Vernunft* (Riga 1781/1787), in *Immanuel Kant, Werke in Sechs Bänden, Herausgeben von Wilhelm Weischedel*, Band II, see also e.g. Höffe (n 19) and Schuhr (n 2) p. 25.

25 For this reason, systematicity is often found as a key notion in definitions of science, see e.g. Kant (1781/1787) A 832/B 860 ff. (for an exposition, Sturm (n 16), pp. 129–182), and, more recently, Hoyningen-Huene (n 3).

26 Whether philosophy is a science or a presupposition for science, is debated, but given the conception of science that the position sketched here builds upon, philosophy – logics in particular – is an integral element of science, as in human reasoning in general. The concept of logic is in this regard by no means simple, see regarding Kant, Huaping Lu-Adler, *Kant and the Science of Logic – A Historical and Philosophical Reconstruction* (OUP 2018).

27 On the difference between consistency and coherence, see e.g. Tuori (n 5) pp. 151–152.

28 The notion of a 'web of belief' is drawn from Quine, but no further link is intended. Another reservation may be in place: A strong preference for a coherence theory of truth is neither intended.

This description applies both to the specific disciplines and within science at large.[29] This is notable to our line of reasoning: Within the web of science, the different scientific disciplines (sociology, medical science, anthropology etc.) are the dominant areas, that are (or at least can be) spun together into a whole by their underlying theoretical assumptions and philosophical starting points. Law for its part is, as we will get back to, a distinct thread in this regard, as it is so intimately involved in the way we structure society and, in that way, engages with so much of what we (not least through other scientific disciplines) claim to know about the world.

e) It follows that science is an extensive enterprise, which includes different exercises, such as collection of data, studies of specific subjects, elaboration of methods and overarching theoretical frameworks, and critical exchanges and double-checking. Contemporary science would therefore not be possible if not as a collective project. Different scientists contribute with different pieces to the puzzle, new generations stand on the shoulders of previous generations, both to learn from insights won, but also to gain new ones. This is partly a practical issue, as none of us have time to cover it all, and a matter of efficiency – why invent the wheel all the time? It also relates to what we may term the limited horizons of experience that each of us has. Rational thought implies a fusion of concepts and empirical impressions. As each of us has an individual and limited empirical basis for our reasoning, engaging with others to grasp other aspects and insight, is essential. The emphasis on this in Kant's concept of rationality is seen in the second of his criteria for rationality, that also capture the basics of science, i.e. '1. Selbst denken. 2. Sich (in der Mitteilung mit Menschen) in der Stelle jedes anderen zu denken. 3. Jederzeit mit sich selbst einstimmig zu denken.'[30]

## 4 *Engaging the Concept of Law*

Now we turn to law, the subject for legal doctrinal studies. Law is a complex phenomenon, which can be described in different manners and is

---

29 See e.g. Sturm (n 16) pp. 135–182 on the 'inner' and 'outer' systematicity in Kant's concept of science.

30 Immanuel Kant, *Anthropologie in pragmatischer Hinsicht* (1798/1800), BA 166, quoted from *Immanuel Kant, Werke in Sechs Bänden, Herausgeben von Wilhelm Weischedel*, Band VI, p. 549.

subject to an extensive (legal) philosophical discussion.[31] However, a starting point that may allow us here to juxtapose (but not to turn a blind eye to) this extensive philosophical discussion, is that law can be viewed as both a rule system, a power system and a meaning system. Of these, law being a *rule system* is likely to be taken as the primary. The basic aim of law is to regulate human conduct through public rules. The rules of law are, opposite to the laws of nature, practical, and tell individuals what to do in public relevant situations (i.e. as narrower domain than morality, which ultimately is an all-encompassing and personal matter). Legal rules may origin from decisions by a legislator or in other way be authorised or acknowledged as a part of the legal order (ultimately by reference to a constitution). Legal rules are most usually paired with sanctions. Simplified, whereas the constitutional stamina of and the substantial justification of the legal rule give it *normative* authority, the possibility for sanctions gives the citizen additional *strategic* reasons for respecting the rule. The last point connects to law as a *system of power*. Legal sanctions imply use of power, criminal law being the most clear-cut example. Criminal law represents hard treatment of individuals, typically in terms of arrest and detention, public prosecution, and deprivation of freedom through incarceration as punishment.

It is very much this combination of a) rules that b) have a certain normative authority and c) is supported by the power system that a political order is related to, that give legal rules their distinct character – this is the *abc* of law. However, to grasp the nature of specific fields or institutes of the law, such as criminal law, we will have to add to this.[32] Criminal law for instance, has specific functions in regard to securing individual freedom, by defining crimes and delivering public blame for crimes that are committed.[33] Several questions remain however unanswered, such as: What is the nature and justification of the authority of law? And, to clarify the stamina of the legal rule is one thing, to clarify the *content* of it is often a far more difficult matter. Even in criminal law, where the principle of legality aims to secure legal certainty for the citizen by requiring accessible

---

31 See e.g. Sean Coyle, *Modern Jurisprudence – A Philosophical Guide* (2nd ed, Hart Publishing, 2017).

32 I differ between institutes (e.g. criminal law) and institutions (e.g. the court). See here e.g. Neil MacCormick, *Institutions of Law – An Essay in Legal Theory* (OUP 2007) p. 12–14.

33 See e.g. Linda Gröning, Erling Johannes Husabø and Jørn Jacobsen, *Frihet, forbrytelse og straff – En systematisk fremstilling av norsk strafferett* (Fagbokforlaget 2019) pp. 1–55.

rules, positive legal rules are in many cases unclear and in need of interpretation. This is a central task for lawyers. Their interpretation, in line with the acknowledged *legal method*, secures that the legal rule is adequately and uniformly understood within the legal order.[34] This brings us to a central point for this article: In particular this method makes law a kind of *bounded* rationality. Law is a specific norm system where there are distinct argumentation rules, authoritative judgements, and institutions for making such judgements, premises that other participants in the legal system must acknowledge to be part of the system. A central aspect of this bounded rationality is that objections such as 'this legislation is not fair', 'this is not how things are in real life', and so on, can be disregarded in daily legal work. The nature and necessity of law as a bounded rationality was aptly captured by Kant:[35]

> The jurist, as an authority of the text, does not look to his reason for the laws that secure the *Mine* and *Thine*, but to the code of laws that has been publicly promulgated and sanctioned by the highest authority (if, as he should, he acts as a civil servant). To require him to prove the truth of these laws and their conformity with right, or to defend them against reason's objections, would be unfair. For these decrees first determine what is right, and the jurist must straightaway dismiss as nonsense the further question of whether the decrees themselves are right. To refuse to obey an external or supreme will on the grounds that it allegedly does not conform with reason would be absurd; for the dignity of government consists precisely in this: that it does not leave its subjects free to judge what is right or wrong according to their own notions but [determines right and wrong] for them by precepts of the legislative power.

However, one should not exaggerate how much bounded this bounded rationality can be. First, even if law is a bounded rationality, it is still open to the *perspective* of the open rationality. We can shift perspective from considering *which* rules that *do* regulate our conduct to trying to *understand* these rules. Then we ask not which rules that regulate our (or others) con-

---

34 See Jørn Jacobsen, 'Det strafferettslege lovskravet i eit metodeperspektiv', in Alf Petter Høgberg and Jørn Øyrehagen Sunde (eds.), *Juridisk metode og tenkemåte* (Universitetsforlaget 2019), pp. 527–561.

35 For the sake of accessibility, I here quote the English translation found in Immanuel Kant, *The Conflicts of the Faculties* [1798] (Mary J. Gregor tr, University of Nebraska Press, 1992). pp. 37–39. A German version accompanies the translation there.

duct, but rather questions such as: Does this rule make sense? Why is there this kind of rule? What is the historical background for this rule? Which factual considerations does it rest upon? What value considerations does it reflect? Is it justifiable from a moral point of view? Is it respected by citizens and upheld by law enforces? By means of such questions, that can be asked by for instance historians, philosophers, sociologists, legal scholars, and even the regular citizen, we try to *understand* this norm and its place in the legal order.

We can also go a step further. To be a *bounded* rationality, this must have the (minimum) characteristics of rationality in the first place.[36] Legal reasoning must, to be comprehensible, conform to basic rationality standards, such as the principle of non-contradiction. Furthermore, the identification of a rule as part of positive law requires in itself a certain pre-understanding of positive law, its character, and the problems it responds to, i.e. general features that cannot be understood through the individual legal rules, but are rather presupposed by them. Also, the interpretation of positive law is in many cases a complex operation which includes for instance drawing on and balancing values. In this regard, different conceptions of the legal method may have different answers to offer regarding the extent to which for instance value considerations are legitimate aspects of legal reasoning, so that different conceptions of the legal method may imply different (broader or narrower) overlaps between the bounded and the open rationality. However, none seem to draw the line very clear-cut and narrowly, and hence is open to considerations that often require a broader perspective on positive law to be applied.[37] Such specific connection points between the bounded and open rationality reflect that law's role in society could neither be justified or well-functioning if law's bounded rationality was in itself not at some level comprehensible from the open rationality point of view.

How to more precisely capture the general (open) rationality features that can be found in law as a bounded rationality is however a complex issue which we will return to. However, regardless of the (for now at least) unclear borderline between bounded and the open rationality, the central

---

36 Cfr. also e.g. Alexy's discourse theoretical approach to law, where law is considered a 'Sonderfall' of the general rational discourse, e.g. Robert Alexy, *Theorie der juristischen Argumentation: Die Theorie des rationalen Diskurses als Theorie der juristischen Begründung* (Suhrkamp 1978) pp. 263 f.

37 The nature of the 'legal method' is debate in legal theory, also in Norway, see for an overview and comment to the discussion, Erik Magnus Boe, *Rettskildelære under debatt* (Universitetsforlaget 2012).

point is that for the citizen, the depth of understanding *need not* be deeper than being able to adopt his or her conduct to the norm. The lawyer, on the other hand, do not *need* to go further than what is needed to establish the content of the legal rule. This practical point of view may thereby let for instance the history of the rule be unexplained. Nor is for instance a theory of negligence of much importance to the judge, once the case can be settled according to positive law. To the legal scholar, however, with one foot in the bounded rationality and one in the open, the matter is more complex.[38] To see why, we should say more on why the bounded rationality of law is a challenge to legal doctrine as a scientific discipline.

## *5 More on Legal Doctrine' Justification Challenge*

The requirements of science do not pose specific challenges to most of legal science's subdisciplines. A legal philosophical elaboration of for instance the concept of justice may challenge viewpoints in positive law, without this being a relevant objection to the study. For a legal historian, the project is to understand law's historical background and development. In pursuing this research interest, the legal historian can draw on a methodological toolbox developed within history science, similar to the way that the legal sociologist may draw on sociology's methodological debates. These may not be free from their own methodological challenges and not necessarily immediately applicable to the studies of *legal* history or sociology, but are still properly anchored in methodological viewpoints that originate from the outside of (and hence not limited by) law's bounded rationality.

For *legal doctrine*, however, the open rationality point-of-view is more of a challenge, as legal doctrine appears to be much more intimately connected to the bounded rationality point of view of law to grasp its very subject of the study. The main problem is that by engaging so closely with the bounded rationality of law, legal doctrine may end up attributing an unwarranted scientific status to positive law, as many critics have pointed to. This appears for instance to be the essence of the German lawyer and philosopher Julius von Kirchmann much-quoted critique, that while the 'sun, moon and stars shine like centuries ago, and the rose is blossoming like in paradise', law is different and more like a wanderer in the desert, as

38 So also to the legislator, whose main task basically is to exchange the public open rationality (via the political domain) into the bounded rationality of law.

'[t]hree words changed by the law-maker may render entire libraries useless'.[39]

It is helpful to elaborate on this critique, which even if we do not agree on all points, may help us to sharpen this important challenge even more.[40] Law, it can be claimed, is a contingent phenomenon, as it to such a large extent depends on *decisions* made by (first and foremost) legislators or judges. Thereby, law, despite its deep structures, does not show the stable character that warrant scientific accounts of it. Human laws are too much shifting, both in time and in space, reflecting that law is politics, and politics is power. Hence, law is inherently influenced by interest, and interests are not necessarily limited by rational deliberation. Utmost, this implies that the status which science generally earns by its commitment to the open rationality, becomes hostage to the decisions of power holders. Legal doctrine becomes not a servant of science, but of power, as it cannot avoid subjecting itself to the bounded rationality. We face the dilemma of the social anthropologist: Either, describe social practices from distance, but then without being able to grasp the meaning of it, or take part in the practice as a participant and thereby grasp the meaning of it, but also lose your scientific objectivity. To this we can add human vanity and weakness to power: That fact that legal scholars so highly value to be quoted by the Supreme Court or to be assigned to legislation says all about which, power or science, that is the strongest. In the next step, the legal doctrine itself fulfils several functions within the legal order and hence reinforces this power system, for instance by producing influential legal interpretations and convincing law students of the 'rationality' of the power system they are about to be socialised into.[41] Legal doctrine's combination of engagement in law, with its inherent symbolic blend of authority, justice and power, and science, with correspondingly strong references to wisdom and truth, makes it a perilous enterprise.

---

39 Translation is from Mathias M. Siems, 'The Taxonomy of Interdisciplinary Legal Research: Finding the Way Out of the Desert' (2009) 7:1 Journal of Commonwealth Law and Legal Education <DOI:10.1080/14760400903195090> accessed 06.07.20 p. 5. German original in Julius von Kirchmann, *Die Werthlosigkeit der Jurisprudenz als Wissenschaft: Ein Vortrag gehalten in der Juristischen Gesellschaft zu Berlin* (Julius Springer 1848).

40 I here emphasise those lines of critique most relevant to our subject, see however also e.g. Smits (n 1) p. 209.

41 See e.g. Nils Jansen, 'Making Doctrine for European Law', in Gestel, Micklitz, Rubin (2017), pp. 229–261, p. 234–239. That legal doctrine 'is even *constitutive* of its object' (p. 233) is however to overstate the point.

Critical viewpoints like these are not fully unwarranted. Law is far from perfect. Legal rules may be irrational, unwise, incoherent, and/or unfair, as both historical and contemporary criminal justice systems too often illustrate. Social acceleration, specialisation, internationalisation, and more, provide difficulties to both legislation and legal practice.[42] Societal challenges such as the war on terrorism have made most civilised legal orders extend their criminal law often far beyond what can be justified by (decent conceptions of) the threat of terrorism and rule of law-principles. The war on drugs is another example. But even at more specific points, contemporary criminal law should raise some eyebrows, as we will get back to. So far and generally: The justification challenge is particularly pressing for criminal law scholarship, given the blend of criminal law's symbolic societal importance, intrusion into the lives of individuals, and extensive history of injustice and political misuse. Legal doctrine should be careful not to swap reason for irrationality and power and lend the stamp of science to criminal law as it develops.

Earlier, without glorifying the past, positive law was often developed by criminal law scholars themselves, which thereby at least to some extent better conformed to the acknowledged principles and concepts, making it possible for the legal scholar to present them in a coherent way.[43] The more recent development, on its hand, drives us towards a choice between 'rationalising' the irrationality in contemporary legislation and continuously patching up the disintegrating 'system', or opting for another strategy, less loyal to positive law. One strategy in this regard is to somehow shift the style of reasoning into something that conforms better to clear-cut scientific practices, such as the empirical sciences. Here, we return to Ross and legal realism, whose prognosis theory sought precisely to mould legal doctrine into a practice compatible with logical positivism's requirement of empirical propositions.[44] This is one attempt to respond to the justification challenge, but as indicated not a successful one. It requires of legal doctrine to fundamentally change its approach to law, as this ultimately normative enterprise is turned into a kind of empirical study. Even more problematic are key ideas in Ross' intellectual enterprise, including logical positivism as theory of science and his non-cognitivism.[45] Even if his engagement with the justification challenge is admirable, he headed in the

---

42 See also e.g. van Hoecke/Ost (n 1), pp. 201 ff.

43 For a more nuanced storytelling here, see e.g. van Hoecke/Ost (n 1) pp. 200 ff.

44 Cfr. sect. 2.

45 For a critique of legal realism, see e.g. Morten Kinander, *The View From Within: An Analysis and Critique of Legal Realism and Descriptive Jurisprudence* (Fagbokfor-

wrong direction.[46] On the other extreme, abandoning the idea of a scientific study of positive law comes at a significant cost: It would imply that positive law, an important dimension of contemporary society, would not be subject to scientific scrutiny.

### 6 *Solving the Justification challenge*

A first step to solve the justification challenge is to consider whether all the premises for the outlined critique are (fully) valid. Perhaps there are more to law than something that can be wiped out by a few words from the legislator and thereby not that a contingent study object after all. This brings us back to the question on the level of conformity of the bounded rationality of law to the open rationality. We cannot settle this complex question here. However, criminal law, with its long history and foundational role in the legal order, brings at least indications of several essential connections. Even if for instance national doctrines of criminal responsibility have their special characteristics, a shared basic structure seems implied.[47] The historical evolution of these doctrines, with Pufendorf's rehearsal of Aristotle's doctrine of responsibility and the infusion of this into German criminal law scholarship as what was to become model for Continental and Nordic criminal law, add substance to this.[48] This kind of foundational conceptual structures inherent in law bring it closer to the kind of 'necessity' that we so easily consider as the core of science.[49] Closely related to such basic con-

---

laget 2004). Specific premises are also criticised, see e.g. the critique of Ross' non-cognitivism, see Jørgen Stubberud, 'En kritikk av Alf Ross' non-kognitivisme' (2004) Tidsskrift for Rettsvitenskap 50. Ross' theory is however also sought rescued by replacing logical positivism with naturalism as philosophical basis, see Jakob V. H. Holtermann, 'Naturalizing Alf Ross's Legal Realism: A Philosophical Reconstruction' (2014) Vol 24 Revus 165, however from a different epistemological starting point that this article sets out from.

46 Cfr. also e.g. Graver (n 11) pp. 232–234.

47 See e.g. Joachim Hruschka, 'Imputation' (1986) Brigham Young University Law Review 669. More generally, see van Hoecke/Ost (n 1) p. 199 on a 'common hard core' of concepts across European legal systems.

48 See e.g. Jørn Jacobsen, 'Pufendorf og den europeiske strafferettsdoktrinen', in Ulrika Andersson/Christoffer Wong/Helén Örnemark Hansen (eds.), *Festskrift till Per Ole Träskman* (Norstedts Juridik, 2011), pp. 247–258.

49 This was not least emphasised by the German criminal law scholar Hans Welzel, see further e.g. Oliver Sticht, *Sachlogik als Naturrecht? Zur Rechtsphilosophie Hans Welzels (1904–1977)* (Schöningh 2000).

ceptual structures are foundational and widely shared normative principles of criminal law, such as the principle of legality and the principle of guilt, and the more general rule of law-principles these relate to. If such foundational principles (*pace* Ross) are accepted as founded in for instance a *Vernuftsrecht* of a Kantian kind,[50] ultimately in the concept of practical reason (correspondingly to the way the concept of theoretical reason founds the empirical sciences), they will provide a robust basis for critically examining positive law. This claim does not presuppose a conception of natural law that determines positive law, i.e. a kind of 'blueprint' that one can compare to positive law (which would be absurd), but rather basic principles which positive law can be judged upon as either normatively necessary, possible or invalid. Also, law has empirical references that can be utilised to relate it to the field of science, such as in the age threshold for criminal responsibility and the perspective of cognitive science. Law also contains and engages several premises of a sociological kind. Hence, even for the non-cognitivist, there are analytical and empirical resources for subjecting positive law to critique.

This can be rephrased in a more general way: Law's rules have *meaning*, as they are the product of beliefs regarding both normative and empirical considerations. These beliefs are also related to more general (also pre-legal) presuppositions, concepts, and principles that give law character of (or at least ambition of being) a system of rules. In this sense, the rules derive their meaning from the broader field of meaning that they belong to, which contains premises of several kinds. Law can thereby also be considered as *a meaning system*, one that (similar to other meaning systems) would not be possible without inherent, intimate references to the open rationality. So even if positive law basically depends on decisions from the legislator, courts, etc., these decisions engage premises of several kinds that science offers knowledge on and that can be utilised to subject positive law to critical scrutiny. This does not imply that these disciplines must offer precise knowledge of the kind often sought for in law ('will an increase in sentencing levels have a deterrent effect?'). Legal doctrine serves a critical function also where it shows that law's presuppositions are naïve compared to the complexity observed within the sciences.

The inherent connection of law's bounded rationality thereby turns out to be significant to the legal doctrinal enterprise, and the key to our alter-

50 For an exposition, see Arthur Ripstein, *Force and Freedom: Kant's Legal and Political Philosophy* (HUP 2009), see also Svein Eng, *Rettsfilosofi* (Universitetsforlaget 2007), pp. 346–436.

native to the traditional Norwegian criminal law doctrine. The suggestion is to view legal doctrine's basic aim as to *identifying positive law with the view of systematising and subjecting it to the critical point of view of the open rationality* for the purpose of securing a *dialogue* between law's bounded rationality and the open rationality of science.[51] This basically implies several stages of reasoning.

To begin with, the identification of positive law, in terms of applying the legal method, *must* be a central starting point also for legal doctrine.[52] The legal doctrinal scholar must master the legal methodology of the given legal order and the interpretive skills of the lawyer. Without this, we would lack (awareness of) the very object for further studies of positive law.[53] Legal doctrine's interpretation of positive law can in this sense be compared to empirical observation as a basis for the empirical sciences: We go into the woods and count the number of insects, observe where the wolves stray or measure temperature changes, as basis for us to explain and thereby understand the given subject. Similarly, legal doctrine goes into the codes, preparatory works, and court decisions to 'find' law, as a presupposition for further studies of it. So, the legal practitioner and the legal scholar share this task, even if their starting points typically will imply some important differences. The legal scholar, whose interpretation of broader parts of law necessarily will involve (some kind of) systematisation, will easily be more in need for and also more capable of interpreting the legal rule in view of basic principles and concepts, while the practitioner will have a better eye for the practical dimension of the rule, viewpoints both relevant to the interpretation. This interpretive engagement with positive law secures legal doctrine, and legal science in general, a unique character so that it *cannot* disintegrate into being a sub-branch of for instance the social sciences.[54] However, to figure out what are the existing rules in an area, for instance the sexual offences, cannot itself claim scientific status. This is (a broader application of) the *legal* operation of the lawyer, and a lawyer is not *per se* a (legal) scientist. To be scientific, studies of law must go beyond the perspective of the bounded rationality and adopt the *knowl-*

51 Compare to e.g. van Hoecke/Ost (n 1) p. 197, considering the aim as describing and systematising the law.

52 At this point too, I share Hagerup's approach, see Hagerup (n 7) p. 21.

53 See also e.g. Smits (n 1) p. 214.

54 Cfr. also more generally Immanuel Kant, *Kritik der Urteilskraft* (Berlin, 1973), in *Immanuel Kant, Werke in Sechs Bänden, Herausgeben von Wilhelm Weischedel*, Band V, § 68 on the importance of considering a science not as 'einen Anbau und als einen Teil eines anderen Gebäudes, sondern als ein Ganzes für sich'.

*edge-point of view* on law of the open rationality.[55] This occurs in two steps, one with a view to systematisation, one with a view to critique.

Similar to the natural sciences, for instance, legal doctrine must elaborate its own principles for systematisation, i.e. develop a theoretical system for interpretation, understanding, systematisation, and discussion of the different norms of positive law, to the extent possible. Whereas grasping positive law requires applying the norms of the bounded rationality and these only, the knowledge framework for systematising law, cannot be subject to the same limits. A legislator cannot *settle* whether for instance the concept of action can give structure to a proper doctrine of criminal responsibility or whether the justification/excuse-distinction is meaningful. Legislation may (and usually do) reflect opinions of such matters, but when legislator do so, it is usually imprinted by historical, traditional, or ideological viewpoints, often in need of rework.[56] So, rather than being limited by law in this regard, doctrinal criminal law scholars must relate to fundamental philosophical premises concerning acts and imputation, practical reason and freedom as foundational premises for criminal law to develop its own take on positive law.[57] By this step, legal doctrine's 'positivistic innocence' is also lost. The dual perspective of the bounded/open rationality is evident already here.

This is not least evident when manifest contradictions appear between the bounded and open rationality. Legal doctrine does then and should indeed pay attention to this. For instance, it may be that specific legal rules, even though they apparently fit into the system of responsibility, are at odds with a broader knowledge perspective. Legal systems where criminal responsibility sets in at 10 or 12 years can exemplify this. Having an age limit for criminal responsibility appears well-argued and a given part of systems of criminal responsibility. However, is the cognitive apparatus of children at that age developed to the extent needed? Research suggests oth-

55 Tendencies in this direction can be found for instance in Graver (n 12) p. 240 where it is claimed that the central aim of legal science in all its aspects is still to describe, analyse and systematise the legal norms *and to consider them in view of their historical evolution or in regard to their social setting*, while the latter (in italics) as argued in this article could be expanded to a broader scientific knowledge perspective – more in line with what Graver (p. 243) generally describes as 'to promote rationality'.

56 See e.g. van Hoecke/Ost (n 1), calling for a general resystematisation of the law.

57 See e.g. Jørn Jacobsen, 'Eit grunnriss av ei strafferettsleg ansvarslære' (2012) Vol 12 Tidsskrift for strafferett 5 and also Linda Gröning, Erling Johannes Husabø and Jørn Jacobsen, *Frihet, forbrytelse og straff – En systematisk framstilling av norsk strafferett*, (2nd ed, Fagbokforlaget, 2019).

erwise.[58] If we acknowledge that, we have also acknowledged the risk relating to a legal doctrine that simply 'forwards' and thereby also in a sense acknowledges this kind of regulation. For this reason, legal doctrine has a responsibility to be critical to law and its premises in general. It will still be law from the point of view of the bounded rationality but should be added to in terms of the critical perspective of the open rationality.[59] This is demanding to legal doctrine, not least as it requires strong engagement with other scientific disciplines, but is still necessary to secure the scientific aspect of legal doctrine.[60] By engaging with other sciences, not least via connecting disciplines such as the sociology of law or law and economics, resources are provided for legal doctrine to critically discuss concepts, principles, and premises in positive law.

The central question can however be said to remain unsolved. How can one in practice combine the bounded rationality of law and the open rationality of science? There is no clear-cut answer to this question, in the sense of a 'manual' to be operationalised. Rather, what we are dealing with here is *a continuous shift of and interplay between different intellectual modes,* a competence that only can be achieved by training on the one hand, in law, and on the other, by learning from the mode of reasoning of the open rationality, for instance as it unfolds within other sciences, philosophy in particular. At the same time, several examples of how the step beyond the interpretation of positive law can be achieved, can already be found in contemporary criminal law doctrine. The proposed approach is by no means

58 See for instance Ray Corrado and Jeffrey Mathesius, 'Developmental Psycho-Neurological Research Trends and Their Importance for Reassessing Key Decision-Making Assumptions for Children, Adolescents, and Young Adults in Juvenile/ Youth and Adult Criminal Justice Systems' (2014) Vol 2 Bergen Journal of Criminal Law & Criminal Justice, pp. 141–163. <https://doi.org/10.15845/bjclcj.v2i2.707> (accessed 07.07.2020).

59 Whether the latter implies an obligation to engage *de lege ferenda*-perspectives, i.e. justified recommendations for the lawgiver can be debated, cfr. Alexander Peczenik, 'A Theory of Legal Doctrine', *Ratio Juris* 14 (2001) p. 75–105, p. 79-80. Legal doctrine may make knowledge-based recommendations but should in case make effort to properly ground these recommendations, which easily calls on the legal doctrinal reseracher to shift perspective to some kind of legal reform research. Relating to Peczenik's works, I add that I prefer not to coin my approach as (another) kind of coherence version of legal doctrine, such as Peczenik is an example of. That easily gives the impression that legal doctrine so to speak *at any cost* shall put the law together in a coherent way.

60 Cfr. Jørn Jacobsen, 'Law, Legal Science and Methodological Pluralism', in Johan Giertsen *et al.* (eds.), *Rett i Vest: Festskrift til 50-årsjubileet for jurist-utdanningen ved Universitetet i Bergen* (Fagbokforlaget 2019), pp. 361–377.

revolutionary but rather quite common, even if not consistently carried through, in much of European and even in Norwegian criminal law scholarship. Scholarship on the legal regulation of intent or *Vorsatz* provides one example.[61] In a Norwegian setting, one may here start by addressing the Norwegian criminal code sect. 22, then relating it to the general system for criminal responsibility, and then consider whether this conceptualisation of intent is, from a broader knowledge perspective, just or well-argued. If justified, the legal doctrine may give its scientific support to the rule as it stands, if not, the legal doctrine should be clear about this and why it is so.[62] To critically scrutinize the concept of intent in this way may require different knowledge resources. It requires us to clarify the philosophy of intention in the first place and which principles a rule of this kind should reflect.[63] Furthermore, it must respond to empirical (e.g. psychological) knowledge of how individuals observe, interpret and interact with the social world.[64] Here, we see how legal doctrine may ground its analysis of positive law in the larger scientific web of knowledge. Precisely by posing questions from a knowledge perspective and engaging the resources from other scientific disciplines as a means to consider the validity of the viewpoints of positive law, legal doctrine may keep its instinctive drive towards the bounded rationality in balance.[65] This seems in fact implied by

---

61 For simplicity, I use 'intent' for what in Continental and Nordic criminal law is known as *Vorsatz*, *forsett* etc. despite intent in Anglo-American criminal law typically being narrower than its Continental counterpart.

62 The notion of 'clouded intent' is one example of a highly problematic element of the Norwegian doctrine of intent, see Jørn Jacobsen, '"Sløret forsett?" Høgsterett mellom teori og praksis i strafferetten', Frode Ulvund and Jørn Øyrehagen Sunde (eds.), *Lovens Speil, Høgsterett 200 år* (Fagbokforlaget 2015), pp. 143–167.

63 See e.g. Nils Jareborg, *Handling och uppsåt: En undersökning rörande doluslärans underlag* (Norstedt 1969) and Antony Duff, *Intention, Agency & Criminal Liability: Philosophy of Action and the Criminal Law* (Blackwell 1990). In the theoretical German criminal law doctrine, the concept of intent has been a core issue, intimately related to the discussion on the act concept. This tradition has also been prolonged into the contemporary discussion on international criminal law, see e.g. Carl-Friedrich Stuckenberg, *Vorstudien zu Vorsatz und Irrtum im Völkerstrafrecht* (De Gruyter 2007).

64 See e.g. Nils Jareborg and Magnus Ulväng, *Tanke och uppsåt* (Iustus 2016).

65 The concept of criminal insanity offers another example, see further e.g. Linda Gröning, 'Tilregnelighet og utilregnelighet: begreper og regler', *Nordisk Tidsskrift for Kriminalvidenskab* 102 (2015) pp. 112–148. Examples can also be drawn from for instance the sanctioning system, where for instance the rules addressing juvenile offenders provide a wealth of examples of legal rules loaded with philosophical, psychological, and sociological premises, see e.g. Ingun Fornes, *Straff av barn. Frihetsstraffene og alternativene* (UiB 2018).

how legal scholars often chose their subjects. These appear often to be chosen due to being intellectually intriguing, rather than for instance due to their practical relevance.

The following clarifications are however important: First, much of what positive law contains is quite neutral from the point of view of a knowledge perspective. Basic concepts, structures and principles do not determine the precise content of a legal order. Precisely what level of alcohol percentage in the blood that is allowed when driving is a matter where the legal doctrine may simply point to this contingency and the solution the legislator has opted for. Second, there is no fixed interaction between the bounded and open rationality. How this emerges in each case depend particularly on the stand of positive law, which thereby set decisive premises for how legal doctrinal studies should be carried out, giving the discipline a dynamic character. Third, it goes without saying that a legal doctrinal investigation can find it hard to live up to the standards of critically examining *all* the different premises involved in a part of positive law and thereby manage to draw on history, philosophy, sociology, medical science, and more in the very same treatise. Here, we should remind ourselves of Carnap's comparison of science to repairing a ship at sea. Not all can be done at once. Also, the collective dimension of science is here of importance. If legal doctrinal scholars know enough at least to pose questions of the kind mentioned, we have come a long way and can invite other legal scientific disciplines to examine them, or build onto studies that have already discussed the matter. The important thing is that legal doctrine is under the obligation to keep positive law (properly interpreted) *open* to the perspective of the open rationality. Fourth, the position advocated does not disregard that legal doctrinal works have many other valuable functions in the legal system. On the contrary, legal doctrine offers qualified, systematic interpretation of law and facilitates for the training of (new) lawyers and guiding judges, prosecutors, and other actors in the legal system, to name a few. This can be considered as ways of channeling scientific knowledge into society, as well as increasing rationality. However, it may only be legitimately carried out when the primary requirements of knowledge production are fulfilled.[66] Stated somewhat differently; in selecting questions to inquire, it is reasonable to take into account social needs for knowledge. When exploring the questions, however, the knowledge interest is no, or should at least not be, other than to acquire knowledge in itself.

66 See also Graver (n 12) p. 235: 'Legal science cannot claim or justify any particular role as participant in the practical life of law and society.'.

## 7 *Epilogue: No Farewell to Criminal Law Doctrine*

This article has addressed the justification challenge legal doctrine faces when judged against the general standards of science. Some may however think that this strenuous effort has been misguided in the first place. It can for instance be claimed that legal science should nevertheless shift its attention away from studies of positive law towards a more progressive point of view, contributing to solving significant social problems.[67] For the criminal law science, for instance, some may think that issues such as the possible role for criminal law in the protection of the environment, how the criminal justice system can more properly deal with the significant number of rapes that occur in society (without offenders being held criminal responsible for the crime), or prevent for the future such large scale financial carelessness of the kind we witnessed in the build up to the financial crisis, are all more important issues than those who traditional doctrinal studies engage with, for instance the conceptual exegeses of favourite legal doctrinal subjects such as the concept of intent or of insanity. In fact, the contemporary development with rising inequality, climate crisis, corruption, devaluation of democracy and rule of law, and so forth, does indeed give also the criminal law scholar reason to ask: *The world is burning, and I am…?*

A fair case can indeed be made for a more multifaceted criminal law science, one that, given criminal law's foundational role within the legal order, to a larger extent engages with issues as the mentioned at some cost of traditional criminal law doctrinal work. Caretaking for the future of the fundamental normative ideas of democracy and rule of law by addressing issues such as the mentioned, typically in collaboration with researchers in other fields of law and in other sciences, is well-argued given how law, science, and democracy are historically and ideologically so intimately linked to each other. Hence, for science it is important to facilitate a society where law, democracy and science continue to play the important roles these institutions have done in Western societies.

However, engaging criminal law science also in such issues is not the same as disregarding or devaluating the importance of legal doctrinal studies. To omit interpretation of positive law from the legal science would not

67 See for instance Edward L. Rubin, 'From Coherence to Effectiveness – A Legal Methodology for the Modern World', in van Gestel, Micklitz and Rubin (2017) pp, 310–350, calling for 'a new methodology, one focused on empirical results and pragmatic strategies' (p. 350).

only be damaging to legal doctrine itself, but also detrimental to other legal scientific disciplines, not least comparative law's comparison of different legal orders, and to other studies relating to law. It would also come at a significant cost for the legal system, as legal doctrinal studies of positive law not only contribute to improve law itself but are also essential for teaching and education of lawyers. Lowering the competence in and quality of the legal system in this way comes at a cost for the citizens as the subjects of law. For such reasons, legal doctrine plays an essential role within the legal science and will continue to do so. Hence, there is an important role for legal doctrine for the future. It remains at the apex of legal science. The call for further dimensions in legal science add to, rather than replace legal doctrine. In fact, it can be viewed as intimately related to the conception of legal doctrine offered here, as this conception underlines the importance of other kinds of studies of (premises in) law. By emphasising legal science's basis in the open rationality, we acquire a solid platform for us to engage in positive law as it is and in the future challenges law and society face.

# The method of (German) criminal law dogmatics*

*Luís Greco*

## *I. The undertaking at issue*

When my friend Shin Matsuzawa suggested I write a contribution on the method of criminal law, I could only but follow his suggestion. Much – and possibly enough – has already been written on this topic,[1] as on many others of criminal law; I have also already commented on it several times,[2] which must have been (one of) the reasons for my friend's enquiry. My previous comments were also one reason for me to follow his enquiry; a return to a previously explored topic is always less time-consuming. I therefore initially planned to offer here what musicians would call a variation on a song already composed.

Well, I sat in front of the computer, drafted a first outline – and did not write further, but turned to other tasks (especially a longer essay on the justification of necessity (*rechtfertigender Notstand*), which will come up quite a bit in the following). Gradually, however, it became clear to me that the idea of providing variations on the familiar was not enough to motivate me to write; man shall not live by bread alone. And so the idea for the present contribution came to life: this contribution will not just be about bread, about another item for one's list of publications, now even in English language, but it will be about something new, unusual, personal – not about the method of criminal law, but about the method of a criminal law

---

* Translation from the German original by Dr. Lucia Sommerer, revised by the author.

1 Detailed bibliographical references can be found in Roxin/Greco, Strafrecht AT I, 5th ed. § 7. My personal favourites are, apart from Roxin's works quoted in the following footnotes, the publications of my teacher Schünemann, which have fortunately been recently compiled in an anthology (Schünemann, Gesammelte Werke, Vol. 1: Rechtsfindung im Rechtsstaat und Dogmatik als ihr Fundament, 2019).

2 See especially in Greco, Lebendiges und Totes in Feuerbachs Straftheorie, 2009, pp. 21 et seq.; id., Strafprozesstheorie und materielle Rechtskraft, 2015, pp. 41 et seq.; and in a number of essays that have been published exclusively in Romanic languages, which will be quoted in the following footnotes.

*scholar*; something like a look behind the scenes, a making of, an open kitchen.

Clearly, this concept has its disadvantages; in particular, it raises the unpleasant suspicion that only someone who is unduly convinced of himself could come up with it. In fact, it would be more suitable for an oral, ephemeral lecture; perhaps this is the psychological explanation for my urge to write this text anyway, i.e. as a replacement for the conferences the pandemic makes me long for. Nevertheless: the subject matter, as personal as it may seem at first glance, is less related to my person than to the occasion for this publication. I am asked by a Japanese friend to write something about "our" method as a representative of the German criminal law scholarship for a non-German audience; as a native Brazilian who only moved to Germany after completing his first law degree in his home country, I am, however, not wholly representative of such scholarship. But what I believe I can represent – in the sense of presenting as well as depicting – is the gap between the external and internal perception of German criminal law scholarship; because this is something I have experienced personally like few others from the day I arrived in Munich in 2001 onwards. It is precisely this insight into the "inside" or the path from the outside to the inside that I would like to try to describe to my primarily foreign readers; an "inside" that will reach as far as into my head.

## *II. Sublime German theory? Or: German criminal law scholarship, seen from within*

I came to Germany as a newly qualified lawyer to learn with and above all from my heroes. The greatest of them, Claus Roxin, had accepted me as an LL.M. student; contact with my teacher Bernd Schünemann, who gave me an assistant position in 2004, developed shortly afterwards. Even from faraway Brazil, I had been an avid spectator of wonderful theoretical battles. Some milestones of which (published in book form, of course, not in magazines) I had delivered to me mainly via internet bookshops – the dispute over the finalistic, teleological theory of action (*finale Handlungslehre*), i.e. Mezger vs. Welzel vs. Roxin;[3] the controversy about guilt, beginning with

3 Welzel, Das deutsche Strafrecht, 11th ed. 1969, which I was fortunately able to find for sale in a German university bookshop in Mainz in 1997. Regarding Mezger I obtained a copy of the Spanish translation of the 2nd edition of his textbook (1933) by Rodríguez Muñoz (Tratado de derecho penal, Madrid, 1955–1957) from a court library in Rio de Janeiro. And I had Roxin's work in front of me in the Por-

freedom of will and guilt based on character (*Charakterschuld*), i.e. with Welzel and Engisch,[4] reaching up to the functional concept of guilt (*funktionalen Schuldbegriff*) and the criticism of it, i.e. with Jakobs, Roxin and Hirsch.[5] When I received the 3rd edition of Roxin's textbook at the beginning of 1999, I was amazed not only by the section on guilt (or rather, as he calls it, responsibility, *Verantwortlichkeit*), but the functional approach as a whole, i.e. overcoming the ontologically oriented approach of finalism, which believed to derive formative traits of the doctrine of unlawfulness and guilt from pre-legal structures.[6] Above all two sections that I did not know from the Brazilian textbooks of the time captured my attention: § 2 on the doctrine of legal goods (*Rechtsgutslehre*), with the attempt to impose limits on the almighty legislator, and § 11 on the doctrine of objective attribution (*objektive Zurechnungslehre*). When I wrote to Roxin in 1999 to ask whether I could do my LL.M. and doctorate under his supervision, I wanted to investigate either the legal good (*Rechtsgut*) or objective attribution. And this is in fact what happened – my master's thesis dealt with the problem of so-called special knowledge (*Sonderwissens*) in the context of objective attribution.[7]

The reason why I chose this issue is obvious. I was fascinated by how it could be that a theory that proudly distinguishes itself from finalistic subjectivism and proclaims a focus shift towards the objective elements of unlawfulness (*objektiver Tatbestand*) through the novel requirement of "illicit

tuguese translation of his collection of essays "Strafrechtliche Grundlagenprobleme" from 1973 (Problemas fundamentais de direito penal, Lisbon, 1993) – there especially his essay "Zur Kritik der finalen Handlungslehre" (originally ZStW 74 [1962], 515).

4 I was able to acquire Welzel, Abhandlungen zum Strafrecht und zur Rechtsphilosophie (1975) via the internet, especially his essay on "Persönlichkeit und Schuld" (pp. 185 et seq.; originally ZStW 60 [1941], 428), as well as Engisch's small but excellent monograph Die Lehre von der Willensfreiheit in der strafrechtsphilosophischen Doktrin der Gegenwart, 1965.

5 Jakobs, Schuld und Prävention, 1976; id., Strafrecht AT, 2nd ed. 1991, § 17. At that time, I only knew Hirsch from hearsay.

6 Finalism derived the finalistic, teleological structure of the offence from the ontological structure of the act as a goal-oriented activity; because a killing finality is part of the act of killing, the description of the killing act by the legal elements of crime also includes the finality, in other words the intention to kill. Intent was thus shifted from the doctrine of guilt, in which it was traditionally placed, to the doctrine of the elements of crime. This conclusion is generally accepted in Germany today, albeit for other reasons, some of which are not least merely didactic.

7 Appearing in essay form in: Greco, Das Subjektive an der objektive Zurechnung: Zum „Problem" des Sonderwissens, ZStW 117 (2005), 519.

creation of danger" (*unerlaubte Gefahrschaffung*),[8] how such a theory could at the same time take into account what the perpetrator knows, i.e. an obviously subjective element. I was especially labouring over an example constructed by Jakobs of a biology student,[9] who, in the course of a moonlighting job as a waiter, recognises a mushroom in the salad he is serving as poisonous, ignores this knowledge that lies beyond his role as a waiter – i.e. this special knowledge – and serves the salad to the unsuspecting guest. Jakobs posits that the biology student did not kill the dead guest, but at best failed to help him – a really objective attribution would have to recognise objectivity as decisive, i.e. the objective social role, in our case that of a waiter, a role which generally does not include special biology knowledge.

What is important in this context is not so much my "solution" to this problem[10] rather than a conversation Roxin had with me in his favourite pizzeria "Bei Mario" in Munich's Adalbertstraße. I told him that I had an idea for a differentiating solution, to which he replied that he always looked closely at the cases that the courts had to decide and asked himself how they differed from each other. What he meant by that, I could not understand at the time, not least because there was no case law on my "problem". At most, there was the discussion about whether ostensibly neutral acts can constitute aiding and abetting (*neutrale Beihilfe*), but this discussion was dealt with under a different heading and with different arguments.[11]

With this brief sentence – which Roxin, who never forgets anything, will probably not remember, because it merely stated what was self-evident to him – everything started to move in my mind – my entire picture of German criminal law scholarship and thus my conception of what constitutes good criminal law scholarship. I began to see a lot of things that had previously gone unnoticed: that the great essays on the timeless questions of criminal law often are based on highly topical occasions, especially deci-

---

8 Roxin, Die Lehre von der objektiven Zurechnung, in: Chengchi Law Review 50 (May 1994), 219 et seq. (229 et seq.).

9 Jakobs, Tätervorstellung und objektive Zurechnung, GS Arm. Kaufmann, 1989, pp. 271 et seq. (273, 286).

10 The problem was solved to my (preliminary?) satisfaction only in Roxin/Greco, AT I, § 11 mn. 57.

11 On this discussion from today's perspective Schünemann/Greco, Leipziger Kommentar zum Strafgesetzbuch, 13th ed. 2020–21, § 27 mn. 17 et seq. In 2004 I produced a small monograph in Portuguese, Greco, Cumplicidade através de ações neutras, Rio de Janeiro et al., 2004.

sions of the German Federal Court.[12] Gradually I, too, began to read these decisions, which are never translated into the Romanic languages. I noticed that the industrious German law students were not entirely familiar with my heroes Feuerbach, Binding, Welzel etc., but they did have structured, differentiated, case-related arguments. I further noticed that even the textbook of my greatest role model did not merely contain statements on guilt and legal goods and objective attribution, on the three- or two-stage structure of criminal liability (*drei- oder zweistufiger Verbrechensaufbau*) or on the systematic status of consent for criminal liability,[13] but that it reflected on and incorporated the entire body of German case law dating back to the time of the Imperial Court of Justice (*Reichsgericht*). I realised that German law was based on an admirable collaboration between theory and practice, between big names and unknown ones, that the stereotype that the German genius was a theoretical one and that practitioners were more likely to be found elsewhere was a caricature.

Nothing is therefore more wrong than the idea, which is not only spread abroad, that German criminal law is exhausted in a series of individual feuds between few great thinkers; I emphasize "not only abroad", because this error in perception seems to be related not only to a distance of geography but also of time. In Germany we, too, tend to shorten criminal law at the turn of the 19th century to the duel between Feuerbach vs. Klein, followed by Feuerbach vs. Grolman,[14] the turn of the 20th century shortened to Binding vs. Liszt (classical vs. modern school of criminal law), the post-war period to Mezger vs. Welzel. Systematically missing in these pictures are the names and faces of the certainly frequently quoted "prevailing opinion" (*herrschende Meinung*) at the time and – especially abroad – the case law. For instance, important works by Mezger and Welzel have been translated into Spanish; the 19 pages long decision BGHSt 2, 190 on the other hand (quite long for a court decision but short compared to scholarly works), is, as far as I know, not yet translated into any Romanic language, even though it played a fundamental role in the development of the dogmatics of guilt and the dogmatics of mistake (*Schuld- und Irrtumsdogmatik*).

12 Cf. especially Greco, Dos formas de hacer dogmatica jurídico-penal, translated by H.Bouvier, in: Discusiones 8 (2008), 177.

13 The questions which primarily (almost exclusively?) interested me when I first read the book.

14 See critical already Greco, Lebendiges (fn. 2), p. 25.

## III. *Exemplification: Foundation and limits of the justification of aggressive necessity. Or: A German criminal law essay, seen from within*

1. As announced, I am writing about myself, but simultaneously about the gap between the external and internal perspectives on German criminal law scholarship. Now I would like to become even more personal; I would like to talk about "method" by trying to make public the thought process behind the coming to life of some of my reflections. For understandable reasons I have to resort to a process that unfolds in my own head.

Even when I completed my doctoral thesis in 2008,[15] Roxin critically noted in his evaluation that I hardly cited any case law; I would try to avoid making the same mistake in the future.[16] Roxin with reference to Radbruch called this interconnectedness and cross-fertilisation of reality and academic reflection the "determination of ideas by matter" (*Stoffbestimmtheit der Idee*).[17] His demand was for theoretical endeavours to trace the "resistance of the matter" (*Widerstand der Sache*),[18] which in fact points to nothing other than what is known in the Anglo-Saxon world as "reflective equilibrium".[19] By this Roxin clearly rejected any attempts to reduce the wealth and breadth of law into much-loved but simple formulas and concepts. Metaphorically speaking, those who use a GPS navigation system may reach their destination more quickly, provided, however, that they know before beginning their journey what their destination will be. This is the difference between the scientist and the tourist. Without metaphor: Deductions alone are not enough; every deduction must be tested with real world cases, which in turn signal by their very "resistance" whether and to what extent the deduction is wrong or incomplete. The scholar's gaze,

15 Greco, Lebendiges (fn. 2).

16 My habilitation thesis (Strafprozesstheorie [fn. 2]) was an attempt in this sense, but when I take into account the reaction of the reviewers (reserved Wohlers, GA 2016, 579; very critical Stuckenberg, ZIS 2017, 445), I cannot describe it as successful.

17 Roxin, Bemerkungen zum Verhältnis von Rechtsidee und Rechtsstoff in der Systematik unseres Strafrechts, GS Radbruch, 1968, pp. 260 et seq.

18 Roxin, Täterschaft und Tatherrschaft, 10th ed. 2020, pp. 536 et seq.

19 Rawls, A Theory of Justice, Revised Edition, 1999, p. 18; this parallel was first drawn in Greco, Methode, Stil, Person: Claus Roxin zum 85. Geburtstag, ZIS 2016, 416 (418; also in: Rotsch [ed.], Zehn Jahre ZIS – Zeitschrift für Internationale Strafrechtsdogmatik, 2018, pp. 1233 et seq).

which wanders back and forth,[20] must move not only from top to bottom, but also from bottom to top, and above all sideways.

2. I am trying to exemplify this with what I am currently working on – an essay (not yet finished) on the justification of necessity (*rechtfertigender Notstand*) (sec. 34 German Criminal Code). I will share with the reader some thoughts that will not necessarily find their way into the soon to be completed essay. The justification of necessity allows the elimination of a source of danger at the expense of legal goods of a party not involved in its creation. Even this seemingly inconspicuous sentence embodies a challenge that can only be understood from a certain (already presupposed) perspective, namely one of taking seriously the status of the individual as bearer of his or her own rights: For how can this be lawful? What does an uninvolved individual have to do with the fact that another person simply had bad luck? This presupposition is for me personally not only convincing in terms of legal morality, but also in terms of positivist legal dogmatics, namely through the German constitution's commitment to inviolable and inalienable human rights (Article 1 para. 2 German Constitution) and human dignity (Article 1 para. 1 German Constitution) – i.e. the axiom in our quite deductive starting point.

The search for an explanation does not stop at the simple "fact" of the existence of sec. 34 German Criminal Code. It further has to do with the issue that we do not want to punish person A for theft when he takes water from neighbour B to extinguish a fire in a building belonging to C; moreover, the fact that we impose on B the duty to tolerate the utilization of his property, i.e. that we not only let firefighter A go unpunished but that we *justify* his behaviour. This train of thought is an inductive one, from bottom to top. Coming from the top down, however, it must be taken into account that B has little to do with C's problems; this means that we owe B a reason why the law decides in favour of A, C and the building and against him and his water.

I do not want to go back over the different answers to this question. Even before I started contemplating necessity, I had argued that there are certain rights that can be called "resistant to the common good" and that could only be withdrawn from their bearer on condition that he or she somehow participated in this withdrawal, that he or she forfeited them, so

20 According to the now famous metaphor of Engisch, Logische Studien zur Gesetzesanwendung, 3rd ed. 1963, pp. 13, 15; on this Pavčnik, Das „Hin- und Herwandern des Blickes" (Über die Natur der Gesetzesanwendung), in: Liu/Neumann (ed.), Gerechtigkeit – Theorie und Praxis. Justice – Theory and Practice, 2011, pp. 157 et seq.

to speak.[21] A now forgotten tradition spoke of rights to which people are entitled simply because they are human beings, and called them innate rights; these rights were contrasted with rights based on a particular historical event, a so-called title, which were called acquired rights. To the first group belong above all life, physical integrity and freedom (of movement), to the second group belong property and assets. From this derives my conviction – again deductively – that necessity should only intervene in acquired rights, in so far as it embodies the deprivation of a right of another without his participating (i.e. structure of the so-called aggressive necessity). The essay on necessity was intended to test this bold thesis, to which the preliminary work had led me, and which had received initial confirmation in *Leite's* very enlightening dissertation.[22]

3. It was necessary not only to fortify the thesis "upwards", by completing and refining some of the premises from previous deductions, but in particular to examine whether it could withstand the "resistance of the matter". Did I really mean it, when I wrote that a minor bodily injury cannot be inflicted, not even when it is a matter of saving a human life? If A has to push aside B, who is blocking the way to extinguish the fire, and B suffers bodily injury – does A make himself liable to criminal prosecution? Does B have the right to defend himself against this? Must one, too, wait for a voyeur's eighth visit appearing at night next to the marital bed over a period of almost two years, and whom the victims only manage to confront once he fled the house, i.e. a situation in which, due to the absence of a "current attack", self-defence (sec. 32 German Criminal Code) is no longer permissible (BGH NJW 1979, 2053[23])?

---

21 Especially Greco, Strafprozesstheorie (fn. 2), pp. 652 et seq.

22 Leite, Notstand und Strafe, 2019.

23 "Current" (gegenwärtig) in the sense of the provision on self-defence (sec. 32 German Criminal Code) is generally and correctly understood more narrowly than the same German word in the context of the provisions on necessity (sec. 34, 35 German Criminal Code). In particular, so-called permanent dangers (Dauergefahren) – conditions which only threaten to turn into damage in the not so near future, but which already require immediate measures of prevention today – are recognised as necessity situations, but not as self- defence situations (Roxin/Greco, AT I, § 15 mn. 27, § 16 mn. 21, § 22 mn. 17). The court therefore did not apply self-defence in the above-mentioned case, but exculpatory necessity (entschuldigender Notstand) on account of the permanent danger, sec. 35 German Criminal Code; of course, this provision only applies in the case of dangers to certain goods, namely "life, limb or freedom". The BGH speaks of a danger to freedom, failing to recognise that in the context of sec. 35 German Criminal Code freedom is and must be understood primarily as freedom of movement (represen-

One idea was initially to limit the sweeping thesis to the infliction of only significant injuries. I decided against it, however, not so much because this standard was vague – sec. 226 German Criminal Code could have been referred to if need be[24] – but rather because of considerations from the top, as well as and especially from the side. The first consideration that came from the top was the fundamental blindness of the qualitatively oriented category of "the innate" towards any kind of quantification. Coming from the side, I had to realize that I was not at all prepared to classify the bullet wounds that the voyeur's buttocks bore as insignificant,[25] and I had to think of numerous imaginary cases, starting with a forced blood draw to save a seriously ill patient, which I – in accordance with the predominant but not uncontroversial prevailing opinion – could not allow to be justified.[26] The prevailing opinion relies on unsatisfying placeholder formulas, in particular human dignity; I thought I had found a more apt justification with the simple thesis that man owes others a part of his property but not of his body, because the body is already his to begin with due to his status as a human being. And again from the top I was able to find support for my thesis, namely that the voyeur can be considered a "disrupter by action" (*Verhaltensstörer,* i.e. anyone who causes, directly or indirectly, harm or damage) and is in this respect no uninvolved person; and that even someone who has to be pushed because he is "in the wrong place" may be held responsible for standing in a certain place – similarly to a "disrupter by situation" (*Zustandsstörer*; i.e. the owner or occupant of a property, even if he is not himself causing the harm), both legal categories also known from German police law. For one specific constellation, too, a legal justification for putting a troublemaker in his place can already be found in sec. 228 German Civil Code (defensive necessity). This concerns the situation that a person who stands in the way of a rescue operation disturbs it and therefore no longer is a mere uninvolved party. His treatment therefore follows different principles and limits; in particular, one no longer has to stop at what is innate.

Of course, thereby I had created the difficulty for me to expound whether innate rights can really be so easily forfeited – I admitted this in

---

tative of many Roxin/Greco, AT I, § 22 mn. 28 seq.). The solution must therefore be a justification of necessity if the offender is to remain unpunished.

24 The norm provides for a qualified form of bodily injury with particularly serious consequences (paralysis, lingering illness, significant permanent disfigurement, etc.).

25 This also speaks against the idea of referring to sec. 226 German Criminal Code.

26 See in detail – in favour of justification – Roxin/Greco, AT I, § 16, mn. 48 et seq.

one footnote and promised a next essay on the reasons for defensive necessity. Let me already say this much here: the undertaking of such expounding seems quite promising to me. On the one hand, again by means of horizontal glances that start off at criminal law – I am thinking of the well-known mountaineering case in which the upper mountaineer cuts the rope that connects him to the lower mountaineer in order to save himself,[27] or the killing of a child (in criminal law terms a fully entitled human being) during birth in order to save the mother from dying, which, thank God, hardly occurs any more these days;[28] our glance must, however, not end with criminal law, as is evident today with the Corona crisis – even the misfortune of being coughed upon is possibly intended to justify a fourteen-day restriction of freedom called quarantine.[29]

4. Whether I, in the way described, will succeed with my initial essay in my quest to give reasons for and thus limit aggressive necessity at the expense of individual positions is to be judged by others in the end. I admit that I had greater difficulty with the issue of necessity *at the expense of collective goods (Notstand zulasten von Kollektivrechtsgütern)*, a problem which is hardly explored in depth academically. For the traditional view, the overriding interest doctrine (*Lehre vom überwiegenden Interesse*), this problem is too self-evident, since this view takes the perspective of society, which is only concerned with minimising an already unavoidable damage as far as possible; for the more modern individualistic views, which seek to give reasons to persons having to give up their rights in the context of necessity, the problem lies in a blind spot, treated as if it did not exist. Above all, it is difficult to discern a clear ranking between the individual and the collective, a ranking which positive law, however, with its "substantial preponderance" in sec. 34 German Criminal Code expects from legal practitioners. This problem poses an unpleasant dilemma: if the collective interest prevails, this gives rise to the bitter taste of collectivism which disregards individuality; if, on the other hand, the individual wins, liberal intuitions are followed, but at the same time the question arises as to whether

---

27 A widespread view justifies this by referring to the idea of a common and joint danger (Gefahrengemeinschaft) – the law must not prohibit the rescue of what can only be saved on its own – which is problematic in various respects (detailed Roxin/Greco, AT I, § 16 mn. 35 et seq.). The correct solution is probably the idea of defensive necessity (very convincing Pawlik, Der rechtfertigende Defensivnotstand, Jura 2002, 26 [30 seq.]).

28 For defensive emergency Roxin/Greco, AT I, § 16 mn. 79.

29 In particular through the respective state ordinances (Landesverordnungen) issued on the basis of sec. 32 of the German Infection Protection Act.

the solution can really correspond to a law based on values such as equality and legal certainty.

Initially I thought that the distinction between the innate and the acquired would provide a clear key to solving this problem.[30] To abandon something that is merely acquired for the sake of the collective – this constitutes expropriation and can be legitimate, if compensation is provided; but the abandonment of what one has been born with cannot be legitimised this way. The deduction was therefore clear: compared to the collective, the innate always wins. What I would still have to think about now was only the acquired.

This deduction was obvious to me at first. In particular, it allowed me to make sense of the court decisions in which a doctor drives drunkenly or speeds in order to give emergency treatment to a patient: here, innate health (or life) would prevail over collective road safety.[31] More recent cases in which narcotics law violations were committed when drugs were used for pain therapy could be resolved in this way, even if the licensing system, which fortunately is provided for by law in Germany and which, as far as I know, works well, were to fail.[32]

But I had to admit that this seemingly inductive support was based on too narrow a foundation. The innocently convicted person must not bribe his prison guard, even though it is the innate freedom that is weighed against the collective integrity of the exercise of public office[33]. Especially the case of Peter Lorenz, in which a politician kidnapped by RAF terrorists was "exchanged" for the release of imprisoned terrorist comrades, seems to be stripped of its tragedy by my simplistic distinction, degraded to an easy case – as if the solution were simply to claim that it was inadmissible to

30 This was also the solution I advocated for in the essay written at the invitation of colleague Puppe in the Legal Philosophy Seminar of colleague Zaczyk (Dec. 2017); because the solution did not satisfy me, I had to brood over the essay for a longer time.

31 E.g. OLG Celle VRS 63 (1982), 449; OLG Düsseldorf VRS 30 (1966), 444; OLG Hamm NStZ 1996, 344; further similar examples in Erb, MK-StGB, 4th ed. 2020, § 34 mn. no. 173; Zieschang, LK-StGB, 13th ed. 2019, § 34 mn. no. 113.

32 Cf. BGHSt 61, 202 (where the danger, however, was "otherwise avertable", namely through the approval procedures under § 3 II BtMG); also BGH NStZ 2018, 226; OLG Braunschweig StV 2013, 708 (709); for sec. 34 German Criminal Code, however, KG NJW 2007, 2425 ("only exceptionally"); for sec. 34, 35 German Criminal Code KG StV 2003, 167.

33 Whatever one posits as the collective legal good protected by anti-corruption laws, see Stein/Deiters, SK-StGB, 9th 2016, vor § 331 mn. 5 et seq.

expropriate Lorenz's life in favour of the "state's claim to punishment"[34] or even in favour of the existence of the state[35]. The tragedy was, however, soon felt by another individual, who was subsequently kidnapped and then murdered, Hanns-Martin Schleyer: for the successful extortion in the Lorenz incident was certainly significant for the decision by the RAF members to repeat the strategy and kidnap once again.

## *IV. Conclusion*

How I solved the problem in the end, or rather how I think I solved it, I will not reveal at this point – not so much (although admittedly a little) because I would like to win you as a reader for my essay on necessity, but rather because the method has been demonstrated with enough examples.

I hope that with these examples I have shed some light on how dogmatic thinking in criminal law unfolds, not only in the cases of necessity, but also with regard to other questions, and not only my thinking but the thinking as well of German criminal law scholarship's native representatives. And I hope I have illustrated how thinking is and must be done in complex networks of differently directed arguments. The convenience of easy formulas, catchwords and isms can usually only be maintained as long as one's own innocence or self-incurred immaturity lasts.

Dogmatics of law is work on law, law is lived freedom and lived respect; dogmatics of law can therefore be little simpler than life itself. Dogmatics of law believe that behind the apparent chaos of life there is often hidden order and reason to be uncovered, and that this effort, in which we all, as theoreticians or practitioners of law, *nolens volens* participate, is worthwhile.

---

34 BVerfGE 46, 214 (222 seq.) referred to this.
35 R. Lange, Terrorismus kein Not Notstandsfall, NJW 1978, 784 (786).

# Law and Science*

*Eric Hilgendorf*
*Faculty of Law, Julius-Maximilians-University of Würzburg*

The relationship between law and science can be investigated from various perspectives.[1] One could inquire into the ways the law restrains or promotes science or the degree to which modern science has altered the law. Biotechnology and digitisation, for example, have challenged the adequacy of existing legal structures, and changed them. Another route of enquiry is how science has affected the laws of evidence and the limits of judicial competence. One could also trace the history of the relationship between law and science or the varied interpretations of these concepts within each country's legal culture.

In civil law countries, the study of law (*Rechtswissenschaft*) is commonly regarded as a science;[2] the relationship between law and science is hardly more problematic than the relationship between, say, sociology and science or biology and science. In comparison, in the United States or Britain a law professor would not be considered a "scientist", because in common law countries, the term „science" is restricted to natural sciences or at least to empirical sciences. It is clear that the study of law is neither. What is typical for the natural sciences and (perhaps) for all kinds of empirical work is the naturalistic perspective. In the following contribution, I want to analyse the relationship between law and its systematic study, on the one hand, and naturalism on the other.

## *Naturalism in Law and Philosophy*

The general naturalistic program draws from the interpretation of contemporary empirical sciences, in particular, from the natural sciences and

---

* This article was published first in Peter Machamer/Gereon Wolters (eds.), Science, Values and Objectivity, Pittsburg 2004, pp. 294 – 309. This version has been slightly modified and updated.

1 Mnookin 2002.

2 Curran 2002, 3.

medicine. It is hardly an exaggeration to say that naturalism is the world view of modern science. Moreover, it is closely connected with the idea of a "unity of sciences," a concept that goes back to the Vienna (and Berlin) Circle of Logical Empiricism. The term *Wissenschaftliche Weltauffassung (scientific world view)*, which Rudolf Carnap, Hans Hahn, and Otto Neurath used in 1929 to characterize the intellectual basis of logical empiricism,[3] is closely related to today's concept of philosophical naturalism.

In German, and, indeed, in European legal philosophy, the term *naturalism* is employed in a variety of ways. In older German legal and jurisprudential literature, naturalism was viewed very negatively, often in the context of positivism, „mechanism“, and even nihilism. Unfortunately, most of these terms were not precisely defined. Naturalism was equated with an alleged "hostility to morality" and warnings of its morally corrosive effects were issued. Reference was made to "the desert-like character of a theory which possesses none of the moral starting points fundamentally necessary for human society" and the tendency of naturalism to "leave both people and their world completely deserted, internally and externally".[4] It comes as no great surprise that naturalism was taken to be partially responsible not only for the downfall of the Weimar Republic but also the reign of terror witnessed during the National Socialist period.

Since the 1970s, the use of such moralistic statements has abated. In most modern theoretical and jurisprudential works, the term *naturalism* does not appear at all, though occasionally the idea of naturalism can still be found in academic legal discussion. In such instances, naturalism has been coupled with "blind" causality and causal theory, and is typically contrasted with "teleological“ or "value-related" jurisprudence. We can conclude that the term, at least as it is portrayed in older German and indeed European literature, has a pronounced polemic character.

In modern analytic philosophy, naturalism stands for the idea that, fundamentally, all phenomena have a natural explanation.[5] Viewed from this perspective, naturalism appears to be something of a simple reformulation of Ockham's Razor as a program for science. A well-known philosopher of science put forward the following minimalistic program for naturalism: Only so much metaphysics as necessary; minimal realism, so that it is possible for a world to exist without human beings; primacy of inanimate matter/energy; construction of real systems from real components; no in-

3 Stöltzner/Uebel 2006, 4 – 29.
4 Von Hippel 1967, 253 (my translation).
5 Nagel 1956; Papineau 2020.

stances that transcend experience; no miracles. Even the intellectual achievements of man do not extend beyond nature.[6]

The modern conception of philosophical naturalism has not yet been integrated into jurisprudence. Some legal theorists' reservations could stem from the fact that some of the points just mentioned — minimal realism, for example—are completely self-evident to lawyers. Other postulates, in comparison, do not have any relevance to the work of lawyers, for example, the axiom of inanimate matter/energy. Legal philosophers and lawyers might also be reluctant to openly accept naturalism because of the older perception of naturalism as a morally and politically dangerous theory.

Unfortunately, lawyers and legal philosophers often simply repeat arguments already raised by philosophers fifteen or twenty years earlier. Why exactly this happens is in itself an interesting question. Many jurists have an inclination to isolate themselves from other disciplines. Interdisciplinary work may also be lacking because of widespread confusion over philosophical terminology, especially when different philosophical schools are involved. Some schools, for example, „German Idealism" or French (and American) "Postmodernism" even seem to regard confused language as a sign of intellectual superiority.[7] Moreover, there is a tendency in contemporary philosophy to dissociate oneself from material issues. Philosophers prefer instead to respond to philosophers' assessments or to philosophers' critiques of other interested parties' assessments. It is not so much the "strife of systems"[8] but this common modern trend of philosophers formulating meta-meta-metatheories that very much hinders interdisciplinary work.

## *Historical Links between Law and Science*

Law and science are more closely linked than they first appear. Increasingly, legal ways of thinking, both in Europe and in the United States, are stimulated by scientific developments and often change course as a result. This was already apparent at the turn of the twentieth century. A distinguishing feature of that period was the movement toward empirical questions. These questions materialized in such influential movements as the

6 Vollmer 1995, 40 (my translation).

7 All the more important is the adherence to scientific standards in philosophy; see Wolters 1994.

8 Rescher 1985.

jurisprudence of interests (Rudolf von Jhering, Philipp Heck), ethnological legal research (Albert H. Post), legal sociology (Max Weber, Arthur Nussbaum), criminology, and research regarding the purposes of punishment (Franz von Liszt). The criminal law in particular is indebted to naturalism for the strong humanizing impulses it brought. These tendencies entered the mainstream of American jurisprudence initially through the writings of Oliver Wendell Holmes, Karl L. Llewellyn, and Roscoe Pound. Scholars emigrating from Nazi Germany (such as Ernst Rabel and Max Rheinstein) brought their ideas on methodology to America, where they blended in with traditional American legal thought.

Medicine is a perfect example of how the employment of a truly naturalistic methodology fuses with a human-oriented discipline. Modern medicine's immense successes since the nineteenth century have only been possible thanks to both naturalism and the decisive application of scientific methods. It goes without saying that we expect good doctors not only to try to cure us in the best way technically possible but also to possess understanding and a basic human touch. However, this is no argument against naturalism: On the contrary, a doctor who wants to help his or her patient will use the best, that is, the most efficient, methods available, the methods approved by science. Medicine clearly shows how a naturalistic method can be combined with the humanistic way of thinking.[9]

My aim below is to demonstrate that a naturalistic program can be integrated both into jurisprudence and without any significant changes to the current legal order. I begin by discussing questions of extra-legal values and norms and their relevance to the legal system. I will then look at two rather different concepts, both of which are very important to most legal systems: human dignity and causation. I will discuss their compatibility with the naturalistic program. After that, I will conclude with a look at techniques of legal argumentation and, more specifically, at statutory interpretation.

---

9 The combination of naturalism and humanism is also to be found in the Vienna (and Berlin) Circle of Logical Empiricism; see Hilgendorf (1998).

### *Values and Norms*

#### *Questions of Value in Law*

Questions concerning the foundation of values and norms are actually more common in jurisprudence than one would expect, judging from a superficial look at legal practice. The most important example is the creation of new legal norms. It is obvious, however, that the moral content of legal norms varies immensely. Minimal changes to the Highway Code or the law of land registration, for example, have much less of a moral quality , say, than consumer protection cases or the criminal law on abortion. In the area of international law, the International Criminal Court statute was drafted in the summer of 1998. In doing that, it was necessary to formulate criminal law norms that could be binding worldwide. It goes without saying that both technical legal problems and problems concerning fundamental norms and values came up and had to be dealt with in the process.

Not only do questions concerning values arise during the creation of new legal norms; they also sometimes arise when attempting to depart from existing norms. Such problems became important in Germany after the end of the Nazi and Communist systems. In both systems pre-existing legal norms seemed to sanction conduct that was not simply illegal but also scandalously immoral from the vantage point of the new legal order. German courts treated such norms as non-legal and therefore invalid. In doing so, the courts referred to the legal philosopher Gustav Radbruch, who shortly after World War II argued that some Nazi laws were so immoral that they lacked the character of law.[10] The main problem with this idea is the question of how *extreme immorality* should be defined without simply referring to the moral prejudices of a given culture or specific groups.

A third example of the importance of fundamental values and norms in jurisprudence is the interpretation of general terms like "*in good faith*" or „*good public policy*". The law seems to refer to a positive standard but does not reveal where to find it. The problem associated with the interpretation of such general clauses is a particularly clear example of how the application of written law is hardly ever truly a simple reconstruction of the standard being set by fundamental values and norms. Even the „arch-positivist" Hans Kelsen pointed out that the application of law nearly always

10 Radbruch 1946, 105–8.

has a political element as well.[11] In a nutshell, questions of value and moral norms are nearly ubiquitous in law. How then are we to find standards of value and norms that are more than just the result of cultural or group prejudices?

*Sociobiological Reasoning in Law?*

Rather than presenting an overview of twenty-five hundred years of moral philosophy, I want to show what a naturalistic answer to questions of values and norms law could look like. Often those making naturalistic moral assertions claim that these are supported by sociobiology. But just because a natural behavior pattern exists, it does not follow that we *should* act in accordance with it. The naivety with which some sociobiologists repeatedly confuse facts and norms is astonishing. Sociobiology, in my opinion, quite often demonstrates some of the problems associated with naturalistic thought patterns. It appears to me that in some cases recourse to "natural" biological factors has not been well thought out.

Let us take a modern textbook example of sociobiology from Franz Wuketits.[12] Here the author attempted to reconcile the decision of a man to live celibate as a priest with the assumption of overwhelming and ubiquitous reproductive interest. The sociobiologist writes that celibate priests make a choice to live without reproduction and families of their own. However, the priestly life is taken to have certain advantages. Indeed, a priest's reputation benefits not only himself but also his parents, brothers, and sisters. Therefore, the sociobiologist argues, the family of the priest profits from his celibacy. This is clearly saying that the priest's reputation promotes the overall reproductive chances of his siblings. The priest thereby still manages to help pass on those genes that he has in common with his siblings. To my mind, this sociobiological argument is not very convincing. What would happen if potential partners of a priest's sister were actually deterred by the sheer fact that her brother was a priest? The only path remaining open to such a sister would lead to the convent. This would appear to be somewhat of a detriment to her reproductive success.

Naturalistic thought does not, however, necessarily lead to reductionism and oversimplification. Explanations of physical phenomena, such as personal preferences and personal values, may take biological factors into

11 Kelsen 1960, 346–54.
12 1997, 174.

account without neglecting other factors such as religion and social influences. The decision taken by a person to become a priest is definitely influenced by many factors. That decision, like all other human decisions, can be analysed naturalistically. There are other areas in which biological research into behaviour could influence the law. For one thing, biological research could make searching for intercultural or even global values easier. Moreover, behavioural biology could uncover genuinely intercultural methods of reinforcing the law and could devise symbols that support the acceptance of legal norms in a universally understandable manner. Biologists exploring human dispositions could explore ways of altering those behaviour patterns that violate legal norms.

It is clear that the law must also pay attention to human nature: law should not demand the impossible (*ultra posse nemo obligatur*). Research that explores the factual possibilities of realizing legal norms also falls within the scope of behavioural biology. It seems possible for the biology of human behaviour to trace hitherto undoubted norms back to their biological roots, thereby making critical analysis possible. One last point: The fact that human behavior is grounded in biological dispositions and is subject to the process of natural evolution by no means makes it impossible nowadays for people to actually decide against their own biological dispositions and, over time, change their own natural development.

### *An Interest-Oriented Concept of Value Foundation*

There is another, indirect way of making sociobiological findings and empirical anthropology fertile ground for lawyers: A legal norm is justified by evidence that the norm is a sufficient, possibly even a neccessary condition for the creation or protection of a positively valued outcome. The question of which conditions are positively valued obviously depends on the wishes and interests of the individuals deciding. A value is arrived at by abstraction from positively valued situations or "states of the world." It follows then that the term *value* as used here is subjective or relative (that is, relative to human beings and their needs).[13]

Moral judgments are not generally arrived at completely freely and arbitrarily but are traceable to a more or less fixed pattern of valuation. Valuations of individuals are therefore assumed to be more or less consistent. The valuation scales in question often vary by only a few degrees from in-

---

13 For a detailed discussion of value theory, see Rescher (1969).

dividual to individual. Even within a large group, uniform values are often to be found. From this we can conclude that, even in large groups or whole cultures, and possibly stretching as far as worldwide, clear homogenous valuations, therewith values, can be pinned down. Certain conditions are valued universally, such as self-survival and personal health, as well as the lives and health of close relatives. Also valued is the satisfaction of core physical requirements, like nourishment and rest. Furthermore, a minimum level of material security would also seem to be universally valued.

Since humans are a product of evolution, it seems to be possible to try to explain our needs and interests biologically. As far as life, health, and core physical requirements are concerned, this does not seem problematic. But this means that certain value dispositions, and consequently values, are the result of natural evolution. Research into and systematization of such natural interests and value standards falls under the umbrella of biology and empirical anthropology. In this sense, there is no categorical or logical gap between the factual and the normative.

It is difficult to avoid using the expression *natural law* when talking about this subject.[14] Still, there are significant differences between the sketch that I have given of universally accepted norms and values and what we understand under the traditional models of "natural law": Biology does not prescribe individual norms, but outlines natural interests, which can help to formulate a common, possibly globally acceptable canon of values. The implementation of such values into moral or legal norms affords the legislature a high level of freedom.

Moreover, such norms cannot simply be arrived at by following natural guidelines; an actual *decision* must be made regarding the realization of a "naturally" existing disposition. It appears that not all natural interests are worth realizing. Moreover, it is obvious that throughout all cultures religion and morality mould people's conduct when they are assigning value. The positive valuation enjoyed by certain behaviours, therefore, consists by no means solely of "natural interests." In spite of this, recourse to natural needs and interests is a means the naturalistic legal philosopher could choose to use in solving law's normative problems. We can ask whether legal and moral norms are compatible with our own natural tendencies and, furthermore, consider the extent to which they provide a suitable channel

---

14 After World War II, German courts cited Roman-Catholic Thomist philosophy of natural law in prosecuting Nazi crimes. The judicature was supported by prominent legal philosophers such as Helmut Coing and Heinrich Rommen (a good example is Rommen 1964).

for conveying our natural interests. It seems, therefore, that you can be a naturalist and still a legal philosopher with more to offer than pure logical formalisms and simple value scepticism.

## *Naturalism in Legal Doctrine*

*In order to review the possibility of transferring naturalistic thinking into law, it is not sufficient to simply consider questions of values and norms, for that is an issue of legal philosophy rather than of law itself. In this section, I discuss the possibility of interpreting practical legal concepts in a way compatible with the naturalistic program.*

### *Human Dignity*

Human dignity plays an immense role not only in legal academia but also in philosophical literature and even mass media. Unfortunately, the term, in spite of or perhaps owing to its widespread use, is extraordinarily ill-defined and metaphysically charged. For this reason, the concept is an ideal candidate for clarification on naturalistic lines. The principle of human dignity provides a basis for many national constitutions in Europe and beyond, including the German Federal Constitution (Art. 1, para. I, *Grundgesetz*), but it is also often involved in much-debated legal policy issues.

Misuse of the human dignity concept is common. Since the widely held understanding of human dignity is so broad and over-interpreted, it is, for example, applied to debates over genetic cell research, where even double or quadruple human cells are viewed as having human dignity. Therefore, all research into such cells often is categorically rejected. On the other hand, such research seeks to find cures that will help improve the human dignity of sick and disabled people. It is obvious then that the "human dignity" argument can be used both for and against genetic cell research, which boils down to the fact that the argument has hardly any value in this debate. To take the idea of "human dignity" seriously, we must make the concept more precise.

The understanding of human dignity in European jurisprudence has two roots, the first being the theological tradition of "man" as "image of God"; the second being the idea of individual autonomy developed during the Enlightenment. According to the definition of human dignity given by German courts, human dignity is infringed if "a person is significantly disparaged as an object or a mere means." This idea is unmistakable from Kant. In many more popularized statements, an infringement of human dignity is defined as the "instrumentalization" of an individual, that is, as using him or her solely as a means to achieve a certain purpose. However, the ban placed on instrumentalization is much too narrow to exhaust all cases that breach human dignity. Let us take the example of a fanatical dictator who tortures to death the last remaining member of a resistance organization in the cellar of his palace. In this case, the dictator is not seeking to misuse his victim for any specific purpose. The breach of human dignity witnessed here does not arise because the torture is a means to an end. Human dignity is infringed because of the *effects* that such treatment has on the victim, who has been locked up, stripped of all rights, and tortured. The expression "instrumentallzation of others" is therefore inapplicable as a general criterion or definition of the violation of human dignity.

From a naturalistic standpoint, human dignity can be defined by an ensemble of subjective rights. These are oriented toward basic human requirements and interests. One could call this the ensemble theory of human dignity.[15] The requirement for the minimum necessary to exist (food, air, space) corresponds to "the right to minimum material existence." The interest in fundamental freedom possibilities corresponds to "the right to autonomous self-development," and the interest in freedom from pain corresponds to "the right to be without extreme pain." The interest in keeping personal information confidential corresponds to "the right to a private sphere," and the interest in intellectual liberty (freedom from brainwashing, for example) corresponds to "the right to intellectual-psychological integrity." The interest in a safe, fundamental legal status corresponds to "the right to fundamental legal equality," and the interest in not being publicly humiliated corresponds to "the right to minimal respect".

The introduction of these seven subjective rights as a definition of human dignity can be interpreted as a *naturalization* of the idea of human dignity. It is, perhaps, worth casting a glance over the advantages and disadvantages of this conception of human dignity: On the pro side, there appears the clear advantage of making a widely held concept more precise. Whether there has been a violation of human dignity can be confirmed in a comparatively easy way by going through the list of subjective rights. But the contra side of the argument also requires attention: The newly gained precision in the terminology corresponds, of course, to a loss in the number of ways the term „human dignity“ can be interpreted. Thus, the concept loses part of its emotional power. This is the price we have to pay if

15 Hilgendorf 1999b, 148–50; 2018, 57–89.

we want human dignity to become a truly legal concept rather than just a philosophical one.

Even more problematic is the question of which type of requirements are formulated to underpin and explicate the content of human dignity: Are we matter-of-factly talking about natural requirements and how such requirements can be used for a "naturalization" of the term *human dignity*? Or are the needs mentioned above culturally shaped or indeed completely dependent on culture and therefore fundamentally culture-specific? For example, as far as the interest in protecting people‘s private sphere is concerned, we are indeed talking about a culturally shaped need that seems to have become apparent only in the last decades, primarily in our Western industrial and media-oriented societies. Other needs, such as the interest in being free from severe pain, seem to have stronger biological roots.

### *Causation*

A further test for the naturalistic program in jurisprudence is the concept of causation. The naturalistic position has been characterized by the thesis that all phenomena can be causally explained, and thus the principle of causation cannot be broken even by a „supernatural“ power. Empirical science has the task of researching natural causal links. In law, causation problems play an immense role when the causal relationship between an action and its result must be examined. In addition to carrying out the offence, the perpetrator actually has to achieve a factual result (such as to cause the *death* of a person or to *damage* something).

In civil law, the test for determining whether a causal relationship exists is called the *conditio sine qua non* formula (comparable to the British/American *but for* test[16]). An action is considered causal when the existence of the end result depends on the action's having been performed. In other words, a causal relationship is said to exist between *A* and *B*, if *A* is a condition necessary for the fulfilment of *B*. This model of causality is compatible with the naturalistic position.[17] Supernatural instances do not play any role in the legal examination of causation. Even causal relationships between psychic and physical factors (and vice versa) are considered unproblematic. The philosophical problems of mental causation are neglected in law.

---

16 See Robinson/Cahill 2012, 124–125.
17 Hilgendorf 1999a.

However, the question of whether *A* was a necessary condition for *B* cannot be answered without considering the empirical relationship between the two. In simple cases, judges can rely on their personal life experiences: If a ball hits a window, and the glass in the window subsequently breaks, then the causal relationship is identifiable without scientific examination. It is a different matter if the issue at stake is, say, whether a particular medication has physically harmed a patient taking it. In such cases, medical experts must deliver their opinions in order to rule out other possible causes that might come into consideration. In the Thalidomide Case, for example, which appeared before the German courts in the early 1970s, it was argued that birth defects suffered in association with use of the drug Thalidomide during pregnancy could possibly also have been the result of the American atom bomb tests carried out during the 1950s and 60s. If that were true, the use of Thalidomide would not have been a necessary condition for the physical deformities. Such problems nevertheless do not hinder the naturalistic interpretation of the concept of causation. Thus, the legal interpretation of causation is perfectly compatible with the naturalistic way of thinking.

### *Legal Method and Naturalism*

Finally, the methods of legal argumentation in German and European law crucial to a lawyer's everyday work need to be investigated visà-vis the question of naturalism.

### *Statutory Interpretation*

The four traditional legal methods of statutory interpretation, otherwise known as "the canons of interpretation, "are methods of examining the text in respect to the wording of the statute, its place in the legal system, its history, and its purpose (teleology). Grammatical interpretation looks at the choice of words and syntax of the written legal norm in question to determine how it should be interpreted. This essentially philological process is in itself compatible with the concept of naturalism. The same is true for the system method of interpretation. Here, the aim is to apply the general sense of the term as found in other legal texts to the interpretation of the terminus in the text in question. Historical interpretation methods look at the views historically held by the legislature: What was the problem at hand? Which solution did the legislature intend? Such questions are empirical and therefore generally create no great problems in terms of naturalistic methods.

The teleological method is much more difficult to analyse. Many textbooks on legal methods claim that teleological interpretation is used to research the „objective sense“ of the law. This explains why this method is often referred to as the "objective teleological" method of interpretation. But what exactly this means is not clear. On the one hand, it can refer to the sense of a law or legal phrase being a clear statement of the aims of the legislature enacting it, in which case the objective teleological method of interpretation coincides with the historical method. On the other hand, it is possible that the „teleology“ is purely the purpose of those applying the law. It is their own purpose that they find in the law. A law text in itself has no "sense." or „purpose“. To speak of an "objective sense" brings us back to the mysticism of Hegel's terminology, to which the „objective teleological method“ of interpretation is in fact closely related. On closer inspection of the practical use of teleological arguments, the confusion seems to resolve. In fact, the debate almost always centres on practical considerations that argue both for and against possible variations in linguistic interpretation. Such variations are then normally supported by considerations of the empirical consequences of specific interpretations of the law. The choice to interpret words in a given way mostly comes down to prognoses. Understood in this sense, teleological methods of interpretation also conform with naturalistic methodology.

Further methods used in statute law and its application normally fall within the categories outlined by the four canons. Application of higher-level legal systems, such as European law or international law, requires conceptual and logical consistency. A consideration of how problems are resolved in other legal systems (comparative law), can essentially be carried out using empirical methods, even if questions of interpretation do often crop up. Legal sociology, legal anthropology, and legal history are all empirical disciplines.

### *The Application of Law*

My final question is whether the practical application of law itself is compatible with a naturalistic program. To apply law practically is not a purely logical process, meaning that statutes alone do not drive the decisions of those who are applying the law. More often than not, the law suggests a mere framework within which those entrusted with applying the law are free to exercise discretion. In doing so, all kinds of considerations are logically possible and actually realized. This means, of course, that concepts contrary to naturalism can play a role as well.

In German law, which I know best, no explicit norm compels those applying the law to conform to the standards of naturalistic argumentation. But it is unimaginable that someone applying the law today would explicitly refer to the will of a god, goddess, or other supernatural entity. A judge arguing openly in a religious or some other metaphysical way would be regarded as irrational. The wide interpretation of fundamental legal concepts makes it possible that such irrational considerations (if they were in fact to arise), could simply be hidden behind such terms as "*human dignity*." As for legal practice, however, I am not aware of any contemporary judgment that oversteps the bounds of naturalistic method.

## *Conclusion*

My aim in this article has been to argue that modern law is compatible with the naturalistic program of science. Empirical biological research into human value dispositions, that is, our natural tendencies to value things or situations as "good" or "bad," can even help us to find a basis for transcultural legal values. Therefore, there is no need to turn to non- or antinaturalistic methods, which are notoriously problematic. It is possible to reinterpret such vague concepts as "*human dignity*" in ways that are compatible with the naturalistic program. Basic concepts such as *causation* are already used by lawyers in accordance with the naturalistic program. This is true as well for the methods of legal argumentation, at least as far as the methods of statutory interpretation are concerned (although case law argumentation was left undiscussed; presumably, the result would not be different). Of course, lawyers applying the law can (and sometimes will) hold private views that are not compatible with the naturalistic program. But in modern legal practice, at least in the West, non-naturalistic beliefs do not seem to exist at all, and if they do, they remain hidden.

*References*

Curran, V. G. 2002.
*Comparative law: An introduction.* Durham, NC: Carolina Academic Press.

Hilgendorf, E. 1999a.
Causality in penal law: Explanation or understanding? A sketch. In *Actions, norms, values: Discussions with Georg Henrik von Wright*, ed. G. Meggle, 265–72. New York: Walter de Gruyter.

Hilgendorf, E. 1999b.
Die missbrauchte Menschenwürde: Probleme des Menschenwürdetopos am Beispiel der bioethischen Diskussion. In *Annual review of law and ethics*, vol. 7, ed. B. S. Byrd, J. Hruschka, and J. C. Joerden, 137–58. Berlin: Duncker & Humblot.

Hilgendorf, E. 2018.
Problem areas in the dignity debate and the ensemble theory of human dignity. In *Human Dignity in Context. Explorations of a Contested Concept*, ed. D. Grimm et al., 57 – 89. Baden-Baden: Nomos.

Hilgendorf, E., ed., 1998.
*Wissenschaftlicher Humanismus. Texte zur Moral- und Rechtsphilosophie des Wiener Kreises*, vol. 12 of *Haufe Schriftenreihe zur rechtswissenschaftlichen Grundlagenforschung*. Freiburg: Haufe.

Hippel, E. von. 1967.
Zur Überwindung des Naturalismus in Recht und Politik. In *Festschrift Fritz von Hippel 70. Geburtstag*, ed. J. Esser and H. Thieme, 245–62. Tübingen: J. C. B. Mohr (Paul Siebeck).

Kelsen, H. 1960.
*Reine Rechtslehre. Mit einem Anhang: Das Problem der Gerechtigkeit.* 2nd ed. Vienna: Franz Deuticke.

Mnookin, J. 2002.
Science and law. In *The Oxford companion to American Law*, ed. K. L. Hall, 714–18. Oxford: Oxford University Press.

Nagel, E. 1956.
Naturalism reconsidered. In *Logic without metaphysics and other essays in the philosophy of science*, ed. E. Nagel, S. Glencoe, II: Free Press.

Papineau, D. 2020.
*Naturalism.* In: Stanford Encyclopedia of Philosophy. https://plato.stanford.edu/entries/naturalism.

Radbruch, G. 1946.
Gesetzliches Unrecht und übergesetzliches Recht. *Süddeutsche Juristenzeitung 1*: 105–8.

Rescher, N. 1969.
*Introduction to value theory.* Englewood Cliffs, NJ: Prentice Hall.

Rescher, N. *1985.*
*The strife of systems: An essay on the grounds and implications of philosophical diversity.* Pittsburgh, PA: University of Pittsburgh Press.

Robinson, P. H. /Cahill, M.T. 2012.
*Criminal law.* 2. ed. New York: Wolters Kluwer.

Rommen, H. A. 1964.
In defense of natural law. In *Law and philosophy: A symposium*, ed. S. Hook, 105–21. New York: New York University Press.

Stöltzner, M./Uebel, Th., ed. 2006.
*Wiener Kreis. Texte zur wissenschaftlichen Weltauffassung.* Hamburg, Felix Meiner.

Vollmer, G. 1995.
Was ist Naturalismus? Eine Begriffsverschärfung in zwölf Thesen. In *Auf der Suche nach der Ordnung. Beiträge zu einem naturalistischen Welt- und Menschenbild*, ed. G. Vollmer, 21–42. Stuttgart: Wissenschaftliche Verlagsgesellschaft.

Wolters, G. 1994.
Scientific philosophy; The Other Side. In *Logic, language, and the structure of scientific theories*, ed. W. Salmon and G. Wolters, 3–19. Pittsburgh, PA: University Of Pittsburgh Press.

Wuketits, F. M. 1997.
*Soziobiologie. Die Macht der Gene und die Evolution sozialen Verhaltens.* Heidelberg: Spektrum.

# *Rechtswissenschaft* revisited

*Heike Jung*

## *I. Why this topic?*

Questioning the scientific character of legal studies seems to be a „no go" for a German (law) scholar. At least, the term „Rechts*wissenschaft*" appears to give a prompt and clear answer as to the German stance in the debate. Von Jhering locutus, causa finita!?[1] You need not be afraid: I do not want to leave this ambitious project by the back door. I have volunteered for it. The German voice should not be missing in the international chorus of those who ponder on the character of law as an academic discipline. Despite the certainty which the term *„Rechtswissenschaft"* insinuates we can produce evidence that this has always been a contested issue, inextricably linked with the wider controversy about the essence of science as such.[2]

In a way, this is a welcome invitation for me to return to some of the German heros of this debate in the 19th century such as von Kirchmann (1802–1884) and von Jhering (1818–1892). The vivid controversy about the integration of the social sciences in the 1970ies has also left its marks.[3] The contempory *„Wissenschaftstheorie des Rechts"* seems to engage primarily in a sub- or intradisciplinary discourse.[4] Still, titles such as *„Selbstreflexion der Rechtswissenschaft"*[5] indicate a never ending interest in rehearsing the theo-

1 Von Jhering, Ist die Jurisprudenz eine Wissenschaft?, ed. by Behrends, Wallstein, Göttingen 1998.

2 E. g. for more details Simon, Jurisprudenz und Wissenschaft, Rechtshistorisches Journal 7 (1988), p. 141–156; idem, Vorwort, in: Simon (ed.), Rechtswissenschaft in der Bonner Republik. Studien zur Wissenschaftsgeschichte der Jurisprudenz, Suhrkamp, Frankfurt 1994, p. 7, 9; Stichweh, Motive und Begründungsstrategien für Wissenschaftlichkeit in der deutschen Jurisprudenz des 19. Jahrhunderts, Rechtshistorisches Journal 11 (1992), p. 330.

3 Cf. Grimm (ed.), Rechtswissenschaft und Nachbarwissenschaften, vol. 1, Athenäum Fischer, Frankfurt a. M. 1973.

4 Typical: Jestaedt/Lepsius (eds.), Rechtswissenschaftstheorie, Mohr Siebeck, Tübingen 2008.

5 Hilgendorf/Schulze-Fielitz (eds.), Selbstreflexion der Rechtswissenschaft, Mohr Siebeck, Tübingen 2015.

retical basis of the legal discipline(s) as such. Hilgendorf/Schulze-Fielitz even invoke a crisis of the German *„Rechtswissenschaft"*.[6]

Contrary to Radbruch´s contention that disciplines which devote too much time to the reflection of their own methodological standards are in bad shape,[7] I tend to think that this is a promising exercise. Engaging in an international discourse on the question might also show that we should not let our minds get obfuscated by terminological niceties, but rather try to address those issues which hide behind the terminological cover.[8]

Theorizing about science is not a German particularity. It has rather, since Kuhn´s groundbreaking studies on scientific progress,[9] become fashionable to ponder on what scientists are doing, on the borderlines of disciplines, on inter- or multidisciplinarity and on new „turns" which claim to do away with disciplinary borderlines in favour of new overarching perspectives.[10] This may reveal a longing for new universal perspectives in a world of science which seems to have lost its traditional bearings.

In actual fact, the „scientific", or should I say the „academic", scene is presently characterized by diversification and fragmentation. In a certain contrast to these introspective *manoeuvres* we register a renewed scepticism with regard to the role of scientists in a democratic society.[11] It has never been self-evident that scholars have more of a say than others in public discourse. Nowadays, with the information-overload generated by internet, scholars have to struggle to get heard. The rise of populism and populist leaders nourish scepticism and disbelief, thus undermining the respect for science and scientists. „Fake news" and the call for a „sound science" add momentum to this „discredibilisation" campaign.

This somber general climate imposes itself on the discourse about the standing and understanding of law as a *„Wissenschaft"*. This calls for a reappraisal of those familiar questions which have already haunted and divided (German) lawyers in the past. Considering that the notion of science is related to discovery and potential progress we have to ask ourselves whether

6 Hilgendorf/Schulze-Fielitz, Rechtswissenschaft im Prozess der Selbstreflexion, in Hilgendorf/Schulze-Fielitz (note 5), p. 1.

7 Radbruch, Einführung in die Rechtswissenschaft, 5. /6. Aufl., Quelle & Meyer, Leipzig 1925, S. 194.

8 Exemplary in this respect Jareborg, Legal Dogmatics and the Concept of Science, in: Festschrift für Frisch, Duncker & Humblot, Berlin 2013, p. 49.

9 Kuhn, The Structure of Scientific Revolutions, Chicago University Press, Chicago 1962.

10 E. g. Bachmann-Medick, Cultural Turns. Neuorientierung in den Kulturwissenschaften, Rowohlt Taschenbuch Verlag, Reinbek bei Hamburg 2006.

11 E. g. Bourdieu, Science de la science et réflexivité, Raisons d´agir, Paris 2001.

and how that applies to law. Isn´t law rather a self-perpetuating system? A technique? Not to say a bureaucracy? Can there be progress in a regulatory program governed by law and what should it look like? And what is the function of the „legal scientist". To think ahead? Yet, into which direction? To produce grand theories? Yet, to what avail? To help promoting the normative aspirations of society? Maybe, but why should this be a pregrogative of a scientist in a democratic society?

## *II. From „art" to science (?): a few glimpses of history*

The Digest classifies the administration of justice as an "art": *„Iuri operam daturum prius nosse oportet, unde nomen iuris descendat. Est autem a iustitia appellatum: nam, ut eleganter Celsus definit, ius est ars boni et aequi. Cuius merito quis nos sacerdotes appellet ...*".[12] Though the reading of the term „art" is not unambiguous, the high rank of justice is underlined by the proximity of judges and priests. Outside the Western main-stream, Arab philosophers like the Northafrican Ibn Khaldūn (1332–1406) indulged in encyclopedic overviews over the sciences, over their methods and their standing in society.[13] Ibn Khaldūn distinguished between the rational sciences which are common to mankind and those sciences which are based on tradition, more precisely on the rules of the Coran and the Sunna. The legal science forms part of the canon of traditional sciences. Its main object is to distill the (religious) laws from the only authoritative text. Hence, whereas the rational sciences are related to reason, law as a science is closely linked to (religious) authority which leaves only a limited margin of manoeuvre for interpretation. Though the embrace between law and religion is particularly close in the islamic tradition, the anchoring of law in religious and metaphysical beliefs is ubiquitous[14] and has only been overcome in modern times.[15]

12 D.1.1.1 pr. up to 1.

13 Ibn Khaldūn, Das Buch der Beispiele. Einführung in die Weltgeschichte, Reclam, Stuttgart 2016, Chapter 6, p. 239 et seq.

14 E. g. Herberger, Recht, in: Ritter/Gründer (eds.), Historisches Wörterbuch der Philosophie, Vol. 8, Schwabe, Basel 1992, S. 222.

15 Cf. the analysis of this process by Habermas, Auch eine Geschichte der Philosophie, 2 vols., Suhrkamp, Berlin 2019. The relationship between religion and reason runs like a silver thread through the whole of his new magnum opus.

It is customary, since von Savigny (1779–1861),[16] to trace back the scientific approach to law to Roman times and to Roman law. It seems to me that this belief in continuity is grounded on a continuity of meaning and purpose which, in actual fact, does not exist.[17] Of course, the role of science, dogma and argument has permeated the whole of the Middle Ages.[18] Yet, according to Simon the „attribution" of a scientific character to law, i. e. the use of the term *„Rechtswissenschaft"*, only took place in the 18th century,[19] during what one might like to call the era of „scientification". In view of Kant´s categorial distinction which amounted to a hierarchical order of „sciences" and a prioritisation of the natural sciences, the lawyers had to struggle[20] though Kant had acknowledged that every doctrine that aims at a systematic and principled body of knowledge should be called „science".[21]

At that time, the discourse centered around the comparison with the natural sciences. Their rise had nourished sort of an inferiority complex as well as a „bandwagon effect" on the part of what we would today call the humanities. Traces of this inferiority complex and the corresponding feeling of superiority cultivated by some representatives of the natural sciences can still be detected today, embodied in the French formula of *„les sciences dures"*. Some contenders in this debate like Feuerbach tried to establish the scientific character of law by way of analogy to the uncontested methods and objects of the natural science. Others like Hugo (1764–1844) flatly denied character of law as a „rational science".[22]

This discussion culminated in von Kirchmann´s legendary lecture on „Die Wertlosigkeit der Jurisprudenz als Wissenschaft" held in Berlin in

---

16 E. g. for a brief rehearsal of von Savigny´s position Stichweh (note 2), p. 340.

17 Cf. Rückert, Denktraditionen, Schulbildungen und Arbeitsweisen in der `Rechtswissenschaft` – gestern und heute, in: Hilgendorf/Schulze-Fielitz (note 5), p. 13 at 16 et seq.

18 Herberger has followed this dogma-discourse for medicine and law in detail. Cf. Herberger, Dogmatik. Zur Geschichte von Begriff und Methode in Medizin und Jurisprudenz, Klostermann, Frankfurt am Main 1981. Cf. in particular chapter 5 on the medieval discussions, p. 161 et seq.

19 Simon, Jurisprudenz (note 2), p. 143.

20 E. g. the illuminating account of the controversial debate by Herberger, Beziehungen zwischen Naturwissenschaft und Jurisprudenz in der ersten Hälfte des 19. Jahrhunderts, Berichte zur Wissenschaftsgeschichte 6 (1983), p. 79–88.

21 Kant, Metaphysische Anfangsgründe der Naturwissenschaft, 1786, Vorrede, A IV f.: „Eine solche Lehre, wenn sie ein System, d. h. ein nach Principien geordnetes Ganzes der Erkenntnis seyn soll, heißt Wissenschaft, und ...".

22 Cf. Herberger (note 20), p. 80.

1848.[23] Impregnated by the dominant fascination for nature and the natural sciences von Kirchmann grounded his argument against the scientific character of law on the lack of objectivity or rather on the importance of *„Rechtsgefühl“* which introduced an element of uncertainty. Contrary to nature, law was, according to von Kirchmann, constantly „on the move“. He put a particular emphasis on the ephemeral character of the positive law. Though his line of thought is somewhat complex and meandering, he is above all remembered for the provocative statement which he actually made in passing: „... *drei berichtigende Worte des Gesetzgebers und ganze Bibliotheken werden zu Makulatur*“.[24]

This amounted to heresy and drew fierce opposition. In singling out the legislator as the „bad guy“ von Kirchmann had already prepared von Jhering´s „defense line“: Actually, his inaugural lecture *„Ist die Jurisprudenz eine Wissenschaft?“* amounted to a grand-scale tour d´horizon of the development of law. In a brief summary of half a page he finally ventured an answer to the question. According to him the systematisation of the given legal order in the light of historical and philosophical insight constituted the scientific character of *„Jurisprudenz“*.[25] In other words: the existence of a meta-level for reflection of the positive law makes up the *„Wissenschaftlichkeit“*. Thus, what is, at least today, rather peripheral in the curriculum of law faculties turns into the decisive criterion when it comes to the qualification of law as a science. The movable character of law is no longer detrimental, but rather a prerequisite as long as development and change are orientated towards perfection (*„Vervollkommnung“*). Contrary to that, von Kirchmann had considered these historical studies to be an „enormous ballast“, since the focus should be put on the present.[26] With his „deconstructionist“ line of thought he was, however, unable or unwilling to give any guidance as to what the present-day law should look like.

In his *„Einführung in die Rechtswissenschaft“*, an influential reader for students, Radbruch devotes a whole chapter to *„Rechtswissenschaft“*, without,

---

23 Von Kirchmann, Die Wertlosigkeit der Jurisprudenz als Wissenschaft. Ein Vortrag gehalten in der Juristischen Gesellschaft zu Berlin 1848, Wissenschaftlicher Buchgesellschaft, Darmstadt 1973 (Sonderausgabe 2012). The original version of the lecture „Die Werthlosigkeit der Jurisprudenz als Wissenschaft“ can be consulted online on the site of the library of the University of Frankfurt a. M.: http://sammlungen.ub.uni-frankfurt.de/1848/urn/urn:nbn:de:hebis:30:2-21092.

24 Von Kirchmann (note 23), p. 25. („Three amending words of the legislator and whole libraries become waste paper.“).

25 Von Jhering (note 1), p. 92.

26 Von Kirchmann (note 23), p. 14 et seq.

however, going into the details of the controversy. Alluding to von Kirchmann's position he proceeds with a description of the lawyers' activity, acknowledging in passing that the scientific character is still not beyond doubt.[27] In his *„Rechtsphilosophie"* he is more explicit suggesting to distinguish between the *„Rechtswissenschaft"* stricto sensu, i. e. the systematic endeavour of interpretation and classification, the systematic search for the objective sense of the positive legal order, and a „social theory" of law in the wider sense which, according to him, comprises history of law, comparative law and sociology of law. Likewise, he distinguishes between the normative and the empirical side, a distinction which somehow cuts across this line.[28]

Radbruch's differentiations hint at the duality of approaches. Whereas one side insists on an „internal justification" which is more or less synonymous with the reflection of legal methodology, others put the emphasis on the idea of a meta-reflection on law and its positive emanations by way of a set of „outside"-parameters which, as an ensemble, allow an „insight" into what law is about. In Germany, this debate centers around the terms *„Kernstück"* and *„Nebenstück"*. The *„Kernstück"*-approach to the question seems to have carried the day.[29] Neumann starts out from this premise in a matter of fact way[30] though, in the end, his illuminating *„Wissenschaftstheorie der Rechtswissenschaft"* reaches far beyond a mere methodological exercise.[31]

L. Constantinesco has attributed this prevalence of legal dogmatics in the German discourse to the historical *„Begriffsjurisprudenz"*, the great affinity to logics and the isolation of the juridical norm from the social and historical reality.[32] German law scholars have indeed for a long time preferred to reflect on the „law in the books" and have somewhat neglected the „law in action"[33], not to mention the interaction with the social reality

27 Radbruch (note 7).

28 Radbruch, Rechtsphilosophie, 5th ed. Koehler, Stuttgart 1956, p. 209 et seq.

29 Cf. Simon, Jurisprudenz (note 2), p. 147: „Die `Kernstück'-Konzeption ist seit der Jahrhundertwende konventionell".

30 Neumann, Wissenschaftstheorie der Rechtswissenschaft, in: Hassemer/Neumann/Saliger (eds.), Einführung in die Rechtsphilosophie und Rechtstheorie der Gegenwart, 9. Aufl., Müller, Heidelberg 2016, p. 351 at 352.

31 Neumann (note 30), in particular the chapter on „Rechtswissenschaft als Handlungswissenschaft" at p. 361.

32 L. Constantinesco, Rechtsvergleichung, Bd. 3. Die rechtsvergleichende Wissenschaft, Heymann's, Köln et al. 1983, p. 11.

33 Dwelling on Roscoe Pound's famous distinction: Pound, Law in Books and Law in Action, Am. L. R. 44 (1910) p. 12.

as such. Due to sociology of law, socio-legal studies and criminology, those who advocate a more comprehensive perspective have gained ground. In France, Carbonnier (1908–2003), one of the most renowned French private lawyers of the last century, will be equally well known in the field of sociology of law.[34] We cannot disregard the fact, however, that, generally speaking, there is still a wide-spread reluctance of lawyers to engage in such operations.

### *III. Making sense of „legal science"*

Though the terms „legal science" and „legal dogmatics" are not totally uncommon in the Anglo-American academic discourse, they still sound somewhat clumsy, not to say awkward. I have no missionary ambition to popularise these terms in the English speaking world and to fuel the ongoing discussion there. Despite some convergence, it cannot be overlooked that the theory of sciences is imbued by national traditions to the extent that a particular labeling might hinder the international discourse of the subject matter. With regard to law as a discipline, this diversity is somewhat related to the boundaries between the different legal systems.[35]

The fact that Anglo-American lawyers and scholars do not cherish the term „science" in connection with law does not reveal a lack of potential for innovation. On the contrary, their interdisciplinary activity, like for example „law and literature" or „law and anthropology", rather tends to be an eye-opener.[36] Yet, they do not rally around the flag of the supposedly unitarian concept of a *„Rechtswissenschaft"*. We already note transatlantic spill-overs of new unorthodox moves which seem to be inspired by a „field"-oriented perspective and attracted by new „turns", accompanied by a pragmatic disregard of classical distinctions.

Traditionally, the high ranking of law was related to its affinity with theology which, along with philosophy and metaphysics, was more or less the leader of the academic disciplines. The rise of the natural sciences has established a new point of reference. Yet, the academic ranking order prevailed. Law, in my Faculty, has taken great pride in having survived the recent university reform as „Fakultät 1". Pride is a key word in our context.

34 Typical of his style of reasoning: Carbonnier, Flexible Droit, 10$^{th}$ ed., Librairie Générale du Droit et de Jurisprudence, Paris 2001..

35 See for the role of boundaries in law Walker, Law Unbounded?, in: Dahlberg (ed.), Law and Society, Iustus Förlag, Uppsala 2019, p. 359.

36 Cf. Hilgendorf/Schulze-Fielitz (note 6), p. 5.

In the German scene, being named a „*Wissenschaftler*" is still a matter of pride. It seems to confer authority. Scientists are part of a community which subscribes to rational quality standards. The constitutional guarantee of Art. 5 subs. 3 of the German Basic Law acknowledges this elevated position of science and gives it a constitutional backing.

For lawyers, the high profile of law as an academic discipline and a traditional member of the family of sciences may function as an antidote against the wide-spread distrust vis-à vis the profession of lawyers. Yet, at times, the „scientification" of law, the learned lawyer, has been the very reason for this distrust. Thus, the authority of lawyers[37] may, in the course of history, have been intermittently fostered and undermined by the supposed „*Wissenschaftlichkeit*" of the discipline.[38] The standing of lawyers in public life seems to depend on their ability to refrain from intellectual conceit and to keep in touch with the reality of social life. The sociology of sciences and of the scientific communities offers illuminating insight into the role of scientists in society[39] which, at least to some extent, accounts for the „the legal scientist" as well.

But what actually constitutes law as a science, or perhaps, in more general terms, what constitutes a science as such? As we have seen, the German discourse favours „method" as the decisive point. This is the proper starting point, since science is primarily about method. Yet, the term „method" needs explanation. The legal method is not an abstract process of scholastic refinement. The innate orientation of law towards the social world and the guarantee of the public peace imply that we have to take into account the facts, reflect the decision-making processes and keep in touch with the consolidated body of knowledge on human behaviour and social development. Law is, in that sense, a communicative enterprise and not a self-contained intellectual *manoeuvre*. Law is, like medicine, an „applied science", i. e. a body of normative knowledge that has to be applied to a concrete set-up, a decision related to human beings.[40] This raises questions of judicial ethics, responsibility, self-reflection and „CAPA"-process-

37 For a more general account e. g. Jung, The authority of lawyers, Oñati Legal Series, Vol. 1, n. 9 (2011) – autonomy and heteronomy of the judiciary in Europe, p. 1.

38 As to the biting criticism of lawyers by Montaigne cf. Jung, Montaigne und die Juristen, in: Festschrift für Wadle, Duncker & Humblot, Berlin 2008, p. 437.

39 E. g. in particular Bourdieu (note 11).

40 Cf. on the comparison of legal and medical thinking Ricœur, Le Juste 2, Éditions Esprit, Paris 2001, p. 245.

es.[41] In short: law is much more than just interpreting statutes. The reference to „*Dogmatik*" with its inherent inclination towards the interpretation of the substantive law does not give a full portrait of the complexity of legal activity.

Therefore we cannot content ourselves with the simple reference to „method". Method is not „*l'art pour l'art*", but requires meaning and purpose. Also, method is not the entrance ticket to an academic enterprise, since a craftsman will also apply a certain method, a technique. And finally: not even the addition „scientific" clarifies the matter, since it may well be doubted that the method applied in legal dogmatics is sophisticated enough to be called „scientific".[42] Either we refer to a certain elasticity of the term „scientific" or we concentrate on the scientific purpose and attitude. We might even combine both „rescue *manoeuvres*".[43] Moreover, the term „scientific" is perhaps still slightly over-determined by the „empirical ideal" of the natural sciences which is not the ideal approach to decipher the socio-cultural aspects of the human world anyway.

I see no point in striking „argumentation" from the list of „scientific" methods; the intellectual input may well pass as an equivalent to the complexity of an empirical design. Eventually, I take Jareborg's reference to purpose and attitude[44] as the missing link to what „*Rechtswissenschaftler*" are in my opinion supposed to do, namely to bring the law forward, to find the better solution („*Das Recht vorandenken.*").[45] This is not about niceties in the process of interpretation, but about helping to pursue and to bring to bear the normative aspirations of mankind and, perhaps, to achieve progress.[46]

---

41 Corrective and Preventive Action.

42 Jareborg (note 8), p. 55. Likewise Stelmach, Kirchmanns Fluch, in: Festschrift für Neumann, Müller, Heidelberg 2017, p. 445 et seq.

43 Both aspects can be detected in the interpretation of Art 5 subs. 3 of the German Basic Law by the German courts and in the German constitutional doctrine; e. g. Wendt, in: von Münch/Kunig (eds.), Grundgesetz, 7th ed., Beck, München 2021, Art 5 note 156 with further references.

44 Jareborg (note 8), p. 55 et seq.

45 Cf. Jung, New Perspectives or More of the Same? Criminal Law and Criminal Science in the 21st Century, Keio Law Review 1993, p. 41 at 61.

46 Cf. Müller-Dietz`s reflections on the potentiality of progress in criminal law: Müller-Dietz, Gibt es Fortschritt im Strafrecht?, in: Jung/Müller-Dietz/Neumann (eds.), Perspektiven der Strafrechtsentwicklung, Nomos, Baden-Baden 1996, p. 31 and, more generally, on progress as a moral dimension Habermas (note 15), vol. 2, p. 789 et seq.

Of course, „progress" is a bold term in connection with law. As far as I am concerned, pursuing for example the perennial issues related to equality justifies the use of this term. Others prefer the term innovation[47] or the neutral „New".[48] Whatever we like or prefer: lawyers are often critisized for their backwards orientation, for their defence of the status quo. We realise, at this stage, that much depends on what we personally associate with law. Those who, like me, relate law to evolution[49] will be inclined to reach out beyond the narrow concept of law as a science, i. e. reach out beyond „*Rechtsdogmatik*". They might want to include socio-historical, comparative and economic aspects as well, the circle of perspectives and subject matters which help getting the bearings for the evolution of law. They will favour the idea of an opening towards other sciences.

Thus the scientific character of law is, in my concept, to some extent contingent upon the sense and the drive of lawyers for interdisciplinarity. Law as a science lives on and depends on the intensity of the input from other sciences.[50] In a way, the lawyers′ scientific standing is a product of teamwork and the lawyers′ ability to entertain productive relations with other sciences which adds a programatic touch to our question. It is not the „*Rechtsdogmatik*", but this overlap with other sciences which guarantees a perpetual process of self-reflection and which enables the „*Rechtswissenschaft*" to help flanking and implementing change. This requires openness and the capacity to connect with other disciplines or other concepts of law.[51] The fact that the so-called „*Bindestrich-Wissenschaften*", like history of law or sociology of law, will share the logics and method of other disci-

---

47 E. g. Hoffmann-Riem, Innovationsoffenheit und Innovationsverantwortung durch Recht, Archiv des öffentlichen Rechts 131 (2006), p. 255. According to Hoffmann-Riem we need more innovation research. Such research is supposed to clarify how the law can contribute to the compatibility of innovation with the common good (ibid, p. 257) which sets a slightly different agenda.

48 Cf. Saliger, Intra- und Interdisziplinarität: Wie kommt das Neue in die Rechtswissenschaft, in: Hilgendorf/Schulze-Fielitz (note 5), p. 117.

49 On Saleilles′ s (1855–1912) similar position cf. Deroussin, Raymond Saleilles: le droit, la méthode et la postérité, in: Audren et al. (dir.), Raymond Saleilles et au-delà, Dalloz, Paris 2013, p. 171.

50 This is the common message of Zheng, Interdisziplinarität der Rechtswissenschaft, in: Festschrift für Neumann, Müller, Heidelberg 2017, p. 483 and of Stelmach (note 42), p. 448. Therefore invoking the solitary autonomy of the legal science (e. g. Martinek, Die Autonomie oder die gescheiterte Interdisziplinarität der Rechtswissenschaft, jM - juris Die Monatsschrift 2018, p. 447) is a misleading directive.

51 Cf. Jestaedt, Die deutsche Staatsrechtslehre im europäisierten Rechtswissenschaftsdiskurs, Juristenzeitung 2012, p. 1 at 9.

plines[52] only goes to show that law is, despite its specific dogmatic core, not an isolated scientific enterprise.

The notion of law as a science will, however, not be prevalent in the public eye which takes note of lawyers at best as trouble shooters and orators, and at worst as a group which rather generates conflicts instead of solving them. This goes to show that the emanations of law are manifold. Not all of them lend themselves to be called „scientific", Yet the „scientific" aspect, i. e. a sophisticated reflection on the world of norms, on their socio-philosophical meaning and relevance as well as on their development, is sort of the intellectual cement that binds the legal world together.

I doubt whether my arguments will convince those who believe in the empirical nature of science or in the idealistic notion of absolute truths. I doubt whether my albeit cautious defence of the scientific character of law will convince contemporary deconstructivists à la von Kirchmann. Yet, I leave it at that. In the academic field the attribution of a „scientific" character is to some extent a matter of self-proclamation. Of course, the self-proclamation must receive some external backing, constitutionally or otherwise. Yet, this needs neither be uncontested nor universal. The standing in the academic field does not depend on the quality of terminological exercises, but on the constant search for knowledge, in other words on intellectual productivity.

## *IV. Some practical consequences*

The academic character of law and legal education is beyond question, irrespective of the intensity of the „*Wissenschafts*-claim". A member of the family of sciences of long standing, the „*Rechtswissenschaft*" has outlived recurrent „deconstructivist" attacks. Of course, theorizing about law as a science seems to be of a very abstract nature, a playground for a group of specialists. Most lawyers will not care. The intellectual hight of this discourse, its certain remoteness from practical life, favours a closed-shop attitude. The fact that the German „*Rechtswissenschaft*" does not get the international resonance that it would like to have may be due to its pre-occupation with such „heavy" stuff or else with the sophistication of the „*Rechtsdogmatik*" which, internationally speaking, accounts for the glory and the misery of the German „*Rechtswissenschaft*".[53]

52 Simon, Jurisprudenz (note 2), p. 148.
53 Jestaedt (note 51), p. 2.

The Germans may entertain a special relationship with their law.[54] This does not mean, however, that legal thinking is a German prerogative. Let me illustrate my point: The German legal language may excel in precision. This is neutralised by a certain bulkiness. Contrary to that the English legal language stands for clearness and vividness and the French for elegance.[55] As regards legal theory, the Anglo-American and Scottish as well as the Nordic legal theory compare favorably to the German one. The style of judicial reasoning at the European courts[56] differs from the elaborate confection by the German Federal Constitutional Court, but let us face it: Karlsruhe becomes equally laconic when the Court arrives at the decisive points.

The internationalisation of the discussion requires a certain re-adjustment of the German position. It seems to me that the classical German departimentalisation (private law, public law, criminal law) is not a promising perspective.[57] Therefore I am not enthusiastic about a sectoral concept of legal sciences which rather weakens the scientific standing of law in general. The international discourse will rather favour, if not demand a more general outlook in combination with the willingness to test and adopt transdisciplinary approaches and new field-oriented perspectives.

Of course, the dogmatic structure of legal thinking should not be watered down.[58] Yet, I doubt whether an exuberant German dogmatics will carry the day;[59] as far as I am concerned this would not even be desirable, since it tends to bind too many intellectual resources with too little effect. I doubt, therefore, that the international community of (criminal) law scholars will appreciate Schünemann´s passionate plea for the supremacy

---

54 E. g. Jung, *Michael Kohlhaas* or the Germans and Their Law, Oñati Socio-legal series (online), vol. 4, n. 6 (2014) – Justice in Literature: New Perspectives on European Legal Culture, p. 1124–1132.

55 In actual fact, English is, whether we like it or not, on its way to become the lingua franca of legal science; cf. Vogel, Strafrecht und Strafrechtswissenschaft im internationalen und europäischen Rechtsraum, Juristenzeitung 2012, p. 25 at 27. This is most noticeable in International Law; cf. A. Roberts, Is International Law International?, Oxford University Press, Oxford et al. 2017, p. 260.

56 As to the European Court of Justice cf. Bengoetxea, The Legal Reasoning of the European Court of Justice, Clarendon Press, Oxford et al. 1993.

57 E. g. Bogdandy, Internationalisierung der deutschen Rechtswissenschaft, in: Hilgendorf/Schulze-Fielitz (note 5), p. 133 at 149.

58 Cf. my own defence of the German Straftatlehre Jung, Making Sense of the German „Straftatlehre". A Personal Account, in: Festskrift till Nils Jareborg, Iustus Förlag, Uppsala 2002, p. 369.

59 Cf. also Bogdandy (note 57), p. 150: „ Bildet die Bewahrung einer spezifisch deutschen Rechtswissenschaft ein Ziel an sich? Kaum."

of the German style of juridical reasoning and his „constitutional upgrade“ of legal dogmatics.[60]

A wider concept of a *Rechtswissenschaft* should also have consequences on the level of legal education and on the research agenda. Law Faculties should develop a renewed sensitivity for interdisciplinary thinking and for new turns on the scientific agenda. This will not only help acquiring funds, but it will also help improving legal education. Lawyers tend to profit from a training which reaches beyond legal positivism and aims at a professionalism which enables young lawyers to cope with complex systems of social regulation. This complexity requires, despite specialisation, the development of an over-all sense of orientation and of social skills as well.[61]

## V. *Conclusion*

I have made up my mind about „science“ and the scientific character of law in a long and, at times, strenuous process of reflection. I have read a lot and consulted colleagues and friends. I am not sure whether such an approach qualifies as „scientific“. At least, I demonstrated a certain perseverance: *„Ich wollte es eben wissen.“* Of course, there is nothing really new in what I have been saying. Yet, I made a few personal discoveries and I have wanted to raise my voice in this continued process of reflection.

Evidently, this is not the type of topic that you can exhaust in ten pages; it already fills libraries. A flourishing „theory of science“ indicates that the quality of „science“ is and has always been, in itself, a matter of research. You should take my intervention rather as the confession of an elderly German law scholar who, in the course of his academic career, has been increasingly attracted by principled questions.

I do not subscribe to Montaigne´s point of view that science is something personal and that it remains a *„point de vue“*.[62] Yet, it is important to acknowledge that individual experiences impose themselves commanding-

---

60 Schünemann, Vom schwindenden Beruf der Rechtswissenschaft unserer Zeit, speziell der Strafrechtswissenschaft, in: Hilgendorf/Schulze-Fielitz (note 5), p. 222.

61 Cf. for the debate on the role of the so-called „Schlüsselkompetenzen“ in legal education S. Jung/Momsen/Saliger/Schmitt-Leonardy (eds.), Strafverfahren und Kommunikationskompetenz, Nomos, Baden-Baden 2018.

62 On Montaigne and the science e. g. Desan, Montaigne. Penser le social, Odile Jacob, Paris 2018, p. 87.

ly on our opinion on the subject matter. Hence it seems worth noting that I would not consider myself to be a passionate „*Dogmatiker*" of the substantive criminal law. I have always been primarily interested in procedure. My background as a criminologist has sensitised me for policy issues and for policy considerations. As regards the use of criminal law, I have rather taken a critical stance, insisting on the legitimacy question.[63] Moreover, the world of comparative law has helped me in understanding the certain relativity of law. Also, working as a part-time judge has left its mark. This may explain why I have opted for a wider notion of *Rechtswissenschaft*, a notion which insists on the interdisciplinary potential and backdrop of the discipline, a notion which also guarantees a productive process of self-reflection.

Finally, I would like to put our topic in a wider perspective. It has certainly not been futile to reflect on the scientific character of law and in doing just that I have learned a lot. This said, we should not disregard the fact that the major battle-field today is actually the defence of science and reason as such. Science and scientists seem to undergo a period of crisis, since they have lost respect in the public debate. Of course, the legitimacy of science and of its role in society has always been a matter of controversy.[64] Of course, science cannot demand to have the last word in a democratic society. Today, however, the voice of scientists will hardly be heard in the mighty storm of social media debates. Observers of public debates in the world of the World-Wide-Web may rather come to believe that the age of reason is passé and that populist irrationality and half-wisdom are about to take over. We should therefore take Habermas´great narrative on the emancipation of knowledge and reason[65] as a reminder that not only liberty, but also the prevalence of reason need to be defended daily. It remains to be seen whether the boost which the coronavirus pandemic gave to the public standing of science and scientists will have a lasting effect.

---

63 Somewhat along the line of what Dubber, The Dual Penal State, Oxford University Press, Oxford et al. 2018, p. 229 et seq. has called „the modern liberal legal-political project"; see also Nuotio, The Dual Penal State à la Markus Dubber, Bergen Journal of Criminal Law and Criminal Justice 6 (2018), p. 178, at 183 et seq.

64 E. g. Bourdieu (note 11), p. 19; Jung, Die postmoderne Kriminologie im Wechselspiel von Professionalität, Demokratie und Rechtsstaatlichkeit, in: Kunz/Bezozzi (eds.), Soziale Reflexivität und qualitative Methodik, Haupt, Bern 2003, p. 153. It is interesting to note that Simon, Jurisprudenz (note 2), p. 156 puts this on top of his research agenda at the end of his article.

65 Habermas (note 15).

# Criminal Law Science: from Legal Technicism to Postmodern Legality. An Italian perspective.

*Massimiliano Lanzi*

## *0. Introduction.*

With this essay, I intend to contribute to the ongoing discussion about the state of art of the Criminal Law Science, and I aim to do so from an Italian perspective.

Criminal Law is facing some material developments which are of course influencing the relevant science; not only in terms of a redefinition of its object and method, but also with reference to the very role that Criminal Law scholarship might play.

First of all, I intend to introduce my essay drafting the meaning I intend to attribute to the terms which are relevant for the investigation. Indeed, notwithstanding the formalistic nature of legal language, we can observe that in Criminal Law Science when it comes to contents some terms might not be univocal in their significance; especially, when translation in languages referred to different systems is involved.

As a second step, I'm going to make some considerations about the method of Criminal Law Science, to track the development, in the Italian Law Theory, of the scientific approach to the Criminal Law.

Then, I intend to turn my attention to the object of the Criminal Law Science, discussing the strict connection between the development of the discipline and the evolution of the Legality Principle: I'll try to draft how and why the changes which occurred in recent time in the shaping of the Rule of Law – in terms of both new sources of law, along with less objective judging rules – have material consequences in the current Criminal Law scientific debate.

## *1. Just a matter of definition... or isn't?*

First of all, it is well established, in any Italian textbook, that the Criminal Law is something different than the Criminal Law Science, the first being the branch of the legal order which comprises all the criminal offences and the relevant punishments; the latter, a subject of the human knowledge, cultivated by those who investigate the Criminal Law[1].

But it would be an error to consider them as one the mirror image of the other.

Considering the object of the discipline, we can observe a perpetual tension between a formalistic idea, as to which the Criminal Law Science must limit its investigation to the *ius conditum*, and a substantial idea, for which even the *ius condendum* and the meta-juridical aspects of crime are relevant.

Facing this issue, we must start from a first definition problem. Coherently with the continental European tradition, in Italy the legal discipline is defined as Penal Law (*diritto penale*) and not Criminal Law (*diritto criminale*). The Italian nomenclature cannot be read literally, of course. Indeed, in that case, we should affirm that the relevant provisions are merely related to the punishment, which of course is not true since they comprise (and maybe with an even predominant weight) the substantial elements of the offence. For this reason, I find definitely suitable, in this essay, to refer to the Criminal Law, rather than to the Penal Law, without causing any misunderstanding as for the relevant contents.

But still, it is not obvious that the Criminal Law scholar should investigate something different and wider than the criminal offence. There are several aspects of the complex "criminal law issue" (or *problema penale*, how it is traditionally recorded in the Italian literature[2]) the inclusion of which within the field of interest of the Criminal Law Science cannot be taken for granted: among the others, the *definition* of crime, the *causes* of crime and the *prevention* of crime; issues and topics of material importance, which are traditionally object of investigation by adjacent subjects, such as sociology, criminology and criminal politics.

Indeed, under this aspect the Criminal Law Science (*Scienza Criminale*) may be considered a wider discipline than the Penal Law Science (*Scienza Penale*), since it embraces all the aspects relevant to understand and consequently to tackle the crime[3].

---

1 A. Cadoppi – P. Veneziani, Elementi di diritto penale. Parte Generale, VII ed., Padova, 2018, p. 12.

2 Among others, see G. Bettiol, Il problema penale, Palermo, 1948.

3 See F. Mantovani, Diritto penale. Parte generale, X ed., Milano, 2017, p. 24, where the Author describes the Penal Law Science (scienza penale) as merely one out of the three elements of the Criminal Law Science (scienza criminale), along with criminology and criminal politics.

Until few years ago it was debated if and how criminal politics, for instance, should be considered within the object of the Penal Law Science. In Italy, the debate was strongly influenced by the Juridical Technicism ("*tecnicismo giuridico*"), the legal theory whose origin can be tracked back to the notorious "*prolusione sassarese*", published in 1910 by Arturo Rocco[4]. This theory played a predominant role not only in the drafting of the still-in-force 1930 Criminal Code[5], but even in the juridical culture of our time. The development of the theory put an end to the dialectical conflict between the Classical School (and its individual liability-based view) and the Positive School (affirming a physiological and innate perilousness of individuals who commit crimes), which characterized the Criminal Law doctrinal debate for several decades, since the mid-nineteenth century. The Criminal Law scholars – in the perspective of the legal Technicism – should rather act as technicians, whose mission is to fully understand the meaning of statutory provisions and the connections among them; this theory had not only the merit of permitting the Criminal Law scholarship to overtake the persistent debate we mentioned between the Classical and the Positive Schools, but also to keep the Criminal Law scholars far away from any politics-related issue: the duty of a criminal law scholar was indeed to "scientifically" manage the tools provided by the legislator, without providing any help in defining strategies and remedies against crime. A well appreciated aspect by the fascist regime, who preferred not to give any room to scholars in the criminal politics[6].

Moreover, on the ground of the method, the legal Technicism promoted a deeply "scientific" view of the Penal Law Science. It was characterised by a constant effort to promote a systematic view of the legal order, in terms of interpreting any legal provision in a way which should be logically coherent with the others and with the system, to be intended as a whole. At the same time, and from this angle, the Criminal Law Science – intend-

4 Arturo Rocco, Il problema e il metodo della scienza del diritto penale, in Opere giuridiche, III ed., Roma, 1933, p. 263.

5 Arturo Rocco, at the time professor of Criminal Law at the University of Florence, was brother of Alfredo Rocco, who later served as Minister of Justice at the time the Criminal Code was published, in 1930. Therefore, the code is commonly known as "Codice Rocco". The most remarkable work of Arturo Rocco is L'oggetto del reato e della tutela giuridica penale, first published in 1913.

6 Under this aspect, a very different approach than the coeval German one, where the jurists, and the jurisprudence especially, were supposed to play an active and creative role in tackling criminal and antisocial behaviours: in is relevant, in this perspective, the amendment of art. 2 StGB and the introduction of a duty of interpretation by analogy, in given circumstances. See below, reference 17.

ed as a wider subject which also includes adjacent disciplines, such as criminology and criminal politics – was perhaps perceived, at the time, as less "scientific", since it embraces issues which lacked such a strictly logical and rigorous approach.

But, on the other hand, the legal Technicism theory was not scientific at all, under a different, but not less important, aspect: since it excluded the criminal politics from its field of investigation, the theory failed to investigate if the legal provisions were efficient in tackling the crime; in other words, if they were suitable for their purposes.

From this point of view, the Penal Law Science (in strict sense) might be considered, nowadays, a less "scientific" discipline than the Criminal Law Science, which embraces a wider and more complete area of investigation.

But over the time, the distance between the two has been reduced more and more; thanks to the development of more modern theories – such as the constitutional theory of criminal law, as I'll explain – it is a consolidated knowledge that the discipline embraces not only the legal provisions which are currently in force, but even how the provisions should be, through an investigation process comprehensive of the history of penal and criminal law, of comparative law and of criminal politics. Therefore, for the scopes of this essay, I can now refer to the "Criminal Law Science" (*scienza criminale*) with no distinction to the "Penal Law Science" (*scienza penale*).

## 2. *The success of the scientific method in Criminal Law Science.*

It is a consolidate belief that Law Theory cannot be regarded as a hard science. It doesn't aim to develop a universal true knowledge; it rather depends by a series of superstructures which influence its contents and, in a way or another, its conceptual schemes[7]. After all, the Law looks at the world in a relativist way, rather than chasing absolute and universal truths.

Of course, things have been different, in the past. In the European experience, we can track the development, starting from the Eighteenth century, of various Natural Law-related doctrines, which see the Law as an absolute and universal value, expression of immutable principles of justice and of a superior moral order. If we start from the belief that a certain discipline might be considered as truly scientific if its suitable to produce uni-

7 A. Cadoppi – P. Veneziani, Elementi di diritto penale, cit., p. 14.

versally reproducibly contents, then those natural law and rationalistic doctrines are scientific in a proper and "hard" way. From their perspective, indeed, it is a black and white world: the crime is, by definition, the evil, the society is the good, and the author of the offence is a negative element of the social system.

The most notable example among those universally valid doctrines is, as for the Italian scholarship, the so called "Classical School" (*Scuola Classica*), which has seen in Carmignani[8], Rossi[9] and Carrara[10] the most eminent scholars. The method is an investigation based upon rational and logic criteria (*criteri di ragione*) expressed by logic deduction from the rational nature of humans or from the hypothetic social contract – as it was theorized by the Enlightenment philosophers – and not from positive criminal law provisions, which are unreliable since subjects to continuous modifications. The influence of the Kantian criticism is evident, apparently to claim the aprioristic nature of human thought, contrary to the empiricism which was dominant in that period[11]. As we know, doctrines of this kind can be deeply appreciated, as for their tension toward a fully rational, refined and universally valid development of the Juridical thought; nevertheless, they have been criticised for their ahistorical attitude, since the social contract, as well as the moral and theological values on which the deductions are based, live out and above the actual reality of society and people.

Natural Law related discipline also lacked a scientific approach and attitude, since they were based on dogmas, which means, following the Cambridge Dictionary: «a fixed [...] belief or set of beliefs that people are expected to accept without any doubts»: as far as an unchallengeable truth is put at the base of a certain theory, it is very hard indeed to appreciate the scientific nature of the same.

It was – as I mentioned before – a great merit of Arturo Rocco and of the legal Technicism the development, in the Italian scenario, of a scientific approach to Criminal Law Science. As for the object of the discipline, in the *Prolusione Sassarese*, Rocco was explicit that criminal scholar's investigation should exclude the prerequisite and the consequences of criminal punishment: from the horizon of interests of the jurist it was banned any reference to legal philosophy and to the natural aspect of the crime. But it

---

8 G. Carmignani, Elementa juris criminalis, first edition in 1808. As for an Italian translation: Elementi di diritto criminale, edited by F. Ambrosoli, Milano, 1863.

9 P. Rossi, Traité de droit pénal, first edition in 1829. As for an Italian translation: Trattato di diritto penale, edited by E. Pessina, Napoli, 1853.

10 F. Carrara, Programma del corso di diritto criminale, first published in 1860.

11 G. Bettiol, Diritto penale, XI ed., Padova, 1982, p. 22.

was especially on the ground of the method that this theory is regarded as a milestone in the scientific development of Criminal Law doctrine. The scientific investigation is carried on under logic-formalistic criteria; a great effort is put, just as in any experimental science, into classification, with a constant ambition to build a logic and well-structured system, where similarities and differences between juridical concepts are well evidenced and arranged.

Though, this dogmatic approach received critics which are well known, and commonly accepted by contemporary jurists. It brought to a system that, even if refined and logically coherent, was far too formalistic and, in some way, sterile. As a mitigation to some excess we can track the different methods proposed, for instance, by the Realism – developed in Italy by Antolisei[12] – for which as to comprehend the norm it is necessary to investigate its scopes, in terms of the social reality in which it is going to be enforced. In similar terms we can appreciate, in the Italian experience, the teleological doctrine of Bettiol, in which the critical interpretation must take into account the material social interest protected by the Law[13]. These innovative doctrines put the basis for the teleological method, in which it is the *aim* of the norms, along with the interaction of the same with the social needs, the key to draft a coherent general structure of the Criminal Law.

While in the view of the legal Technicism the evolution of Criminal Law was only referred to the explicit will of the legislator, the affirmation of the teleological method in Criminal Law Science makes the interpretation more evolutional, in terms of taking into account, in a more realistic way, the social developments and changes which might occur in the time.

This is the way the *aims* of the norm entered into the horizon of modern Criminal Law scholarship; in order to mitigate the rigid formalism affirmed between the end of XIXth and the start of XXth sec. But still, in this perspective the aims come to our attention on the ground of the scientific method, as a path to find a right balance between the need to preserve the coherence and logical structure of the Criminal Law as a whole, and the development of the social reality for which those norms are drafted. The logical structure of the legal order cannot forbid the evolution "in action" of the Law, and the teleological method gives to the jurists – scholars, judges and lawyers in general – a tool as to find a useful application of

12 F. Antolisei, Per un indirizzo realistico nella scienza del diritto penale, in Riv. It. Dir. pen., 1937, p. 121.

13 G. Bettiol, Diritto penale, cit., p. 83 ss.

criminal law provisions, adequate to the actual time. At this stage, it is still a matter which refers to the relation between the jurists and the legislator; in terms of having the first a duty to give to the will of the latter the most suitable and correct application.

In recent times, the *aims* of the norm have assumed a relevance which goes forth the ground of the scientific method. They rather affect the very object of the discipline, and the Criminal Law scholarship indeed is currently involved in a debate on how this is changing the actual perception and meaning of the Principle of Legality.

### 3. *A new puzzle of sources for the Criminal Law.*

The investigation on the actual contents of the *nullum crimen sine lege* principle is at the origin of the science of the Criminal Law. Indeed, we can track the modern shape of the Criminal Law Science back to the Englightment period, when scholars perceived the need to investigate the *jus puniendi* in all its aspects: its fundaments and limits, its methods and implementation measures[14]. In other words, the development of a Criminal Law Science runs side by side with the investigation upon the structure and the meaning of the Rule of Law, and since then scholars put a huge effort in studying the relations between Criminal Law and ideology, in a perpetual dialog between a formalistic and a substantive idea of the Legality Principle[15]: the first, supporting the knowledge of the crime as a fact qualified as criminal offence by a legal provision; the second, the definition of crime as an antisocial behaviour. Some of the most important issues of the Criminal Law discipline are at stake in this dialog: certainty of the law and guarantee for individual freedom, on one side; social justice and prevention of crime, on the other. The most relevant examples are well known and have been deeply investigated by modern Criminal Law scholarship. The formalistic idea of the Legality Principle has been remarkably affirmed in Europe, at first, by the French *Déclaration des droits de l'homme et du citoyen*, in 1789. On the opposite shore, we can find examples of radical substantial models in the Soviet Union (at least, until the reforms following the XXth Congress of the Communist Party of the Soviet

---

14 P. Nuvolone, Il sistema del diritto penale, II ed., Padova, 1982.
15 F. Mantovani, Diritto penale. Parte generale, cit., p. 23.

Union, in 1956)[16], and in the National Socialist Germany, after the reform of s. 2 *StGB* in 1935[17]: here we find the explicit will to reach a substantial justice (*die materielle Gerechtikeit*) as defined by ambiguous sources such as the revolutionary consciousness of the judge, in the Soviet Union, or the sound perception of the people (*gesundes Volksempfinden*).

In the Italian experience, we see that the formalistic model was recognized at first by the Constitution of Piedmont dated 1848 (*Statuto Albertino*) and by several pre-unitary criminal codes; and then, by the first criminal code of unified Italy, the *Zanardelli* Code, published in 1889. Then, an hyper-formalistic model of the Legality Principle prevailed; supported, in the Criminal Law Science, through the Juridical Technicism theory, whose influence can be tracked in the 1930 criminal code and in its art. 1, which confirms the rigid formalistic idea of the Rule of Law. Even if, in this case, the prevalence of a formalistic legality didn't mean the preference for an individual-freedom-oriented criminal law system; rather, it was the expression of an authoritative State which didn't admit any source of law different than the central State statutes[18].

As a reaction to the hyper-formalism of the legal Technicism, and to the positivist normative doctrines in general, the modern Criminal Law scholarship felt the need of a return to values which stay above the legislative provisions. We already went through important authors as Bettiol and Antolisei, with a deep values-oriented approach and interest; they made clear that each legal norm has an aim of protection of some relevant social interest, and that the jurist should find the way as to guarantee the actual protection result notwithstanding the reality might have been changed since the norm itself was drafted. The teleological method, as I mentioned above, affirms the duty of an evolutionary interpretation. Then, that scenario was enriched by the affirmation of the duty, for jurists, to give material application to general obligations and principles which can be tracked in higher sources; namely, the Constitution, even with reference to the contents merely implicitly affirmed. The constitutional theory of Criminal Law affects the method of Criminal Law Science, since positive norms are instruments, needed to give concrete application to principles and values expressed by the Constitution; and it consequently effects as well the ob-

16 K. Grzybowski, Soviet Legal Institutions: Doctrines and Social Functions, 1962, p. 172 ss.

17 L. Preuss, Punishment by analogy in National Socialist Penal Law, in Journal of the American Institute of Criminal Law and Criminology, vol. 26, n. 6, 1936, p. 847–856.

18 F. Mantovani, Diritto penale, cit., p. 5.

ject of the discipline, since the scientific investigation is no longer confined to the *ius positum*, rather looking at the system how it should be, and the border between juridical science and criminal politics is no longer obvious[19].

Nevertheless, those values are not aprioristic or immanent as they were depicted by the Natural Law and are not even the one which might be assumed from the norm itself, as the teleologic method affirms; they rather come from the norms of the Constitution and from the whole of concepts, values and principles referred to it, which are mutable and evolutive themselves due to the need to follow social changes and to be adapted coherently with these. Criminal Law undertook a path which brought, in recent time, to a deep redefinition of its essence, in terms of a switch *from norms to principles*, as it has been focused by contemporary scholars[20].

Under this angle, the enforcement of Criminal Law has now become mainly an interpretation problem, which cannot be confined any longer to the systematic and rational-logic method drafted by the legal Technicism, nor it can be predominantly based on the correct definition of the will of the legislator, in terms of actual aim of the norm; it is rather a values-oriented process, in which any interpreter expresses a content of values which are relevant to the issue[21].

Nothing new, some might say. It is indeed a well-established knowledge that the «*Weltanshauungen*» of the interpreter play a material role in the output of his interpretation. The complex of ideologies and personal believes proper of the person has its weight within the interpretation process; and, I might say, there is nothing extraordinary in that, since it is a mere consequence of the human nature of the interpreter. It is possible indeed to track a natural tendency of the interpreter – especially of the jurisprudence – to give room to the "substantial sources" of the Law, in terms of the complex of social and cultural believes which stays above the "formal source"[22].

The issue assumes now a rather new significance, since it is no longer confined to the influence played by values as a merely and unavoidable

19 F. Bricola, voce Teoria generale del reato, in Nov. Dig. It., Torino, 1974.

20 See among others, in the Italian literature, M. Ronco, La legalità stratificata, in Riv. It. Dir. Proc. Pen., 2018, p. 1387, in which it is outlined the material difference between judging under principles and judging under general and abstracted norms.

21 D. Pulitanò, Tra jus facere e Jus dicere, in Criminalia, 2016, p. 205.

22 See F. Palazzo, Corso di Diritto penale. Parte generale, Torino, 2005, p. 94 ss., about the interaction among formal and substantial sources of the criminal law.

consequence of being jurists human people; rather, it has been affirmed a relevant proper *duty* of the interpreter, since through the lines of law provisions it must be given tangible application to values and principles which have a proper juridical base: national constitutions and international treaties and conventions, among others.

In the Italian experience, the case law of the Constitutional Court of the last 30 years is significant, under this aspect. Indeed, since the '90s we can track the development of a well consolidated principle, as to which the single judge cannot challenge the constitutional validity of a certain law provision any time it is possible to interpret it in a way that conflicts with the Constitution; rather, only in those cases in which it is impossible to interpret it respectfully to the Constitution[23]: it was consequently affirmed a duty of "compliant interpretation" (to the Constitution) of ordinary law provisions, by each judge.

Another important step in the same direction was the reform in 2001 of art. 117 of the Italian Constitution, under which it is now provided that the legislative power is exercised by the central State and by the Regions (within their area of competency), in respect of the Constitution, of the European Union Law and of the international obligations. The case law of the Constitutional Court played, once again, a first standing role, and in 2007 two now-popular decisions (n. 348 and 349) stated that within those «international obligations», binding for the legislative power, there are those set forth by the European Convention of Human Rights, in the way they are interpreted by the relevant European Court of Human Rights of Strasbourg. Therefore, the duty of "complaint interpretation" – drafted by the Constitutional Court – takes into account not merely the Constitution but also the provisions of the ECHR and the relevant case law of the Court of Strasbourg, along with the law of the EU and the relevant case law of the European Court of Justice. The multitude of the sources of law originates a puzzle that the single judge has the incumbent to compose, making him, in several circumstances, the immediate creator of the actual rule to be applied[24]. This process is even emphasized by the circumstance that those different sources rarely set forth precise and immediately enforceable rules; they have rather a programmatic nature, expressing values and political aims, in the light of which the political role of the interpreter of the national law becomes quite obvious. National Criminal Law, notwith-

23 Corte Cost., 22 October 1996, n. 356, in Giur. Pen., 1997, I, p. 85.

24 See, in the Italian scientific literature, V. Manes, Il giudice nel labirinto, Roma, 2012.

standing being traditionally moved by a conservative and formalistic attitude, has entered into the "postmodern world", in which the sources of law along with the actual rules are no longer uniform and well ordered, but rather spread, pluralistic and complex[25].

With this respect, the contemporary Science of Criminal Law is no longer confined to the systematic investigation of the "Law in the books". The augmented perception of the role of the interpretation – and of the role played, in this sense, by different actors, both national and supranational – has determined a renovated interest, even among academic scholars, for the Jurisprudence as a decisive actor in drafting the actual borders of the Criminal Law; indeed, as said before, if sources along with legal rules are spread and uncertain, the judge is often called to a reconciliation activity which makes him a leading protagonist in the creation of the rule to be applied in the given single case.

We can recall, under this aspect, those theories as to which the legal rule itself is not the one drafted by the general disposition, rather the one contained in the actual *norm*, as expressed by the jurisprudence and applied by the judge in the given case[26]. In the past, some wrote that just few new words by the legislator could make entire libraries totally outdated[27]: now, we can provocatively say that a new decision of a Supreme Court might have the same effect.

Along with this process, we can recall, in the Italian experience, that a recent reform of the criminal procedural code (art. 618, sec. 1 *bis*) gave to the decisions of the *Sezioni Unite* of the *Corte di Cassazione* (the most eminent composition of the High Court) a greater weight within the internal system, since their law principles are binding for the common sections of the Court. A reform that – even if limited to make the decisions of the *Corte di Cassazione* steadier – was read as a step in the direction of a *stare decisis*-oriented model[28].

---

25 See D. Harvey, The Condition of Postmodernity: An Enquiry into the Origins of Cultural Change, Oxford, 1991. In the Italian literature, see R. E. Kostoris (edited by), Percorsi giuridici della postmodernità, Bologna, 2016.

26 It is indeed a key point of the contemporary Criminal Law theory debate. See M. Donini, Europeismo giudiziale e scienza penale. Dalla dogmatica classica alla giurisprudenza fonte, Milano, 2011.

27 See J. Von Kirchmann, Die Wertlosigkeit der Jurisprudenz als Wissenschaft, Stuttgard, 1848.

28 P. Ferrua, Soggezione del giudice alla sola legge e disfunzioni del legislatore: il corto circuito della riforma Orlando, in dir. pen. proc., 2017.

It has been a quite shocking development for some of the academic culture of the time, and it imposed the investigation of the "Law in action" as an essential part of the Rule of Law[29]. This evolution, which I just briefly depicted, has not merely affected the recognition of the sources of law in the present scenario; it rather influences the very contents of legal rules, and brings the need to investigate the legitimacy of the current Criminal Law system.

## 4. *From objectiveness to case-by-case justice.*

Following these developments, we can see that Legality Principle is now turning in the direction of a substantive model, in which the aim to provide protection to juridical relevant interests and to give actual application to general principles from sources of different level and nature, is predominant to the strict respect both of the separation between the powers of the modern State and of the letter of statutory provisions. The aim to be taken into account by the interpreter, in this new scenario, is not the one affirmed, with respect to the method, by the teleological interpretation criteria. Indeed, it is no longer the one contained in the single provision, but it can be rather tracked from different and heterogenic sources, positioned at different hierarchical levels and might not be corresponding to the one pursued by the national legislator at the time the provision was introduced.

As far as we assume that the achievement of political interests through the declination of juridical binding norms can, or even *must*, be done "in action" by the jurists, we are eroding a traditionally considered monopoly of the legislative power. As a consequence, the strict letter of the legislative provision is increasingly considered as a starting point, rather than the finish line for the enforcement of Criminal Law measures.

In this liquid scenario[30], the general criterion, which can be tracked even in several decisive judicial decisions, is a clear preference of the "substance" above the "form", driven by the ambition to reach, in each decision, a "fair" or "just" result. Much has been the influence of course, on this ground, of the case law of the ECtHR, which indeed is strongly single-

---

29 Among the first to investigate the issue, see A. Cadoppi, Il valore del precedente nel diritto penale: uno studio sulla dimensione in action della legalità, Torino, 1999.

30 The reference is to Z. Bauman, Liquid Modernity, Cambridge, 2000.

case oriented, since it is institutionally asked to verify the respect of the conventional obligations in the single given case.

With this respect, we can observe the progressive development of quantitative and single-case oriented criteria and rules for the enforcement of Criminal Law. The ambition of the logic-formalistic model as to reach a completely coherent and well-ordered system "in the books", has been substituted by a case-by-case approach, which is well appreciated especially by the jurisprudence, since it leaves the single judge freer to decide the single case coherently with practical needs and social expectations.

There are several examples in recent years we can go through.

The "sufficiently close connection, in substance and in time" criteria, elaborated by the ECtHR case law with reference to the scrutiny of eventual breaches of the *ne bis in idem* (double jeopardy) principle, when an *idem factum* is punished through both an administrative and a criminal punitive proceeding[31].

The application of individual fundamental rights following the recognition of the *substantial punitive nature* of a given legal provision, regardless to the formal classification used under single national law[32].

The affirmation of a "substantive" sentencing which, even if different than a "formal" sentencing, is supposed to be enough – under the case law of the ECtHR, promptly followed by the Italian Jurisprudence of the Constitutional Court and of the *Corte di Cassazione* – to apply certain kind of punitive measures: different kinds of seizure of proceeds of crime, among others[33].

The affirmation of a duty of disapplication of domestic provisions when the national judge finds them unsuitable, in many severe cases, to protect the financial interests of the European Union[34].

Moreover, the establishment of extremely broad and unpredictable criteria for the application of some very harsh forms of confiscation by dis-

---

31 A. and B. v. Norway [GC], app no 24130/11 and 29758/11 (ECtHR, 15 November 2016). The criterion has been rapidly adopted within the national law: see Constitutional Court, 2 March 2018, n. 43, in Cass. Pen., 2018, 6, p. 1940.

32 See the Engels criteria, starting from Engel and o. v. The Netherlands, App no 5100/71 and o. (ECtHR, 23 November 1976).

33 As for the European Court of Human Rights, see G.I.E.M. and o. v. Italy [GC], App no 1828/06 and 2 o. (ECtHR, 8 June 2018); as for the national jurisprudence, see Corte Cost., 26 March 2015, n. 49, in Foro It., 2016, 5, I, p. 1623; and Cass., SS.UU. pen., 26 June 2015, n. 31617 (Lucci), in CED Cass. 2015; and Cass., SS.UU. pen., 30 January 2020, n. 13539, in CED Cass. 2020.

34 Case C-105/14 Taricco and Others [2015] EU:C:2015:555.

proportion, capable to seize the entire assets of a person convicted for several severe crimes[35].

It is interesting to observe that legal theorists traditionally consider the process of "objectivation" of legal rules as the most qualifying point in the establishment of the modern legal order[36]. Nowadays, we see a rather opposite process since, in order to achieve a "just result" in the single case, rules *must* be flexible, as to consent the judge to operate a case by case evaluation, and objectiveness is recessive.

Therefore, we understand that the liquid model is not merely referred to spread sources of law, but even to the uncertain contents of the legal rules to be applied.

I assumed that the confine between a formal and a substantial model of legality relies on being a crime what is set forth by a legal disposition or merely an antisocial behaviour. Well, it's clear that when the judge is asked to put order in a puzzle of different and heterogenic sources of law and to achieve a just result in the given case through less objective rules, the result is to apply criminal sanctions through a substantive evaluation which takes into account social requirements and expectations, making a distance from formal legality.

But still, it is of course a substantive model rather different than some which were affirmed in the past. Indeed, as for its contents, it doesn't imply a criterion of "free justice" as it happened in the totalitarian States; neither, as for the method, it can be developed through an uncontrolled creative role attributed to the interpreters.

It is not a "free justice" model, since the relevant interests and concepts shouldn't be freely deduced from unspecified and general values (as it was the sound perception of the people or the *Fuhrerprinzip*, in the German *Neue Staat*; not even the substantial interest of the people as it was provided for in the criminal code of the Soviet Union). Rather, those concepts have, at least, a legal base in national constitutions and international conventions, whose interpretation is hierarchically subject to legitimacy control by the Jurisprudence, at different levels.

---

35 See, among others, the criteria established by Corte Cost., 21 February 2018, n. 33, in Cass. Pen., 2018, 9, p. 2816, under which all the disproportionate assets possessed by the D. must be seized if he/she embodies the "criminological" prototype considered by the norm and if the assets were acquired in a period "reasonably closed" to the commission of the crime.

36 Among others, see S. Romano, L'ordinamento giuridico, first published in 1918. Recently republished in Macerata in 2018, pp. 31–34.

And it is not even an uncontrolled creative role, since there is at least one aspect of the formal Legality Principle which has been preserved, perhaps because it has been considered the only which deserved to be saved from the sinking ship of the Enlightenment – based formal model: the *foreseeability* of criminal liability. This is how both the ECtHR and the Court of Justice of the EU gave relevance to the Rule of Law in criminal matters, in several important decisions[37]. Even the development "in action" of the Criminal Law provisions is subject, at least, to this control of legitimacy.

Notwithstanding these reassurances, I believe that the Criminal Law Science can't avoid to confront itself with this new scenario, in order to understand how this development has affected its current and prospective role.

## 5. *The approach of Criminal Law Science to the new legality model.*

This new model of legality has several relevant consequences for the Criminal Law Science.

This recent substantial model gives far greater space of manoeuvre to jurists, in terms of identifying goals and requirements of the actual Criminal Law, giving them as well the chance to elaborate and provide the jurisprudence with relevant rules and criteria to be applied. For the scholar, it means perhaps a greater weight in the development of Jurisprudence and in the creation of actual legal rules. And it is doubtless, on this regard, that the higher steadiness of precedent decisions is suitable to make the legal system more certain and ordered, even in its scientific contains. If the influence of the Criminal Law Science is a criterion to define the scientific level of the Criminal Law, we might say that, due to the substantialist approach I outlined above, the Criminal Law is nowadays more "scientific" than before.

It is not the first time that jurists claim a primate in defining the contents of legal rules and disciplines. The Classical School used to assume that Criminal Law is composed by "juridical concepts", which are the real

37 Contrada v. Italy (no. 3), App no 66655/13 (ECtHR, 14 April 2015), in relation to art. 7 of the European Convention of Human Rights; Case C-42/17, M.A.S. and M.B., [2017], ECLI:EU:C:2017:936, in relation to art. 49 of the Charter of fundamental rights of the European Union.

source of law and prevail to written norms, which can be deemed as correct or incorrect accordingly to their suitability to actualize those concepts.

In the present model, those "juridical concepts" – to which the ordinary statutory rule is recessive – are rather of a different nature; they don't come from the theoretical thought of erudite scholars: as I mentioned, they show the ambition of the contemporary jurisdictions to achieve just practical results, giving direct application to political goals and principles set forth by hierarchically superior norms.

Also, the hierarchical application of criminal law under higher principles makes the language of Criminal Law Science more universal than before; not because – as it was under Nature Law related doctrines – we track the legitimacy of the punitive system in dogmas and immutable universal values; but rather because it has been conventionally decided, and accepted by a vast majority of the countries of the world, to share common goals, among whom to provide all people with common and equal rights. Under this aspect, the establishment in the last 60 years of international and cross-national courts is playing a role into drafting common language and concepts, influenced by – and, at the same time, influencing – the Criminal Law scholarship.

Another issue is that, considering that law provisions are tools to obtain a certain result (the prevention of crime), it is actually very positive – in scientific terms – the vast focus upon criminal politics, since it permits scholars to give their contribution as to reach better results. It is obvious that, in this liquid scenario, the object of Criminal Law Science is not only how the law *is* (*lex lata*), but also how it *should be* (*lex ferenda*): to rationalise the past, on one hand, and to programme the future, on the other.

But, on the other hand and under different aspects, this substantive approach, based on a remapping of the sources of law along with the development of case-by-case judging rules, has definitely made the Criminal Law less certain and consistent than before, and, at the same time, it can render the life of Criminal Law Science extremely hard.

First of all, it can be more difficult than before, from the point of view of a scholar, to systematize in a coherent way the whole complex of the system. Far from suggesting a return to the very formalistic approach of the Juridical Technicism, we must consider that the scientific approach itself, as for the legal doctrines, has been traditionally considered as the attitude to organize the complex of knowledge, related to a certain category of facts: which, in the Criminal Law area, are the statutory provisions[38]. In-

38 G. Bettiol, Il problema penale, cit., p. 16.

deed, it has been the development of such an attitude which founded the Criminal Law Science, marking the separation from the Civil Law Science, on one side, and from the legal philosophy, on the other.

I believe that the scientific nature of Criminal Law Theory is at stake, as long as theoretical and systematic forms will be replaced by case-by-case substantial rules, in which of course the political aims become more relevant than the need of maintaining the coherence of the whole discipline. And the more is the ambition for a "substantial justice" immediate result, the more is the tendency to consider forms as mere encumbrances or obstacles in pursuing it. This is something that cannot happens in the Criminal Law area, where indeed *form is substance*[39].

This takes to a second point, which is related to the legitimacy of the State's power of enforcing criminal punishment. The Criminal Law system finds its legitimacy in being controlled and governed by the Rule of Law, in the light of two different requirements: certainty of the law, on one hand, and legitimacy of the source, on the other[40].

The foreseeability of the legal (penal) consequences of actions is definitely not enough to guarantee the certainty of the law; indeed, they are just two different things.

As I wrote, the substantialist changes in postmodern law often makes the crime qualified by its antisocial attitude, rather than by its formal legal qualification. In these terms, the foreseeability of the criminal punishment happens to be coincident with the understanding of the antisocial character of the fact; which is actually quite obvious by anyone who undertakes an antisocial behaviour. The certainty of law should operate in a rather different way, since it consists on a formal and objective *ex ante* knowledge of what is considered a criminal offence, and what is not. Any case-by-case

39 T. Padovani, Jus non scriptum, e crisi della legalità nel diritto penale, Napoli, 2014.

40 See. F. Palazzo, Corso di diritto penale, cit., p. 89. It is an established knowledge that the Legality Principle pursues different goals. It has a protective nature, since it is finalized to guarantee the citizens not to be punished but under an accessible legal provision. It also has, at the same time, a political nature, since it defines the constitutional balance between different powers of the state, locating the legitimate source of that provision. In the opinion of some scholars, only the first one represents the undeniable content of the Rule of Law, while the latter is modifiable from period to period, depending also on the reliability socially attributed to the different institutions, in the given historical period: indeed, in the present heterogeneous and "liquid" multinational and multilevel context, the second aspect of the Rule of Law (the political definition of the source of law) is definitely recessive, as the jurisprudence of some international courts testify.

rule doesn't match with this requirement, and the mere foreseeability criteria might be ineffective to guarantee the certainty of the law, in case there isn't a strong effort as to make the legal rules and requirements for criminal liability objective and general.

In these terms, the issue goes straight to a further point, related to the legitimacy of the source of criminal law.

I wrote above that the direct application of principles through general norms makes the role of the interpreter explicitly political; the crime politics carried out by the jurists in this liquid law scenario is no longer confined in influencing the legislator in order to emend statutory provisions, it is rather related to an effort in order to directly reach, through the enforcement of Criminal Law, the political goals set forth by heterogenic spread sources. This process is suitable to take the Criminal Law system out of any legitimate control, and to alter significantly the role of Criminal Law Science, whose method wouldn't be any longer to investigate the discipline and to contribute to a gradual and coherent development of the system, rather to take part into an immediate reach of general interests, out of any democratically controlled mediation.

In my opinion, in the light of these considerations, the primate of statutory norms and the ban of creative interpretation (along with some instrument as to make, at the same time, steadier and necessarily evolutive the most relevant interpretations) – in other terms, the respect of the forms – are the only reasonable remedies as to obtain a certain and objective Criminal Law system: in other terms, to guarantee the substance and the contents of the discipline. These are the reasons for which it is said that in Criminal Law the form is the same as the substance; there isn't any difference between the two, since any rule or practical result which differs from the form can't be even considered as part of that system. The more the rules are parcelled out and poor of objectivity and the more actors intervene in shaping the contents of those rules, the weaker is the democratic control of the system and the greater is the lack of legitimacy of it.

Indeed, it's very hard to believe that the democratic nature of the source of the law doesn't play any longer any role in providing the penal system with the required legitimacy.

When individual liberty is at stake, the mediation operated by the legislator, in terms of identifying the general ends and providing the relevant most suitable legal tools to be applied, is indeed essential. It is a process that cannot be finalized without the active contribution of the jurists – judges and scholars – whose work allows those provisions to effectively reach their goals; but it can't be the jurists who autonomously identify and reach, in a creative way, the same goals[41].

I believe that this problem goes to the very core of the issue at stake in the present essay; because the science of the Criminal Law has been developed since Legal Theorists ceased to give the legitimacy of the criminal punishment for granted. In other words, it all began when the "*why to punish?*" became a question which deserved a detailed investigation[42].

As above-mentioned, the affirmation of a science of the Criminal Law is strictly connected to the development of the Principle of Legality. Indeed, the arguments between formal and substantial legality is at the centre of the contemporary scientific debate on Criminal Law.

In the present and in the next future of Criminal Law science, I believe that the legitimacy of the state punishment will remain an hot issue which cannot be taken for granted; and that the Criminal Law Science should put an effort as to valorise the retention of the forms of a democratically controlled, certain and objective system, which – as experience teaches – is the only way to preserve, at the same time, the underlying substantial contents and to impede that Criminal Law, at same point, becomes rather an arbitrary tool of social control, and the criminal punishment nothing but an arbitrary punitive reaction to antisocial behaviours or even just to antisocial attitudes.

41 The legality principle, also under the aspect of the legitimacy of the source of law, was defined as an essential and inalienable part of the constitutional identity of the State by several recent decisions of the Italian Constitutional Court, such as 26 January 2017, n. 24, in Guid. Dir., 2017, 8, 27; and 31 May 2018, n. 115, in Cass. Pen., 2018, 9, p. 2776.

42 See P. Nuvolone, Il sistema del diritto penale, cit., p. 3.

# Transformation of criminal law science in China: Description and Discussion*

*Liang Genlin***

## *Introduction*

Criminal jurisprudence is a normative science of law concerning about crime and its legal consequences. "As a practice-oriented science, in order to adapt to the need of criminal justice and draw more new inspiration from judicial practice, criminal law science must build its own system, as it is the prerequisite of a robust and well-organized criminal law doctrine to arrange all the relevant knowledge in a systematic way. Otherwise, the application of law would always remain dilettantism subjected to coincidence and arbitrary decisions."[1] The core task of criminal law science is to systematically design a structure of qualifying a criminal offence according to the positive law in which each problem has its logical place in accordance with its functional requirements, so as to build a logically self-consistent and functionally self-sufficient knowledge system. Therefore, criminal law science usually refers specifically to the theory of structure of crime.

Since the 1950s, Chinese scholars have introduced the "four constituents" theory of crime construction from Soviet Union. "Four constituents" theory has overwhelmingly dominated Chinese criminal law theory and judicial practice after continuous development, enrichment and improvement from the 1980s to the 1990s. In the meantime, it has seemed that the study of structure of crime in China "has been finished

---

* This paper is originated from the theme report delivered by the author at the second Sino-German symposium on criminal law in Beijing, China in 2013. The author further describes and comments on the transformation of the criminal law science in China based on his understanding of the characteristics and functions of the criminal law science.

** Professor, Peking University Law School. Translated by Dr. Chen Eryan, Peking University Law School.

1 Franz von Liszt, Lehrbuch des Deutschen Strafrechts, Band I, 26. Aufl., S. 2.

shortly after the starting"[2], which is so confusing that some Chinese scholars ever remarked with regret: "The study of 'four constituents' theory of crime construction seems to have come to an end, since almost all of the problems related to this theory have been studied and settled."[3]

However, since the beginning of the 21st century, with the continuous accumulation of local criminal law knowledge and experience as well as the perpetual introduction of foreign criminal law theories, the topic of structure of crime, which focuses on re-ordering the various conditions of crime and establishing their interrelationships for the purpose of providing the judges with an applicable guidance for conviction, has reawakened the enthusiasm of Chinese scholars. In this research boom, based on different knowledge backgrounds and value judgements, Chinese scholars adopt various completely different paths to the improvement or construction of the structure of crime: Some of them seek to expand the theoretical content within the framework of the traditional system to achieve knowledge growth and system improvement; others advocate a thorough transformation in research paradigms, methods, logic and systems, or even reconstructing criminal law system through returning to the origin of the modern criminal law theory, namely the classical structure of crime founded by Ernst von Beling. The construction, the argumentation and the controversy of various concept or structure of crime have greatly promoted the rationality and normativity of the Chinese criminal law theories. The overall pattern and academic situation of Chinese criminal law study have significantly changed compared with the 1980s and 1990s, which makes it possible for Chinese scholars to initiate academic dialogues with the scholars from foreign countries including Germany and Japan at an international level.

The main concern of this article is to describe and evaluate the modern transformation of Chinese criminal law science, especially the theory of structure of crime. The author will also take a position on how to build a criminal law science in China, which is not only in line with the systematic and logical construction of the step-up level structure of crime, but also provides reasonable explanation for criminal law theory as well as practical guidance for criminal justice.

2 Li Haidong, Theories of Criminal Law (Fundament of Concept of Crime), Law Press, 1998, p. 2.

3 See Liang Genlin, He Huixin, "Chinese Criminal Law Science in the 20th Century (Part 1)", Peking University Law Journal, No. 2, 1999.

### *I. Learning from Soviet Union: Main Points of the "Four Constituents" Theory of Crime Construction*

On January 1, 1980, the first criminal code of the People's Republic of China came into effect, since then China has committed to the path of rule of law. Chinese criminal law scholars combined the legislation with the actual needs of punishing criminals and protecting individual rights under the background of reform and opening-up, further enriched and developed the "four constituents" theory of crime construction, through which the "four constituents" theory of crime construction has become a widely prevailing view in both theoretical field and judicial practice.

It is generally accepted that the publication of the textbook "Criminal Law" edited by the famous Chinese criminal law scholar Professor Gao Mingxuan published in 1982 is the most important symbol which indicates that the "four constituents" theory of crime construction has been the predominant concept of crime in both academic and practical fields. According to the definition in this textbook and several other textbooks edited by the Ministry of Justice and the Ministry of Education, "the structure of crime is the combination of all necessary objective and subjective elements stipulated by the Criminal Code of China, which determine whether an act can be evaluated as a crime."[4] Correspondingly, the "four constituents" theory of crime construction is typically characterized by its structure consist of two general parts that can be further divided into four basic interrelated aspects. To be more specific, "the so-called 'two general parts' are the objective part and the subjective part of a crime in accordance with the principle of the unity of objectivity and subjectivity. And the 'four basic aspects' are the four necessary elements for the construction of a crime, which include the following elements in sequence: the object of a crime-the objective side of a crime-the subject of a crime-the subjective side of a crime. All of these four elements are indispensable for establishing a crime."[5]

The crime construction in the context of the "four constituents" theory is the legal standard for conviction as well as the only reliance of criminal liability. "Crime construction encompasses many different subjects of criminal law study that extend from the definition of crime to criminal liability. Based at the theory of crime construction, the criminal law science

---

4 See Gao Mingxuan (eds.), Criminal Law, Law Press, 1984, p. 96.

5 Gao Mingxuan, "Reflections on the Theory of Crime Construction in China", Law Science, No. 2, 2010.

with Chinese characteristics centered on the fundamental order of 'crime-responsibility-punishment' has been founded. In other words, the logical order in Chinese criminal law science is shown as follows: firstly, the theory of concept of crime focuses on the issue of 'crime', whose core task is to judge whether a conduct can be qualified as a crime; secondly, the theory of criminal liability focuses on the issue of 'responsibility', whose core task is to find out whether a perpetrator should be held responsible for his unlawful act; finally, the theory of punishment focuses on the issue of 'penalty', whose core task is to determine the appropriate penalty for the responsible criminals. To sum up, 'crime-responsibility-punishment' is the logical structure of Chinese criminal law science, while 'conviction-determining responsibility-sentencing' is the operational orientation of Chinese criminal justice, correspondingly."[6]

## *II. Following the Example of Germany and Japan: Introduction of the Step-Up Level Theory and the Doctrine of "Reconstruction"*

Since the beginning of 21st century, with the comprehensive introduction of the criminal law knowledge from Germany and Japan, especially the knowledge about the concept or structure of crime, the theory of structure of crime in China has been experiencing a systematical and functional transformation. On the basis of rethinking and criticism of the systematical and functional deficiencies of the "four constituents" theory, Chinese scholars made efforts to construct the step-up level theory of structure of crime in China, following the example of Germany and Japan. Professor Chen Xingliang, a representative for the construction of the three-layered structure of crime, and Professor Zhang Mingkai, a representative for the construction of the two-layered structure of crime, are the most important leading pioneers in the process of the transformation in China. Of course, it was not only Chen and Zhang who made contributions to the transformation of criminal law system and knowledge in China, but also many, especially young and middle-aged criminal law scholars. This article only takes the concept put forward respectively by Chen and Zhang as two examples to show how the step-up level theory has been rapidly developing and widely spreading in contemporary China.

6 Gao Mingxuan, "Reflections on the Theory of Crime Construction in China", Law Science, No. 2, 2010.

### 1. *Construction of Three-Layered Structure of Crime of Professor Chen Xingliang*

Chen focused on the basic defects of the "four constituents" theory of crime construction from the structural and functional perspective, describing it as "crime construction without elements of the offense (Tatbestand)", "crime construction without justifications and excuses", "crime construction without attribution", "crime construction without levels", and concluded that these structural and functional defects are sufficient reasons for abandoning the "four constituents" theory in China.[7] Chen strongly advocated the farewell to the Soviet model[8] and the construction of a new system based on the doctrine of the three-layered structure following the example of Germany and Japan, which consists of "elements of the offense" (Tatbestandsmäßigkeit), "wrongfulness" (Rechtswidrigkeit) and "culpability" (Schuld). In such a system, factual judgement is to be made before value judgement, objective judgement before subjective, formal judgement before material, and typical judgement before individual.[9] In the heated debate between the "four constituents" theory and step-up level theory, Chen is therefore recognized as the leading figure of the doctrine of "reconstruction", namely abandoning the "four constituents" theory and rebuilding a three-layered theory in China.

However, the transformation of Chen's concept of crime and criminal law methodology was not accomplished overnight. As a criminal law scholar who had learned the "four constituents" theory systematically and comprehensively from the previous generation, Chen also did his research within the context and framework of "four constituents" theory in early years. Since the 21st century, however, under the influence of German and Japanese criminal law doctrine, he has gradually detached himself from the "four constituents" theory and eventually parted ways with it.

In his book "Essential Criminal Law Science" published in 2001, Chen has come to the conclusion: "Crime construction should adopt a dichotomy structure and be divided into two parts, namely the entity of crime and the guilt of crime. The entity of crime is the objective aspect of a crime, while the guilt of crime is its subjective aspect. They constitute a unity of

7 Chen Xingliang, "Crime Construction: From Four Constituents to Three-Layered Theory", Peking University Law Journal, No. 1, 2010.

8 Chen Xingliang, "Farewell to the Soviet Model of Criminal Law Knowledge", Tribune of Political Science and Law, No. 5, 2006.

9 Chen Xingliang, "Crime Construction: From Four Constituents to Three-Layered Theory", Peking University Law Journal, No. 1, 2010.

objectivity and subjectivity."[10] In this book, Chen defined the so-called "entity of crime" as "the objective factual elements of a particular crime that are found in the special part of the criminal code",[11] and the "guilt of crime" as "the subject fault of the perpetrator, which is the blameworthiness of the act in the presence of 'entity of crime'".[12]

In his book "Normative Criminal Law Science" published in 2003, Chen further developed his theory of crime structure on the basis of the dichotomy structure mentioned above, which consists of (1) the "entity of crime", which is the objective element of a crime, (2) the "guilt of crime", which is the subjective element of a crime and is regarded as the substance of a crime together with the "entity of crime", and (3) the "quantitative level of crime", which is the quantitative element of a crime based on the "entity" and the "guilt".[13] According to this structure, the "entity of crime" comprises act, object, result, causality, and other objective conditions of the act; the "guilt of crime" comprises criminal liability, form of responsibility (intention, negligence) and other subjective conditions of the act (motivation, purpose, etc.). The "quantitative level of crime" including amount and circumstances is a quantitative condition, which indicates the degree of the infringement of legal goods, when the conditions of the substance of a crime are fulfilled.[14]

At the same time as Chen published this book, the textbook "Criminal Law" edited by him was published as well, which is the first criminal law textbook in China compiled according to the three-layered structure of elements of the offense, wrongfulness and culpability.[15] The publication symbolized that Chen bade farewell to the "four constituents" theory of crime construction. Since then, under the support of many scholars, especially young and middle-aged scholars, Chen has been committed to thoroughly

10 Chen Xingliang, Essential Criminal Law Science, The Commercial Press, 2001, pp. 220–221.
11 Chen Xingliang, Essential Criminal Law Science, The Commercial Press, 2001, p. 226.
12 Chen Xingliang, Essential Criminal Law Science, The Commercial Press, 2001, p. 296.
13 Chen Xingliang, Normative Criminal Law Science, China University of Political Science and Law Press, 2003, p. 85.
14 See Chen Xingliang, Normative Criminal Law Science, China University of Political Science and Law Press, 2003, pp. 61–62, 76–77, 95–96.
15 See Chen Xingliang, Criminal Law, Fudan University Press, 2003.

criticizing the "four constituents" theory,[16] advocating the methodology of criminal law doctrine (Strafrechtsdogmatik),[17] promoting the farewell to Soviet model,[18] and constructing a three-layered structure of crime.[19] And the book "Doctrinal Criminal Law Science" written by him in 2010 further emphasizes his firm support for the three-layered theory and the doctrinal methodology.

Chen has systematically analyzed the development of the structure of crime in Germany in the past hundred years, which extends from the classical structure of Ernst von Beling/Franz von Liszt and the neoclassical structure of Hellmut Mayer/Edmund Mezger, to the structure of neoclassical-finalism founded by Hans Welzel, and to the rational teleological structure of Claus Roxin. He has finally come to the conclusion that the three-layered system is the basic logical structure of crime in Germany because of its logicalness and plausibility in spite of the differences in the four phases of development, and can provide a well-ordered pattern for analyzing an offense.[20] In his opinion, "the task of the theory of structure of crime lies in systematizing the legal prerequisites of a crime and establishing its internal logical connections. Hence, whether a theory of structure of crime can be evaluated as scientific, depends on whether it is logically plausible."[21] And such plausibility manifests itself, when factual judgement is made before value judgement, objective judgement before subjective, formal judgement before material, and typical judgement before individual.[22]

---

16 See Chen Xingliang, "Structure of Crime: Comparation, Description and Discussion", in Chen Xingliang (ed.), Criminal Law Review, Vol. 14, China University of Political Science and Law Press, 2004.

17 See Chen Xingliang, "Methodology of Criminal Law Doctrine", Chinese Journal of Law, No. 2, 2005.

18 Chen Xingliang, "Farewell to the Soviet Model of Criminal Law Knowledge", Tribune of Political Science and Law, No. 5, 2006.

19 Chen Xingliang, "Crime Construction: From Four Constituents to Three-Layered Theory", Peking University Law Journal, No. 1, 2010. Chen Xingliang, "Step-Up Level of Structure of Crime", Chinese Journal of Law, No. 4, 2010. Chen Xingliang, "Rethinking and Reconstruction of Basic Concept in Structure of Crime", Chinese Journal of Law, No. 2, 2011.

20 Chen Xingliang, Doctrinal Criminal Law Science, Chinese Renmin University Press, 2010, p. 116.

21 Chen Xingliang, Doctrinal Criminal Law Science, Chinese Renmin University Press, 2010, p. 135.

22 Chen Xingliang, Doctrinal Criminal Law Science, Chinese Renmin University Press, 2010, pp. 135ff.

*2. Construction of Two-Layered Structure of Crime of Professor Zhang Mingkai*

Besides Chen, Zhang has also contributed much to the transformation of the Chinese criminal law knowledge and the construction of the step-up level theory. While Chen completely rejected the traditional "four constituents" theory and built his new theory only by one step at a single leap, which is a more radical solution for reconstruction of crime structure in China, Zhang has instead taken a step-by-step, milder and thus less-opposed solution that is presented in detail in the first to fifth edition of his textbook "Criminal Law".

In the first edition, Zhang fully adopted the "four constituents" theory of crime construction and explained the structure of crime within the framework of the object of a crime, the objective side of a crime, the subject of a crime, and the subjective side of a crime.[23] However, in the following editions (2nd edition-5th edition), Zhang has changed his theory successively from the "three constituents" theory of "the objective side of a crime, the subject of a crime, the subjective side of a crime and the grounds for exclusion from punishment", to the "two constituents" theory of "the objective elements of offense (unlawfulness) and the subjective elements of offense (culpability)", to the two-layered structure of "elements of unlawfulness and culpability", and eventually to the two-layered structure of "unlawfulness and culpability".

In the second edition, Zhang pointed out that the common prerequisites of crime construction are the objective side of a crime, the subject of a crime, and the subjective side of a crime.[24] In addition, he dealt with the so-called "overall elements of crime construction" with regard to the "particularly serious circumstances" regulated in Chinese Criminal Code, as well as the grounds for exclusion from punishment separately outside the structure of crime. Such arrangement of position indicates that Zhang did not include the grounds for exclusion from punishment into the structure of crime in this edition. Therefore, it can be concluded that the theory of crime construction of Zhang had not yet gone beyond the basic scheme and method of the "four constituents" theory at that time.

However, in the third edition, Zhang has greatly changed his theory of crime construction from the "four constituents" theory to the step-up level theory. With regard to the change, Zhang explained that "there are two common prerequisites of crime construction: (1) the objective elements of

---

23 Zhang Mingkai, Criminal Law (Part 1), Law Press, 1997, p. 109.
24 Zhang Mingkai, Criminal Law (2nd edition), Law Press, 2003, p. 135.

offense, which indicate and lay foundation for the unlawfulness of an act (infringement of legal goods), and thus can also be referred to as elements of unlawfulness; (2) the subjective elements of offense, which indicate and lay foundation for the culpability of an act (blameworthiness), and thus can also be referred to as elements of culpability.[25]

While in the third edition, Zhang developed the prototype of his two-layered structure with the "two constituents" theory, but has not yet completely detached himself from the "four constituents" theory, the fourth edition published in 2011 symbolizes that Zhang has already completed the transformation of structure of crime to the two-layered theory. He described the changes as follows: "In this book, the two-layered structure of crime consisting of unlawfulness and culpability is adopted. The element of unlawfulness is not the only requirement for a crime, but merely one of it; it shows the infringement of legal goods caused by the act. The issue of justifications is involved in this level. On the other hand, the element of culpability shows the blameworthiness of the unlawful act. The issue of excuses is involved in this level."[26]

The fifth edition continues the two-layered structure and explicitly divides it into wrongfulness and culpability. "Unlawfulness means that an act not only meets the statutory description of a criminal offense but is also illegal. The statutory elements of a crime constitute to type of illegality that indicates the infringement of legal goods caused by the act. If an act conforms to the statutory elements of a crime, then it is unlawful unless there is a presence of a justificatory defense. There is no need to positively test the illegality. Therefore, the elements of the offense and unlawfulness belong to the same level in the crime structure."[27] "Culpability means the unlawful act is blameworthy...The elements of culpability consist of positive elements (such as intention, negligence, purpose) and negative elements (such as the mistake of law and the fairness of expecting the defendant to act otherwise under the circumstances)."[28]

Owing to the great contributions made by Chen and Zhang, many young criminal law scholars now – although consensus has not been reached on every detail – share the view that the structure of crime in China should be reconstructed into a step-up level pattern following the example of Germany and Japan. And the step-up level theory has influenced the

---

25 Zhang Mingkai, Criminal Law (3rd edition), Law Press, 2007, p. 108.
26 Zhang Mingkai, Criminal Law (4th edition), Law Press, 2011, p. 105.
27 Zhang Mingkai, Criminal Law (5th edition), Law Press, 2016, pp. 103–104.
28 Zhang Mingkai, Criminal Law (5th edition), Law Press, 2016, p. 104.

judicial practice, especially the judgement of the difficult cases, to a certain extent.

### *III. Preservation and Improvement of the "Four Constituents" Theory*

Since the representatives of the step-up level theory have strongly criticized and completely rejected the "four constituents" theory, the supporters of the "four constituents" theory, the most important representative of whom is Professor Gao Mingxuan, strive to defend and justify this theory. On one hand, Gao admitted that the traditional criminal law science is not perfect and in lack of dynamic perspective for analyzing crime, responsibility and punishment beyond the static description of crime. The doctrine of responsibility is relatively weakly developed in comparison to the doctrine of crime and of punishment and cannot connect these two fields in a proper way. Therefore, Chinese traditional criminal law science should be further improved.[29] On the other hand, Gao maintained that the "four constituents" theory of crime construction was chosen in China for historical reasons and is therefore "rational from the perspective of history"; that this theory adapts to the actual needs in China and is therefore "rational from the perspective of practice"; that this theory is logically precise, compatible with the law of recognition and the nature of the crime and is therefore "rational from the internal perspective"; that this theory is relatively stable compared with the German and Japanese three-layered theory, fit in with Chinese criminal procedure and is therefore "rational from the comparative perspective".[30]

When it comes to the doctrine of reconstruction insisting on abandoning the "four constituents" theory and completely introducing the three-layered theory, Gao defended himself from the perspective of urgency, necessity and feasibility: "The change from the current system to another system requires urgency, necessity and feasibility. Urgency would only exist, if Chinese criminal law system were to lag behind the demand of the time and the trends of the world, if German, Japanese, or other new criminal law theory were the irresistible trend of the future, and if we were to be criticized by criminal law scholars around the world for not adopting the

---

29 See Gao Mingxuan, "Rationality of the 'Four Constituents' Theory and Preservation of Chinese Criminal Law System", China Legal Science, No. 2, 2009.

30 See Gao Mingxuan, "Rationality of the 'Four Constituents' Theory and Preservation of Chinese Criminal Law System", China Legal Science, No. 2, 2009.

new criminal law system. This is certainly not the case. Besides, necessity would only exist, if the new system were clearly superior to the old one, and the one system were not longer able to solve the new problems in reality. This is not the case, either. Furthermore, the concept of reconstruction would be not feasible, unless we have intellectually well prepared and got trained for the adoption of the new system. However, in the absence of adequate preparation, it is difficult to affirm the feasibility for the reconstruction. Therefore, the doctrine of reconstruction is not acceptable. Admittedly, it is necessary to learn from others. However, we should not lose ourselves and lose our own direction during study."[31]

Therefore, Gao calls for "adherence to the current 'four constituents' theory of crime construction and the Chinese criminal law system of crime-responsibility-punishment". At the same time, he also asks for the improvement of the "four constituents" theory through acknowledging its disadvantages, changing the static research methodology, deepening the doctrine of criminal responsibility, focusing on practical problems in reality, as well as balancing the system-oriented thinking and the problem-oriented thinking.[32] Gao is recognized as the most important exponent of the view of "preservation and improvement" that is supported by many Chinese criminal law scholars and, above all, the criminal judges.

## *IV. The Doctrine of Modification Between Preservation and Reconstruction*

The doctrine of "modification" derives from the improvement of the "four constituents" theory within its own framework at the end of the 1980s. In the 1990s, this doctrine has come to a peak. As Gao stated, the doctrine of "modification" of the "four constituents" theory in the 1980s-1990s "was aimed at technically revising and reprogramming Chinese traditional crime construction theory within its basic framework and pattern. The so-called 'two constituents' theory, 'three constituents' theory, 'five constituents' theory, and even the new 'four constituents' theory as achievement of the doctrine of 'modification' came out one after the other, and then quickly lost their significance."[33]

---

31 Gao Mingxuan, "Rationality of the 'Four Constituents' Theory and Preservation of Chinese Criminal Law System", China Legal Science, No. 2, 2009.

32 See Gao Mingxuan, "Rationality of the 'Four Constituents' Theory and Preservation of Chinese Criminal Law System", China Legal Science, No. 2, 2009.

33 Gao Mingxuan, "Reflection on Theory of Crime Construction in Chinese Criminal Law, Law Science, No. 2, 2010.

Since the 21st century, with the introduction and influence of German and Japanese criminal law doctrine and step-up level structure of crime, Chinese criminal law scholars have been attempting to find a compromise between the "four constituents" theory and the three-layered theory, as well as to introduce concepts, logic, and methods of the step-up level structure of crime within the basic framework of the "four constituents" theory, so as to reconstruct the "four constituents" theory in the way that materially changes its logic and function to varying extents, while its formal pattern and scheme remain untouched.

For example, Professor Li Hong asserted that the structure of crime in China should not be reconstructed in accordance with the German and Japanese step-up level structure. The defects of the "four constituents" theory do not cause fatal threat and can be overcome by meliorating, to be exact, by carrying through an object-preferred step-up notion.[34] In this regard, Li made the following proposal: First of all, in the "four constituents" theory, a strict distinction should be made between the objective and subjective requirements. Secondly, as for the constituent "the subject of a crime", a distinction should be made between the subject of the act, which should be included in the objective requirements, and the criminal capability, which should be included in the subjective requirements. Thirdly, the justificatory defenses such as self-defense and necessity are to be classified as objective requirements, while the reasonable expectation is to be classified as subjective requirement. According to Li's "two-layered step-up crime construction" in his textbook, the objective requirements of crime construction include object, perpetrating act, result, identity of the perpetrator, causality, time and place, etc., while the subjective requirements of crime construction include criminal capability, intention, negligence, mistakes, reasonable expectation, etc.[35] The arguments for this scheme are as followed: this two-layered step-up crime construction not only carries out the principle of legality, but also persists in continuing the Chinese criminal law research; the division between objective and subjective requirements meets the demand of separate and step-by-step characteristics of crime construction; and the combination of formal and material assessment in the objective requirements is compatible with the prevailing view that crime construction is the only standard of criminal liability.[36]

---

34 See Li Hong, "The Structure of Crimes in China not to be Restructed", Chinese Journal of Law, No. 1, 2006.

35 See Li Hong, Criminal Law, Law Press, 2012, pp. 66–67.

36 See Li Hong, Criminal Law, Law Press, 2012, pp. 66–67.

In contrast to Li, Professor Zhou Guangquan recognized the defects of the "four constituents" theory comprehensively and expressed full approval of the step-up level structure of crime, however, in his textbook, he did not completely detach himself from the "four constituents" theory, but instead continued to use its basic scheme, dividing the requirements of crime into three aspects: objective elements of crime, subjective elements of crime, and exclusion of crime.[37] The objective elements of crime include the constitutive elements of the objective side of a crime, such as perpetrating act, result, causality, time, place and approach of act, etc. With respect to the subjective elements of crime, issues such as intention, negligence, mistakes, lack of blameworthiness, motivation and purpose are to be discussed. And the exclusion of crime refers to justifications and excuses.[38]

## *V. Discussion on transformation of criminal law science in China*

The author approves of the step-up level structure of crime, especially the three-layered theory consisting of elements of offense, wrongfulness and culpability, in consideration of its logical self-consistency and functional self-sufficiency. However, the author also admits that there is still a long way to go to introduce and build the step-up level structure of crime in China, although the step-up level theory has already occupied a place in Chinese criminal law research, since not only many criminal law scholars strongly and convincingly opposed this theory, but also the judges and lawyers mostly do not accept its method of thinking. In other words, the step-up level theory in China is now met with an awkward situation that it is vividly debated in academic communities, but is hardly accepted in judicial practice.

Apart from time, institution, environment, communication and other objective and non-scientific reasons, it is necessary for the supporters of the step-up level theory to reflect on the defects associated with the introduction of German and Japanese knowledge and method, and the problems caused by construction of the Chinese step-up level theory, so as to develop

37 See Zhou Guangquan, Criminal Law General Part, Chinese Renmin University Press, 2016, pp. 85 ff.

38 See Zhou Guangquan, Criminal Law General Part, Chinese Renmin University Press, 2016, pp. 88 ff.

it further and eventually complete the transformation of structure of crime in China.[39]

### 1. *Ambiguity of the Step-Up Level Theory as Reference Model*

Chinese scholars have firstly learned the step-up level theory from the neighbor Japan. It is only in recent years that they gradually began to pay attention to theories in the birthplace of modern criminal law doctrine, namely Germany. The structure of crime of Japan and of Germany are both stepped-up, however, there sill exist many significant differences between them in terms of the theoretical structure and the fundamental standpoint. Even within Japan or Germany, the concepts of structure of crime also vary widely. In Japan, there is a major controversy of theoretical system between worthlessness of conduct (Handlungsunwert) and worthlessness of result (Erfolgsunwert). In Germany, although such a controversy has been eliminated and the dualistic theory combining worthlessness of conduct and worthlessness of result has become the prevailing view, there is still a distinction within the dualistic theory about whether worthlessness of conduct or worthlessness of result the dominating factor is, which has given rise to various schemes of crime structure. When it comes to the relationship between elements of offense and wrongfulness, some consider that the elements of offense should be separated from the level of wrongfulness out of respect for the guarantee function of the elements of offense for principle of legality, through which the three-layered structure of elements of offense, wrongfulness and culpability comes into being. Others tend to combine elements of offense and wrongfulness under the definition of unlawfulness (Unrecht) based on the standpoint that elements of offense are the foundation for the existence of wrongfulness, and build the two-layered structure of unlawfulness and culpability. Furthermore, taking into account the act as the basis of the offense and the particular importance of the objective conditions of criminal liability (objektive Strafbarkeitsbedingungen), there exist even more concepts of crime structure, such as the three-layered system of act, unlawfulness and culpability; the four-layered system of act, elements of offense, wrongfulness and culpability; the two-plus-one layered system of unlawfulness, culpability and objective conditions of criminal liability; the three-plus-one layered of ele-

39 See Liang Genlin, "Structure of Crime and Construction of Criminal Law Science", Chinese Journal of Law, No. 1, 2013.

ments of offense, wrongfulness, culpability and objective conditions of criminal liability; the three-plus-one layered of act, unlawfulness, culpability and objective conditions of criminal liability; the four-plus-one layered of act, elements of offense, wrongfulness, culpability and objective conditions of criminal liability, etc. Among these different types of crime structure, the significance and functions of the elements of offense, wrongfulness, culpability and objective conditions of criminal liability are also different, and their interrelationships are even more complicated and confusing. In this regard, although the supporters of step-up level theory in China have reached an agreement on introducing the step-up level theory in place of the "four constituents" theory, there is still no consensus on which specific structure among these various types of step-up level theory should be introduced and adopted as the reference model, which not only prevents the development of step-up level theory in China, but also leads to difficulties in communication to some extent.

### 2. *Preference for Theory Restricted by the Educational Background of Scholars*

The various types of step-up level theory in Germany and Japan provide many beneficial theoretical resources for the construction of step-up level system in China. However, most Chinese scholars simply adopt the German or Japanese theories without profound analysis or critical reflection. The point of view on which theory to be introduced usually depends on the educational background of the scholar himself. As a result, it is common to see that those who have ever studied in Japan tend to introduce the Japanese theories, while those who have studied in Germany prefer to the German theories, especially the doctrines suggested or supported by their own foreign supervisors. Such academic continuity from teachers to their own students further prevents a consensus when designing the structure of crime in China.

### 3. *Influence of Personal Value Concept and Individualized Research Style of Scholars*

The different value concept and research style of the scholars are necessary preconditions for the free development of academic research and the emergence of different schools of criminal law. But they also constitute an obstacle to the construction of a uniform structure of crime in the meantime.

For example, as the representatives of supporters of step-up level theory in China, Chen and Zhang have totally different value preference and research style. Chen advocates the doctrine of formal interpretation and the classical three-layered theory for the sake of the primacy of formal rationality and legal formalism.[40] His serious and even rigor research style[41] leads him to pay more attention to logical plausibility than to functional sufficiency in system designing. Although he has built a crime construction system of "entity of crime – guilt of crime – quantitative level of crime" based at the regulations in Chinese Criminal Code, shortly afterwards, he has turned to the more systematic and logically plausible theory, namely the structure of crime consisting of "elements of crime – wrongfulness – culpability". In contrast, as mentioned above, Zhang prefers the doctrine of material interpretation and the concept of crime with emphasis on materiel justice in accordance with material rationality and legal instrumentalism. The gradual, step-by-step strategy, by which he builds up his step-up level theory, is closely linked with his personality and research style. And the reason why he prefers to the two-layered theory instead of the three-layered theory simply lies in his persistence in the doctrine of material interpretation and his point of view that "the elements of offense are the foundation for the existence of wrongfulness, thus the elements of offenses can not be fulfilled without wrongfulness".[42]

### 4. *Lack of Thorough Understanding of German and Japanese Criminal Law Theories*

The step-up level theory emphasizes the scientific combination, structural function as well as the systematic order of the elements of crime, which is also its advantage. In the past hundred years, the concept of crime in Germany has changed considerably in its structure, system, function and methodology from the classical structure of crime, the neoclassical structure of crime, and the neoclassical-finalism structure of crime, to the current functional, teleological structure of crime. Through this process of development, not only the paradigm of criminal law research has become systematized, logical and normative, but also the knowledge of criminal

40 Chen Xingliang, "Advocate for the Doctrine of Formal Interpretation", China Legal Science, No. 4, 2010.

41 Chen Xingliang, Enlightenment of Criminal Law, Law Press, 1998, p. 259.

42 Zhang Mingkai "Persistence in the Doctrine of Material Interpretation", China Legal Science, No. 4, 2010.

law has been more precise. Although Chinese criminal law scholars have introduced the Japanese three-layered theory several years ago, they are still lacking in full understanding of the German theory which is much more complicated, profound, hard to understand, and has a closer relationship with philosophy and history compared to the Japanese theory. Besides, neither the interrelationship among the elements within the concept of crime nor the constraint on crime structure theory from history, culture, philosophy and reality has been discussed and analyzed in depth. The misunderstanding or even misrepresentation of German theory occurs from time to time. Without thorough understanding of German and Japanese criminal theories and the process of development, it would be nearly impossible to build up a scientific step-up level theory in China.

### *5. Lack of Adjustment to Theory and Practice in China*

The step-up level theory is not limited to a specific country or penal code, but is universally applicable to all countries, as it is a method aimed at creating a model for conviction, preventing the unlimited and arbitrary jurisdiction, and protecting both legal goods and human rights.[43] However, the concrete structure and standpoint of the step-up level theory are closely linked with the culture, history and social context, which means that the concrete answers to the specific criminal law questions are not necessarily universal within the framework of the step-up level theory. Hence, it can not be simply introduced in each country without any change. Instead, the introduction of step-up level theory should be adapted to the concrete regulations in Chinese Criminal Code and the actual needs of Chinese society, while maintaining its consistency in aspect of definition, logic and system; otherwise it would be neither inapplicable nor unpractical in China.

In my opinion, when adapting a foreign theory to the Chinese criminal law, its compatibility with the context of Chinese society as well as the current stage of the criminal law study in China should firstly be considered. Under the special context of Chinese society in the 21st century, if the step-up level theory were still to be established on the basis of the more than 100-year-old classical crime structure of Germany without consideration of the development of German and Japanese criminal theories about elements of crime and their interrelationships over the past hundred years, or

43 See Fan Wen, "Criminal Law Without Borders", Chinese Journal of Law, No. 1, 2010.

even without taking into account the traditional problems and current challenges in modern China, then the structure of crime built in this way would be unhelpful for the establishment and improvement of the rule of law and justice, in spite of its perfect logic, system and argumentation.

Furthermore, when adopting the German or Japanese step-up level theory in China, not only the general principles of epistemology and methodology together with the basic requirements of the rule of law are to be emphasized, but also its legal foundation derived from Chinese Criminal Code should be paid more attention to. Just as German and Japanese three-layered theory are usually based on the principle of legality, protection of legal goods and principle of culpability as the most important criminal law foundations, the construction of Chinese step-up level theory should be connected with the regulations in Chinese Criminal Code as well. Actually, the current provisions on the purpose of criminal law (Article 1), the task of criminal law (Article 2), the principle of legality (Article 3), the adaption of punishment to offense and responsibility (Article 5) already imply the three-layered structure of elements of offense, wrongfulness and culpability. In this sense, the step-up level theory can be regarded as the immanent requirement of Chinese Criminal Code. However, Chinese scholars pay too little attention to the compatibility between the step-up level theory and the Chinese Criminal Code. And the abstract construction without consideration of the current Criminal Code would weaken the legitimacy of Chinese step-up level theory to a certain extent.

Finally, the step-up level theory is not only a criminal law methodology, but also a knowledge system of domestic criminal law. Therefore, it is both national and international. It cannot be developed independently of specific provisions in domestic criminal law. It is also inadvisable to criticize or even reject the specific regulations of domestic criminal law, simply because that they do not conform to the logic and system of the step-up level theory stemming from foreign countries. For example, Chinese criminal law differs from German and Japanese criminal law in its "exception clause" regulated in the general part of Criminal Code, which is the necessary component of the definition of crime, together with the amount of crime as the prerequisite for conviction in the form of "relatively large amount", "serious consequences" and "serious cases" specified in the special part of Criminal Code. When constructing the step-up level structure of crime in China, criminal law scholars should take these differences into account, recognize the function of the "exception clause" and locate it properly in the structure of crime. It is totally wrong to exclude the "exception clause" and the amount of crime from crime structure simply because they do not fit into the three-layered theory, or merely locate them in the objective conditions of criminal liability beyond wrongfulness and culpability. In my opinion, the function and systematic position of the amount of crime is one of the most important questions to be solved for the sake of adopting the step-up level theory in China.[44]

44 See Wang Ying, "The Systematic Position of Circumstances of Offense", Chinese Journal of Law, No. 3, 2012; Wang Qiang, "Amount of Crime: Element of Offense or Conditions of Punishment?", The Jurist, No. 5, 2012; Liang Genlin, "Exception Clause, Amount of Crime, and Criminalization of Pickpocket", Chinese Journal of Law, No. 2, 2013.

# The Role of Philosophy within the General Theory of Crime

*Michael Pawlik*

## I. *The Autonomy of Legal Discourse and Its Limits*

According to Arthur Kaufmann, philosophy and legal dogmatics (*Rechtsdogmatik*) are in the 'relationship of alterity'.[1] This dictum can count on broad approval within today's jurisprudence. In the words of Kaufmann's teacher, Gustav Radbruch, legal dogmatics are best understood as 'the science of the objective meaning of positive legal systems'.[2] As a 'monitor of those conditions under which legal principles can be implemented in case decisions',[3] dogmatics function as a 'stop rule for reason-seeking reasoning'.[4] Against this background the recourse to philosophy is under suspicion of arbitrariness: it turns out to be 'a capricious quotation from a confusing abundance of speculative texts'.[5] Philosophical arguments are either mere embellishments of genuinely dogmatic considerations or, in the end, bad arguments *ab auctoritate*.[6]

At first glance, these concerns seem to be compelling. As Niklas Luhmann states, in the course of the 19th century (at the latest), it became obvious that the evolution of ideas was shifting from the level of society as a whole, represented by the upper class, to that of the individual social subsystems. '[I]n Königsberg and Berlin [...] attempts are being made once again to reconcile the world of ideas anew with a philosophical concept of science. In fact, however, the reflection efforts of the functional systems take the lead.'[7] This excludes direct recourse to the semantic resources of

1 Arthur Kaufmann, '*Rechtsphilosophie. Rechtstheorie, Rechtsdogmatik*' in Arthur Kaufmann et alii (eds), *Einführung in die Rechtsphilosophie und Rechtstheorie der Gegenwart* (8th edn, 2011) 3.
2 Gustav Radbruch, *Rechtsphilosophie* (Studienausgabe, 2nd edn 2003) 106.
3 Niklas Luhmann, *Ausdifferenzierung des Rechts* (1981) 396.
4 Niklas Luhmann, *Das Recht der Gesellschaft* (1993) 387.
5 Christoph Engel/Wolfgang Schön, '*Vorwort*' in C Engel/W Schön (eds), *Das Proprium der Rechtswissenschaft* (2007), X.
6 Luís Greco, '*Neue Wege der Vorsatzdogmatik – Eine Auseinandersetzung mit drei neuen Monographien zum Vorsatzbegriff*' [2009] ZIS, 815.
7 Niklas Luhmann, *Die Gesellschaft der Gesellschaft*, vol 1 (1986) 553.

other social communication systems. Thus, philosophy can directly solve only its own problems and not those of law,[8] and law can only be derived from the reference to other law; recourses to social evaluations and interests 'only stimulate self-contact, in which only law can identify itself as law'.[9]

However, the dynamics of the development of criminal law dogmatics in Germany do not only, indeed not even primarily, result from inner-dogmatic problems. Admittedly, the prevailing doctrines of the theory of crime recommended themselves also by the fact that they promised relief from the pressure that newly discovered dogmatic problems exerted on the outdated concepts of the theory of crime. Thus, the normative understanding of guilt (*normativer Schuldbegriff*) played into the hands of the neo-Kantians, the subjective elements of injustice (*Unrecht*) favoured the finalist position, and the doctrine of objective imputation (*objektive Zurechnung*) benefited the normativist movement. Nonetheless, it is a commonplace in the sociology of knowledge that established styles of scientific thought display extraordinary creativity in harmonising *prima facie* contradictory findings with their own systems, provided they do not simply ignore them.[10] Taking this into account, the pressure of inner-dogmatic problems has never been so great that it would have *forced* abandoning the more or less functioning previous system and the departure to uncertain new shores.

Moreover, the dogmatic problems that gave rise to profound reorientations in German criminal law theory were mostly of a rather marginal nature. For the most part, their significance for the everyday application of criminal law was so minimal that the theoretical effort that was put into them must have seemed downright absurd in the eyes of practitioners who were concerned with their everyday business. Such astonishment is even greater when one considers that every change of a scientific theory involves a risk that can be pre-calculated only to a limited extent. A new theory is initially little more than a promise of a better scientific future.[11] Admittedly, the proposed innovation may prove superior to its predecessors in solving the problem it was conceived to address. However, its consequences for other parts of the theory as a whole can never be fully assessed in advance. If the above-mentioned new approaches nonetheless met with posi-

---

8 Christoph Menke, '*Zwischen Literatur und Dialektik*' in Joachim Schulte/Uwe Wenzel (eds), *Was ist ein ‚philosophisches' Problem?* (2001) 128.

9 Niklas Luhmann, *Gesellschaftsstruktur und Semantik*, vol 2 (1993) 102.

10 Classical Ludwig Fleck, *Entstehung und Entwicklung einer wissenschaftlichen Tatsache* (9th edn, 2012), 40 ff.

11 Thomas Kuhn, *Die Struktur wissenschaftlicher Revolutionen* (2nd edn, 1976) 37 f.

tive responses from the majority of scholars, as they did, their success cannot be attributed solely to their dogmatic superiority. But to what else?

As long as one's own view is limited to the internal perspective of legal dogmatics, it is impossible to answer this question adequately. The finding just mentioned becomes intelligible, however, as soon as one realises that the insistence of criminal law scholars on their disciplinary independence is counteracted by their efforts to preserve what Munich philosopher Dieter Henrich calls their 'identity balance'.[12] This need is inextricably linked to the structure of modern societies that emerges between the 17th and 19th centuries: the transition from stratification to functional differentiation, as Luhmann analyses it.[13] In stratified societies, society is represented in the form of a social hierarchy.[14] Under these circumstances, belonging to a social class had a multifunctional effect: it bundled advantages and disadvantages in virtually all functional areas of society.[15] In functionally differentiated societies, however, the overall system does not require a hierarchical order of relationship between the functional systems.[16] Rather, it lies within the logic of functional systems to give every participant in social life access to all functions, as long as the function itself does not preclude it.[17] Ontologically, this is made possible by the discreditation of former cosmic thinking,[18] and it is legitimated by the postulate of the equality of all human beings.[19] Since then, society no longer presents itself to individuals as a well-ordered whole into which they must fit, but 'as a complexity with which one has to cope individually in a contingent and selective manner'.[20]

In this situation, all members of society are confronted with the highly demanding tasks of coordination and integration. They must relate their actions to a multiplicity of social systems and combine the requirements of these systems in a personal behavioural synthesis.[21] Admittedly, human persons are beings of great complexity who can understand and orient themselves in different social systems at the same time. In particular, a cer-

12 Dieter Henrich, *Denken und Selbstsein* (2007) 221.
13 Niklas Luhmann, *Gesellschaftsstruktur und Semantik*, vol 1 (1989) 72 ff.
14 Niklas Luhmann, *Die Gesellschaft der Gesellschaft*, vol 2 (1997) 679.
15 Ibid 679.
16 Ibid 746.
17 Luhmann (n 13) 168.
18 Charles Taylor, *Ein säkulares Zeitalter* (2012) 110 ff.
19 Luhmann (n 13) 168; Taylor (n 18) 362.
20 Niklas Luhmann, *Gesellschaftsstruktur und Semantik*, vol 3 (1989) 225.
21 Niklas Luhmann, *Grundrechte als Institution* (3rd edn, 1986) 53.

tain amount of self-distance from one's professional role is part of the everyday behavioural repertoire of modern individuals. Nevertheless, the individual cannot limit himself to operating with what French philosopher Vincent Descombes calls a 'plurality of business cards'[22] without coordinating the various requirements for each and every role. Otherwise, he could not be identified as the unique bearer of these different partial identities. Instead, he would be *quelque façon nul*, a creature that is unable to explain how he routinely manages to switch back and forth between the diverging identities.[23] For this reason, the individual must submit to the 'effort of integration with regard to himself',[24] which today is categorised under the name of identity formation.[25] He must give his life coherence and a direction with which he can identify.

This requirement becomes all the more urgent the more a particular activity shapes the overall identity of an individual. It is, therefore, particularly important for those whose job is the application of criminal law. The task of criminal law dogmatics is to justify in the best way possible why a citizen, when certain legal requirements are fulfilled – and only then! – may be compelled to endure the evil of punishment.[26] Because the dogmatics of criminal law are to be used as a basis for the decision on the exercise of state coercion, and because criminal punishment is the symbolically and often physically most severe sanction known to our legal system, the dogmatist of criminal law has a responsibility that goes far beyond that of the ordinary humanities scholar.[27]

Bearers of this responsibility are not only judges, but also include academic criminal law dogmatists. Since legal dogmatics help to shape the content of the law and since in German legal culture, with its extraordinarily close interrelation of theory and practice, the courts are expected to deal with the positions of dogmatics, they too exercise power.[28] Which professor does not consider it a success if the courts take up his ideas? Moreover, present-day jurisprudence is aware that legal interpretation is never strictly bound by the words of law; legal interpretation always has a creative side. Members of the legal profession, therefore, do not act as impersonal

22 Vincent Descombes, *Die Rätsel der Identität* (2013) 42.
23 Ibid 45.
24 Ibid 35.
25 The argumentation outlined here is developed in more detail in: Michael Pawlik, Critical Analysis of Law 7:1 (2020), 1 ff.
26 Michael Pawlik, *Das Unrecht des Bürgers* (2012) 26 ff.
27 Ibid 43 f.
28 Ibid 44 with further references.

'mouths that pronounce the words of the law' (*Montesquieu*), but inevitably make individual evaluations[29] for which they are individually responsible.[30] For this reason, legal professionals must be concerned with integrating their interpretations of criminal law as well as possible into their role-spanning self-image as reflected subjects of their lives. The more individual criminal lawyers succeed in this integration, the more willing they will be to accept personal responsibility for the infliction of pain that occurs as a result of this activity.

To sum up, modern dogmatics of criminal law operate in a field of tension between disciplinary autonomy and an exaggerated need for integration, arising from the conflict between the two major social trends of professionalisation on the one hand and individualisation on the other. In everyday business of dogmatics, this tension is and should usually remain unnoticed. Of course, lawyers dealing with highly specialised questions from the field of white-collar criminality do not need to begin each of their statements with general discussions on the meaning and justification of punishment and criminal law. Rather, they may rely on the fact that the methodological and legal assumptions on which they base their argumentation are sufficiently legitimised. As American legal philosopher Ronald Dworkin has shown, however, the aforementioned tension is ever-present in latent form, and sometimes, especially in hard cases, it comes to light unexpectedly in a bold argumentative sleight of hand.[31]

## *II. Is the General Theory of Crime a Scientific Discipline?*

In our legal system, there is no shortage of specialists in the numerous legal sub-disciplines. As I have shown, however, a criminal legal system also needs a sub-discipline that is concerned with defusing of the above-mentioned tension. This sub-discipline is, in my understanding, the General Theory of Crime (*Allgemeine Verbrechenslehre*).[32] Its task is to support the dogmatics of criminal law by placing its evaluations and argumentations in a reflective relationship to broader conceptions of world interpretation and life orientation. The scope of this mediation is not limited to the ex-

---

29 Eg Karl Larenz/Claus-Wilhelm Canaris, *Methodenlehre der Rechtswissenschaft* (3rd edn, 1995) 25 ff; Kurt Seelmann, *Rechtsphilosophie* (5th edn, 2010) 116 ff.

30 Pawlik (n 26) 44.

31 For more details see Michael Pawlik, '*Ronald Dworkin und der Rechtsbegriff*' (1992) 23 Rechtstheorie 289 ff.

32 Pawlik (n 27), 16.

ceptional situation of avoiding blatant divergences, but goes beyond that to improving the interpretation of everyday law.

Whether this activity is granted the designation of 'science' depends largely on the understanding of science and is, therefore, subject to historical fluctuations. In the last decades of the 19th century, reservations grew in Germany about the conventional General Theory of Crime, which was, because of its focus on logical-systematic deductions, accused of ignoring the social and economic causes of the conflicts with which it dealt.[33] In particular, the rising crime rate in the wake of rapidly advancing industrialisation[34] was perceived to be threatening and seen as an indication that the conventional position was inadequate and had to be replaced with a modern view, i.e., one that was oriented to the methodological self-image of the natural sciences. According to this view, an expedient, effective fight against crime required precise knowledge of the causes of crime and the effects of punishment, which could only be achieved through the application of scientific methods.[35] Accordingly, in his inaugural lecture in Berlin in 1899, Franz von Liszt limited the actual '*scientific* task of criminal law scholarship' to 'the causal explanation of crime and punishment';[36] for only a causal explanation could claim the title of scientific knowledge.[37]

---

33 On this political subtext of the controversy about the concept of science, see for example Görg Haverkate 'Jurisprudenz: Wissenschaft als Politik' in Roland Simon-Schaefer/Walter Zimmerli (eds), *Wissenschaftstheorie der Geisteswissenschaften* (1975) 293; Dieter Simon, 'Zwillingsschwestern oder Stammesbrüder?' (1992) 11 RJ 356; Franz Wieacker, 'Zur praktischen Leistung der Rechtsdogmatik' in Rüdiger Bubner (ed), *Festschrift für Hans-Georg Gadamer*, vol 2 (1970) 315. The same uneasiness, albeit articulated under different political auspices, was behind the demand made in the late 1960s and 1970s to transform jurisprudence into a social science (Hubert Rottleuthner, *Rechtswissenschaft als Sozialwissenschaft* [1973] 7 ff, 245 ff; extensive further evidence can be found in Ralf Dreier, 'Zum Selbstverständnis der Jurisprudenz als Wissenschaft' Rechtstheorie 2 [1971], 37 footnote 3).

34 On the contemporary perception and discussion of this finding: Arnd Koch, 'Binding vs. v. Liszt – Klassische und moderne Strafrechtsschule' in Eric Hilgendorf/Jürgen Weitzel (eds), *Der Strafgedanke in seiner historischen Entwicklung* (2007) 129 with further references.

35 See von David von Mayenburg, 'Die Rolle psychologischen Wissens in Strafrecht und Kriminologie bei Franz von Liszt' in Mathias Schmoeckel (ed), *Psychologie als Argument in der juristischen Literatur des Kaiserreichs* (2009) 115 ff.

36 Franz von Liszt, *Strafrechtliche Aufsätze und Vorträge*, vol 2 (1905) 289.

37 Ibid 289.

Also, legal realism, as it is powerfully represented by Shin Matsuzawa in this volume, denies that dogmatics and even more so a philosophically based General Theory of Crime are sciences. This narrow understanding of legal science has never been particularly influential in Germany. Beginning with neo-Kantianism and its emphasis on the equivalence of all intellectual manifestations, it has aptly been pointed out that the question of whether legal dogmatics and legal theory are sciences is mainly a matter of definition.[38] One *may* follow the empirical focus of legal realism's understanding of science, but one does not *have to.* Rather, according to the more recent philosophy of science, it may be considered sufficient that the General Theory of Crime 'pursues by rational means a certain epistemological task that is meaningful in this world',[39] namely the integration of modes of thought and justification in criminal law in an overarching horizon of meaning.

Moreover, the assumption that legal realism's approach is a non-metaphysical one, whereas the resort to philosophical categories inevitably results in metaphysical abysses and subjectivist arbitrariness, is mistaken. To begin with, legal realism also makes use of metaphysical presuppositions. Anyone who speaks about 'reality' refers to an ontic category. Statements of this kind are constantly made in all areas of human life, including science, but are rarely reflected upon.[40] Ontology as one of the traditional branches of metaphysics tries to fill these gaps. It asks 'about the *meaning* of being, i.e., about the *meaning* of speaking of (real) existence'.[41]

One of the most important findings of recent ontology is the analysis of so-called 'institutional facts'. From GWF Hegel to John Searle, it has been argued that facts of this kind are rooted in collective practices and cannot be reduced to individual acts of consciousness.[42] An approach, as advocated by Matsuzawa, that focuses primarily on the psyche of judges neglects this insight. Of course, dogmatic statements or court judgements cannot

38 For this and for further details see *Pawlik* (n 26), 5 f.

39 Franz Bydlinski, *Juristische Methodenlehre und Rechtsbegriff* (2nd edn, 1991) 77.

40 Anne Sophie Meincke, 'Von der Wirklichkeit des Wirklichen. Eine kritische Verteidigung der Metaphysik als philosophischer Disziplin' in Christopher Erhard et alii (eds), *Wozu Metaphysik?* (2017) 96; Uwe Meixner, *Einführung in die Ontologie* (2004) 16; Christof Rapp, *Metaphysik* (2016) 22.

41 Pirmin Stekeler-Weithofer, 'Was ist... wirklich? Zur Notwendigkeit von Metaphysik in der Gegenwart' in: Christopher Erhard et alii (eds), *Wozu Metaphysik?* (2017) 42.

42 Survey representations in Ludger Jansen, *Gruppen und Institutionen* (2017); Brian Epstein, Social Ontology, in: Edward Zalta (ed): *Stanford Encyclopedia of Philosophy* (accessed 22.05.2020).

be produced without the involvement of consciousness; but that which gives them their specific communicative quality is beyond the realm of individual consciousness. This is so because interventions of criminal law scholars are not private events but rather contributions to an ongoing debate, and they are presented with the claim of general acceptability. To achieve this aim, individual participants in the discussion must orientate themselves to the expectations of their communication partners; for 'what is a valid reason for something', as Ludwig Wittgenstein remarks, is 'decided not by me',[43] but by the addressees of my utterance.[44]

For this reason, Matsuzawa's charge that representatives of a philosophically informed General Theory of Crime would introduce their 'unwashed subjectivity', as Friedrich Nietzsche's friend Franz Overbeck called it, into the science of criminal law is exaggerated. If I want to be regarded as a scholar who deserves to be taken seriously, I must present my argument in a way that corresponds to the expectations of my scientific discipline. Even if I go beyond positive law, I must, therefore, explain the relation of my considerations to the established interpretations of positive law. While there is room for subjective creativity in my argumentation, there is none for individual arbitrariness.

### *III. The Affinity of the General Theory of Crime with Philosophy*

The fact that the General Theory of Crime deals with the whole of criminal law – its disciplinary identity, its style of thinking, and the 'master narrative' to which it is committed – explains the harshness that is inherent in debates about it, a harshness that is sometimes bizarrely disproportionate to the immediate practical significance of the problems being debated. The considerable variability of the prevailing basic concepts of criminal law theory is, against the background just outlined, equally unsurprising. As long as the General Theory of Crime does justice to its role as mediator and translator, it is almost a matter of necessity that every substantial change of the cultural background convictions brings about a redefinition of the fundamental patterns of interpretation of said theory.

The effort to connect the thoughts of criminal law dogmatics to an overarching understanding of the reality of human life is a genuinely philosophical undertaking – 'philosophical' not in the sense of being the exclu-

---

43 Ludwig Wittgenstein, *Über Gewißheit* (7th ed, 1990) no 271 (73).
44 Josef Kopperschmidt, *Argumentationstheorie zur Einführung* (2000) 69 f.

sive property of the philosophy departments, but in the sense of a reflective approach to a fundamental problem of orientation. According to a cheeky but accurate remark by American philosopher Richard Rorty, philosophy is 'not something anybody can ever walk away from; it is an amorphous blob whose pseudopods englobe anyone attempting such an excursion.'[45] Rorty's allusion to the inevitability of philosophy also applies to the General Theory of Crime. Insofar as it relates the evaluations and modes of argumentation of the dogmatics of criminal law to the standards and demands of its cultural environment, every General Theory of Crime, however unphilosophical it may appear, exhibits philosophical traits. Moreover, it owes its specific intellectual profile to its underlying philosophical conception.

The comprehension of the position and task of philosophy on which this thesis is based is admittedly quite demanding and by no means self-evident. In the second half of the 19th century, a self-concept began to spread within philosophy that was anxiously mindful of strictly distinguishing its own activity, which was regarded as scientific, from mere 'world views' (*Weltanschauungen*), which were considered to be solely a matter of personal confession and incapable of being the subject of science. It is almost palpable how regretful some proponents of this line of thought found the meagreness of this definition of philosophy. Heinrich Rickert, one of the most important representatives of philosophical neo-Kantianism, explicitly understood his discipline as a 'science of the world as a whole',[46] which for this very reason had to do with the 'overall meaning of life in the world'.[47] Nevertheless, a scientific philosophy 'must refrain from giving what is not very significantly named "world view", for this concerns the human being as a whole and is always determined by atheoretical motives, so that its theoretical foundation and logical universality is inaccessible to every thinker'.[48] For Rickert, therefore, fully fledged philosophy must confine itself to providing conceptual clarity about the diversity of actually existing world views, and thus become a theory of world views;[49] it can describe the various offers of meaning, but cannot take position on them.

In the 20th century, the mainstream of philosophical thought has definitely become accustomed to seeing philosophy primarily as a *therapeutic*

45 Richard Rorty, *Philosophie als Kulturpolitik* (2008) 253.
46 Heinrich Rickert, *Philosophische Aufsätze* (1999) 151.
47 Ibid 255.
48 Ibid 319.
49 Ibid 319.

discipline.[50] In the words of Wittgenstein, the philosopher treats a question 'like an illness'[51] that requires treatment and cure. It is characteristic of the therapeutic understanding of philosophy that 'we do not want to learn anything *new* with it'.[52] The result of philosophy is 'not "philosophical sentences", but the clarification of sentences'.[53] According to this understanding, the problems of philosophy are 'not to be sought *alongside* but *within* the sciences, as their confusions or omissions in the theory of justification'.[54]

It is an important and useful task of philosophy to elucidate the depth structure of criminal law concepts and arguments. The current German dogmatics reveal an unreflected use of language in numerous instances. For example, physical health and integrity, and even life are called 'things'[55] that are assigned to certain 'carriers'; some scholars do not even shy away from calling a 'functioning body' 'the means of transport' 'which transports the "spiritual ego" through life'.[56] This tendency to an unreflected reification of legal goods (*Rechtsgüter*) is in urgent need to be cured by Wittgenstein's proof that the having of a certain status is to be understood differently than the having of objects.[57] The same applies to Wittgenstein's statements about the influence of metaphors on our thinking.[58] Metaphors such as those of the 'camp' (*Lager*) in the dogmatics of fraud or those of 'standing on the side of wrongdoing' in the dogmatics of necessity (*Notstand*) lead to a dangerous distortion of the general standards of imputation which are substituted by ad hoc plausibilities mainly guided by pure intuition.[59]

---

50 Gunnar Hindrichs, *Das Absolute und das Subjekt* (2008) 222; Kurt Wuchterl, *Methoden der Gegenwartsphilosophie* (3rd ed, 1999) 74 ff.

51 Ludwig Wittgenstein, 'Philosophische Untersuchungen', no 255, in: Wittgenstein, *Tractatus logico-philosophicus/Philosophische Untersuchungen* (1990) 221.

52 Ibid, no 89 (152).

53 Ludwig Wittgenstein, 'Tractatus logico-philosophicus 4.112', in Wittgenstein, *Tractatus logico-philosophicus/Philosophische Untersuchungen* (1990), 32.

54 Friedrich Kambartel, *Was ist und soll Philosophie* (1968) 17.

55 Ralph Ingelfinger, *Grundlagen und Grenzbereiche des Tötungsverbots* (2004) 38.

56 Thus Lars Wortmann, *Inhalt und Bedeutung der Unzumutbarkeit normgemäßen Verhaltens im Strafrecht* (2002) 91.

57 See Gerhard Gamm, *Philosophie im Zeitalter der Extreme* (2009) 191 f.

58 Also on this subject ibid 192 f.

59 For more details see Michael Pawlik, *Das unerlaubte Verhalten beim Betrug* (1999) 213 f (on *Lagertheorie*); Pawlik, *Der rechtfertigende Notstand* (2002) 299 ff (on *Nötigungsnotstand*).

As important as the therapeutic role of philosophy may be, it does not exhaust the functions of this discipline. The venerable view, going back to Plato and Aristotle, according to which at the centre of a 'good and great philosophy [...] is a vision of the world in general and of our position in it',[60] is still justified, even in a society of individuals. In the words of Wilhelm Dilthey, 'in the recognition of reality, the determination of values, the setting of purposes', a unique self expresses itself,[61] which is not satisfied with 'letting the most diverse areas, about which something is to be known or in which knowledge can be demanded, suddenly stand side by side'.[62] This self therefore requires the formation of a summarising view, that undertakes to 'connect our individual knowledge [...] and to unite it with a general insight into the world'.[63] If this demand is not fulfilled by philosophy, it will assert itself in a less reflected form.

As an integrative discipline in the sense just explained, the General Theory of Crime participates in this philosophical task. The General Theory of Crime should, therefore, make use of the numerous philosophical insights that have been developed over the centuries. These insights are valuable not only from a distanced, historicising perspective. In fact, they can contribute to the best possible solution of *today's* fundamental problems of criminal law. Philosophy deserves a place within the General Theory of Crime, not as a repository for dated vestiges of the past, but as an aid to the best possible articulation of our self-understanding as individuals who *also* practice criminal law dogmatics but whose overall identity is richer than that.

## *IV. A Glance Back at the History of Ideas (1): The Self-Conception and Practice of the General Theory of Crime*

The General Theory of Crime seeks, as described above, to connect the thinking of criminal law dogmatics with a comprehensive understanding of the reality of human life. This statement may at first sound highly speculative. However, on closer examination, it merely invokes what the General Theory of Crime in Germany has practiced since Paul Johann Anselm Ritter von Feuerbach. Feuerbach's doctrine of punishment and attribu-

---

60 Holm Tetens, *Philosophisches Argumentieren* (2nd edn, 2006) 257; similarly Dietmar von der Pfordten, *Suche nach Einsicht* (2010) 37.
61 Wilhelm Dilthey, *Das Wesen der Philosophie* (2008) 123.
62 Dieter Henrich, *Werke im Werden* (2011) 123.
63 Von der Pfordten (n 60), 37.

tion, despite his turning away from Immanuel Kant's *apriorism* towards an empirical doctrine of law,[64] is inconceivable without Kant's concept of law and state;[65] the Hegelians' doctrines of action and imputation are based on Hegel's metaphysics of will;[66] the neo-Kantians' insight into the teleological character of criminal law concepts is based on Wilhelm Windelband's and Rickert's introduction of the concept of value into philosophy;[67] and Hans Welzel's finalist theory of action is based on the reception of a large philosophical tradition that reaches from Samuel von Pufendorf to Nicolai Hartmann.[68]

However, it would be short-sighted to see philosophy in the material sense I have described at work only when explicit reference is made to philosophical authors. Rather, philosophical concepts underlie even those doctrines of crime that would not classify themselves as philosophical. For example, Claus Roxin, in the name of a well-understood criminal policy, wants to undo the banishment of the 'dimensions of the social and political from the sphere of the legal';[69] criminal law functionalism wants to orient criminal law specifically towards the normative identity of society.[70] This is precisely the way of integrating the dogmatics of criminal law into a larger context of thought and conviction that constitutes the philosophical aspect of the General Theory of Crime.

In terms of content, of course, it makes a great deal of difference whether a theoretical foundation of criminal law uses the categories of Hegel's philosophy of law (the position of the 19th century criminal law Hegelians), or whether it takes into account the ontological structures of reality (Welzel's view), or whether it is aligned with the postulate of preserving the social system (the position of the functionalists). Despite their differences in content, however, these approaches have one thing in common: they all assume that a General Theory of Crime is based on the re-

---

64 See Reinhard Brandt, 'Feuerbach und Kant. Anmerkungen zu ihrem Staatsund Strafrecht' in Arnd Koch et alii (eds), *Feuerbachs Bayerisches Strafgesetzbuch* (2014) 171 ff.

65 Wolfgang Naucke, *Kant und die psychologische Zwangstheorie Feuerbachs* (1962) 62 ff.

66 Eckart von Bubnoff, *Die Entwicklung des strafrechtlichen Handlungsbegriffes von Feuerbach bis Liszt unter besonderer Berücksichtigung der Hegelschule* (1966) 52 ff; Pawlik (n 26) 290 f.

67 Sascha Ziemann, *Neukantianisches Strafrechtsdenken* (2009) 108 ff, 134 ff.

68 Oliver Sticht, *Sachlogik als Naturrecht?* (2000) 261 ff.

69 Claus Roxin, *Kriminalpolitik und Strafrechtssystem* (2nd edn, 1973) 9.

70 Günther Jakobs, 'Das Strafrecht zwischen Funktionalismus und "alteuropäischem" Prinzipiendenken' (1995) 107 ZStW 843.

flection of an intellectual material that is located outside of the traditional discourse on criminal law.

That these framework convictions change over time is not surprising, but rather natural. Every text is based – in the words of Bochum philosophical historian Kurt Flasch – on a 'pre-individual context of images, themes, concepts, valuations and ways of life'.[71] For this reason, it is not the exception, but rather the rule that it will be grinded by the sands of time: questions, terminologies, and procedures become obsolete; evidence shifts; new experiences can no longer be adequately articulated with the existing theoretical material.[72]

Thus, one may perceive, with Karl Löwith, post-Hegelian philosophy to be a 'barbaristion of thought';[73] one may, with Windelband, assign to the 19th century a 'low level of philosophical achievement';[74] and one may – especially with regard to criminal law – consider von Liszt to be the far weaker thinker in comparison to Christian Reinhold Köstlin or Hugo Hälschner. Nevertheless, it would be naïve to attribute the process of turning away from comprehensive philosophical systems – for which the dramatic title 'collapse of idealism' has become established[75] and of which von Liszt is regarded as the main proponent in criminal law – to the inability of single individuals to maintain the theoretical level reached. The aversion to speculative thinking associated with Hegel, which in the eyes of its critics sought to force progress into an arbitrary and rigid philosophical system, was joined by a massive loss of plausibility of the central Hegelian category of free will. Thus, the opening of criminal law scholarship to research in criminal statistics, which von Liszt in particular pursued,[76] emphatically demonstrated the strong influence of biological and social factors on an individual's tendency to delinquency. What is more, Hegel's 'free will that wills the free will' (*der freie Wille, der den freien Willen will*)[77] did not find any noteworthy resonance either in the most widely discussed scientific theories of the time, Darwinism and Positivism and the world views that emerged from them, or in the reality of most people's lives, which were shaped by the experience of far-reaching heteronomy that was

71 Kurt Flasch, *Theorie der Philosophiehistorie* (2005) 123.
72 Henrich (n 63) 182.
73 Karl Löwith, *Von Hegel zu Nietzsche* (9th edn, 1986) 96.
74 Wilhelm Windelband, *Präludien*, vol. 2 (6th edn, 1919) 5.
75 Herbert Schnädelbach, *Philosophie in Deutschland 1831–1933* (6th edn 1999) 21 ff.
76 Programmatically von Liszt (n 36) 324 f.
77 GWF Hegel, 'Grundlinien der Philosophie des Rechts' in Hegel, *Werke in zwanzig Bänden*, vol 7 (1986) para 27 (79).

later formulated by Max Weber in the famous formula of the 'steel-hard shell'.[78] Against this background, Hegelianism almost inevitably appeared as a relic of a past epoch that has finally come to an end.

However, the attempts to place dogmatic considerations in an overarching horizon of understanding are not limited to the spectacular new interventions in the General Theory of Crime. Rather, I would assert that *each* legal institution of the general part (*Allgemeiner Teil*) of criminal law and *each* of the central offences of the special part (*Besonderer Teil*) has its own framework theory. In many cases, these theories reflect the great controversies in the General Theory of Crime; as an example, I would point out the importance that the doctrine of objective attribution (*objective Zurechnung*) is accorded today in the interpretation of numerous offences of the special part.[79] In other cases, however, these framework theories have developed largely independently of the 'great' controversies and are, therefore, subject to a relatively independent rhythm of development. Michel Foucault's critique of the 'idea of a single break suddenly, at a given moment, dividing all discursive formations, interrupting them in a single moment and reconstituting them in accordance with the same rules'[80] also applies to an all too sweeping understanding of the history of criminal law dogmatics.

This is illustrated by the right of necessity (*rechtfertigender Notstand*), which under strict conditions justifies perpetrators who attack innocent bystanders in order to save themselves. In the late 19th and early 20th centuries, this right was introduced on the grounds that it helped to secure the largest possible total stock of goods for society.[81] This consideration stems from collectivist thinking, the roots of which lie in a rather toxic mixture of an authoritarian thinking that exaggerates the political community in relation to the individual and capitalist utility calculations. How firmly this pattern of justification is anchored in German criminal law theory is shown by the fact that it survived all of the upheavals of the General Theory of Crime in an attenuated and refined form, and it continues to live on to this day in the form of the legitimising figure of the 'prevailing interest' (*überwiegendes Interesse*).[82] This example, to which a number of others could be added, shows that the framework of criminal law dogmatics is – once again, in Foucault's words – 'not *a* science, *a* rationality, *a* mentality,

78 Max Weber, *Gesammelte Aufsätze zur Religionssoziologie*, vol 1 (1988) 203.
79 Evidence in Pawlik (n 26) 46 footnote 155.
80 Michel Foucault, *Archäologie des Wissens* (1972) 175.
81 For more details see Pawlik (n 59 – *Notstand*) 34 ff.
82 Ibid 45 ff.

*a* culture; it is a tangle of interpositivities whose limits and points of intersection cannot be fixed in a single operation'.[83]

The irreducible diversity of integrating narratives running parallel to one another indicates that talk of *the* best possible identity balance and *the* horizon of understanding to which criminal law dogmatics should be adapted should not be harmonistically misunderstood. The horizon of understanding of a single individual who, in addition to many other things, is also a scholar of criminal law is usually a conglomerate of different convictions that at best do not contradict each other, but by no means can occur only in this combination and no other.[84] A neo-Kantian background, for example, can be connected both with a National Socialist conviction – the case of Edmund Mezger[85] – and with a liberal attitude – the case of Alexander Graf zu Dohna.[86] All the more so, it will not be possible to agree on the sole authoritative nature of a certain horizon of understanding within a community as long as is not trimmed for conformity from the outset.[87] On the contrary, even the most honest efforts to achieve general acceptability are confronted with the insight, which is inevitable under today's living conditions, that there is, as Canadian social philosopher Charles Taylor states, a great and presumably growing number of points 'which intelligent, reasonably undeluded people, of good will, can and do disagree on.'[88] This 'fact of reasonable pluralism'[89] is 'not a temporary state [...] that will soon disappear', but 'a permanent feature of the public culture of a democracy'.[90] Under these conditions, the integration goal of the General Theory of Crime can only be represented in a quasi-bracketed form. However carefully a contribution to the General Theory of Crime may be reasoned, it is neither a cognition of the truth – for example, the cognition of a *Zeitgeist*[91] – nor a normatively compelling act of evaluation, but rather a tentative, highly individualised balancing act.

---

83 Foucault (n 80) 159.

84 Fleck (n 10) 60 f.

85 For more details see Gerit Thulfaut, *Kriminalpolitik und Strafrechtslehre bei Edmund Mezger (1883–1962)* (2000) 12 ff, 123 ff; Francisco Muñoz Conde, *Edmund Mezger – Beiträge zu einem Juristenleben* (2007) 3 ff.

86 For details see Alfred Escher, *Neukantianische Rechtsphilosophie – teleologische Verbrechensdogmatik und modernes Präventionsstrafrecht* (1992) 28 ff, 39 ff.

87 John Rawls, *Politischer Liberalismus* (2003) 107.

88 Taylor (n 18) 28.

89 Rawls (n 87) 215.

90 Ibid 106.

91 In this sense Günther Jakobs, 'Das Selbstverständnis der Strafrechtswissenschaft vor den Herausforderungen der Gegenwart' in Albin Eser et alii (eds) *Die Deutsche*

## V. A Glance Back at the History of Ideas (2): The Contribution of Philosophy to the General Theory of Crime

The endeavour to integrate dogmatic considerations in one – not necessarily *the one* – overarching horizon of understanding is, according to the above, one of the typical characteristics of German criminal law scholarship. However, the extent to which criminal law scholars have been willing to listen to professional philosophy varies considerably.

Dogmatics of criminal law in which the conviction prevails that they are by and large up to date have less of an affinity for philosophy than when they are in an identity crisis, or when they are concerned with coming to terms with political disasters, to which the usual dogmatic instruments are evidently not tailored. The former was the case in Germany at the beginning of the 19th century;[92] the latter occurred first after 1945 and then again after 1989.[93] No less significant is the change in philosophical cycles. It was Henrich who declared proudly that philosophy is 'more sensitive than any other academic subject [...] to the living conditions of its time'.[94] However, the extent and depth of philosophers' efforts to focus their attention on understanding these living conditions are subject to major changes. It makes a great deal of difference whether a philosophy claims to identify 'the speculative idea' in all forms of nature and spirit[95] and doesn't consider itself too noble for following this idea up to its specifications in the theory of action and of imputation, or whether it is, like neo-Kantianism, of the conviction that so far 'nobody has yet "mastered" the world by thinking',[96] and, therefore, from the outset limits itself to

---

*Strafrechtswissenschaft vor der Jahrtausendwende* (2000) 47; Jakobs, 'Strafrecht als wissenschaftliche Disziplin' in Engel/Schön (eds), *Das Proprium der Rechtswissenschaft* (2007) 106 – for more details see Pawlik, 'Das Strafrecht der Gesellschaft. Sozialphilosophische und sozialtheoretische Grundlagen von Günther Jakobs' Strafrechtsdenken' in Urs Kindhäuser et alii (eds), *Strafrecht und Gesellschaft* (2019) 217 ff.

92 See Sylvia Kesper-Biermann, *Einheit und Recht* (2009) 102 ff, 411 ff.

93 After the Second World War, the quest for philosophical reinsurance led to a – admittedly rapidly fading – enthusiasm for natural law justifications (see Lena Foljanty, *Recht oder Gesetz* (2013)). Of particular significance for legal practice was the reception of the Radbruch formula by the highest German courts, which was taken up again after 1989 (for more details see Giuliano Vassalli, *Radbruchsche Formel und Strafrecht* (2010) 51 ff).

94 Dieter Henrich, *Die Philosophie im Prozeß der Kultur* (2006) 126.

95 GWF Hegel, 'Enzyklopädie der philosophischen Wissenschaften I' in Hegel, *Werke in zwanzig Bänden*, vol 8 (1986) 15.

96 Rickert (n 46) 316.

give 'a consistently justified summary of the epistemological activity branching out into the abundance of detail'.[97] The possibilities of connection that such a philosophy opens up for criminal law dogmatics are from the outset much narrower than those offered by Hegel's comprehensive system of knowledge.

The fact that there is no going back to a system such as Hegel's is, indeed, practically undisputed in philosophy since the middle of the 19th century.[98] I am also convinced of the indispensability of Windelband's statement that a knowledge 'flowing from thousands and thousands of sources all over the world' will 'never again be reduced to a simple comprehensive formula'.[99] But it is not only the rapid expansion of the manifold individual sciences that has narrowed the scope of philosophical reflection. Also, the abandonment of Hegel's system claim by his successors[100] and the insight into the irreconcilability of the antinomies that permeate human life in modern society[101] make it inevitable to reduce the expectations towards the world- and existence-illuminating power of philosophical thought. The aforementioned tendency of newer philosophy to limit itself to the therapy of conceptual and argumentative ambiguities probably has its most important motivation in this experience of disillusionment.

As I have tried to show, however, such a position would throw the baby out with the bathwater. By retreating into a citadel of supposedly unimpeachable scientificality, this mode of philosophising does not meet the claims that are directed at philosophy from human life itself, and that helped it reach cultural significance in the past.[102] In my opinion, the only option left to a philosopher aware of this situation – admittedly risky and akin to walking on a tightrope – is to hold on to the traditional task of integrating particular knowledge and convictions into a superordinate system of categories, but not to grant any single proposed solution – not even one's own – the status of a timeless insight of reason, a definitive solution to the mysteries of life. Philosophising from this perspective remains obliged to the regulative idea of truth, but it takes place – in the words of Flasch – only as a 'process in which individual thinkers create dissonances that their successors try to make bearable by continuously forming theo-

97 Windelband (n 74) 11.
98 Schnädelbach (n 75) 20 f.
99 Wilhelm Windelband, *Präludien*, vol 1 (6th edn, 1919) 119.
100 See Schnädelbach (n 5) 51 ff.
101 Henrich (n 12) 56, 361; Herbert Schnädelbach, *Kant* (2005) 13 ff.
102 Henrich (n 62) 150 f.

ries, which in turn create new conflicts'.[103] That every penetration into the whole of a subject area inevitably leaves behind unresolved remnants that provoke contradiction and new approaches[104] is thus one of the insights of a philosophy that has become completely reflexive, which a philosophically aware science of criminal law simply cannot ignore. I will return to this point at the end of this essay.

To state that a direct recourse to Hegel, as well as to Kantian universalism of reason, is no longer possible today is one thing. It is another to note how much the interest of post-Hegelian philosophy in legal (especially criminal law) questions has declined in comparison to the zenith of critical and idealistic thinking.[105] Already, neo-Kantians had little interest in Kant's practical philosophy; they were primarily interested in his epistemology. Also, the great thinkers of the first half of the 20th century – Husserl, Martin Heidegger, the logical empiricists, and Wittgenstein – skated over practical philosophy.[106] The same applies, with certain reservations, to many post-war tendencies that have shaped the discussion – analytical philosophy, structuralism, and postmodernism: there seems to be no room for the world of orderly repression embodied by criminal law between the retreat to an analysis of ordinary language that 'leaves everything as it is'[107] and steep theses, such as Jacques Derrida's critique of all violence.[108]

The renaissance of political philosophy, represented by John Rawls and Jürgen Habermas, has also largely bypassed criminal law. Apparently, criminal law is located on too archaic a level of human existence for it to be of serious interest to theorists, who have placed sophisticated problems such as distributive justice and democratisation at the centre of their thoughts. Where the transfer of these approaches to criminal law is nevertheless attempted, it quickly loses itself in noble fictions. Thus, the supporters of discourse theory declare the right to participate in democratic decision-making as the basis of criminal law obligations. According to them, the obligation to avoid wrongdoing is only legitimate if the wrongdoer 'has the right and the possibility to assume the role of citizen and as such to make use of its deliberative abilities in such a way that it publicly

103 Flasch (n 71) 94.
104 Eg Robert Spaemann, *Gott und die Welt* (2012) 135.
105 See with further evidence Pawlik (n 26) 28 footnote 21.
106 Gamm (n 57) 10.
107 Thus the programmatic formula of Wittgenstein (n 51) no 124 (163).
108 Jacques Derrida, *Gesetzeskraft* (1991) 11 ff, 99 ff.

takes a stand against the norm'.[109] 'Without such procedures, there is no obligation to follow the norm, and the violation of the norm does not inflict guilt.'[110] Literally understood, this means that, from Roman law to the Prussian penal code of 1851, all criminal law is illegitimate. Such exaltations have the unfortunate tendency to disregard the basic political and regulatory prerequisites of human existence. Of incomparably greater existential importance than the right to democratic participation is the individual's prospect of being able to live safely and in peace in everyday life between election dates. In accordance with Thomas Hobbes, I am, therefore, convinced that the citizens' duty to obey must be tied to this primary task of the state, not to its democratic constitution.[111] From the point of view of discourse theory, such a sentence is certainly sacrilege – but is such a denial of reality really convincing? From my point of view it is not.

This does not mean that criminal law theorists would not find anything in contemporary philosophy that would be of interest. On the contrary, in recent years, criminal law theorists have resorted to contemporary philosophical literature, ranging from the debates on causality[112] and the doctrines of action,[113] intent,[114] and emergency,[115] to the concepts of criminal wrongs, guilt, and punishment.[116] As valuable as these contributions are, they offer only punctual clarifications, which – not least because they

---

109 Klaus Günther, 'Welchen Personenbegriff braucht die Diskurstheorie des Rechts? Überlegungen zum internen Zusammenhang zwischen deliberativer Person, Staatsbürger und Rechtsperson' in Hauke Brunkhorst/Peter Niesen (eds), *Das Recht der Republik* (1999) 95.

110 Klaus Günther, *Schuld und kommunikative Freiheit* (2005) 256.

111 For more details see Pawlik (n 27) 107 f footnote 594 with extensive evidence.

112 Ingeborg Puppe, 'Der Erfolg und seine kausale Erklärung im Strafrecht' (1980) 92 ZStW 863 ff.

113 Urs Kindhäuser, *Intentionale Handlung* (1980) 153 ff; ders., 'Der Vorsatz als Zurechnungskriterium' (1984) 96 ZStW 5 ff.

114 Jochen Bung, *Wissen und Wollen im Strafrecht* (2009) 57 ff; Carl-Friedrich Stuckenberg, *Vorstudien zu Vorsatz und Irrtum im Völkerstrafrecht* (2007) 40 ff.

115 Reinhard Merkel, 'Zaungäste? Über die Vernachlässigung philosophischer Argumente in der Strafrechtswissenschaft (und einige verbreitete Mißverständnisse zu § 34 S. 1 StGB)' in Institute for Criminal Science Frankfurt am Main (ed), *Vom unmöglichen Zustand des Strafrechts* (1995) 171 ff.

116 Regarding the logic of the concept of crime especially Urs Kindhäuser, *Gefährdung als Straftat* (1989) 45 ff; Kindhäuser in Harald Koch (ed), *Herausforderungen an das Recht: alte Antworten auf neue Fragen?* (1997) 86 ff. – On the discussion of the criminal law concept of guilt, particularly Reinhard Merkel, *Willensfreiheit und rechtliche Schuld* (2008). – On the theory of criminal justice Florian Zimmermann, *Verdienst und Vergeltung* (2012).

come from very different schools of thought – do not show any internal connection. For this reason, neither individually nor as a whole do they allow for the development of an overarching horizon of understanding that is sufficiently substantial to address the problem of identity balance that I presented at the beginning of this essay. Detailed analyses of specific problems may please the small circle of immediately interested scholars who do not care that the debates they conduct can hardly be made comprehensible to the rest of the world. But they are neither suitable nor intended to offer those who are professionally concerned with criminal law an attractive perspective to adjust their dogmatic activities to the other aspects of their practical identity.

## *VI. The Task of Today's General Theory of Crime*

In light of this situation, the General Theory of Crime must set out on its own. As I have tried to show, it cannot evade this task. The starting point of such an endeavour is relatively clear.

The transition from stratification to functional differentiation, mentioned at the beginning of this essay, imposes the burden of having to understand themselves as subjects of their own lives not only on criminal law scholars, but on *all* members of modern societies. This task was indeed made easier by the influence of collectives (well into the 20th century) into which they could place themselves and through which they could gain meaning in life – from religion and nation to race and class. The decades following the Second World War, however, saw a privatisation of standards of the meaning of life, probably unprecedented in history.[117] As a result, individuals have become the first and final authority in the question of whether their lives are successful or unsuccessful.

But the prospect of having to cope alone with the consequences of a life that in one's view has failed is only bearable if one simultaneously has the power to steer it in another direction. Accordingly, the main task of the law, especially criminal law, lies in safeguarding the concern that all people should be able to lead their lives according to their own insights. The state and its criminal law cannot guarantee its citizens meaningful lives.[118] But criminal law is capable of enabling individuals, under the condition of

117 Cf only Ulrich Beck, *Risikogesellschaft* (1986) 205 ff; Peter Gross, *Die Multioptionsgesellschaft* (1994) 57 ff.
118 Daniel Hildebrand, *Rationalisierung durch Kollektivierung* (2011) 270.

strict reciprocity, of course, to shape their own existences free from paralysing fear and oppressive heteronomy.[119] In my opinion, this is the horizon of understanding to which each General Theory of Crime must be oriented, both in the architecture of its overall system and in its treatment of individual questions.

In implementing this program, the General Theory of Crime should guard against the illusory claim that it must reinvent the entirety of criminal law. Such a claim would be incompatible with a reflective understanding of what practical philosophy – and thus a philosophically informed General Theory of Crime – can and should achieve: synthesising existing belief structures, not reinventing them. The source of this view is none other than Kant. To the reproach that his *Critique of Practical Reason* did not contain a new principle of morality, but only a new formula, Kant replied: 'But who would want to introduce a new principle of all morality, and be as it were the first to invent it? as if before him the world had been ignorant, or in continuous error of what is one's duty.'[120]

This is an expression of a decidedly anti-elitist attitude. As philosopher Otfried Höffe, one of today's leading Kant experts, has pointed out, with Kant, unlike Plato, it is not esoteric special knowledge that counts, 'but only that general reason which everyone, albeit faintly, has at his disposal'.[121] Although philosophers have access to more subtle methodological instruments than do laypersons, they cannot, by virtue of their profession, claim a deeper moral insight for themselves.[122] According to Kant, enlightening the ordinary moral consciousness about itself does not mean exposing it to rebuking or unmasking criticism, but rather helping it to understand itself better. The thinker is 'indeed the active center and the accountable master, but not the constructor of the whole of his own knowledge. That is, he masters the construction of this whole, but he does not create it.'[123] Taking this to heart, in my book *Das Unrecht des Bürgers*, I have tried to integrate numerous individual developments that are emerging in today's dogmatics of criminal law into a unified concept[124] – no less, but no more either.

119 For more details see Pawlik (n 26) 99 ff.

120 Immanuel Kant, *Kritik der praktischen Vernunft*, 'A 15 Note' in Kant, *Werke in zehn Bänden*, vol 6 (1983) 113.

121 Ottfried Höffe, *Kants Kritik der praktischen Vernunft* (2012) 31.

122 This position finds approval from quite different philosophical camps; see only on the one hand Henrich (n 12) 94; on the other hand Rorty (n 45) 320.

123 Henrich (n 62) 107.

124 Pawlik (n 26) 19 ff.

However, these relieving factors do not alter the fact that a General Theory of Crime that takes the line of thought outlined in this chapter seriously recognises the inherent tension between the time-relatedness of its execution and the timelessness of its claim. On the one hand, reflexive criminal law scholars are aware that history, fragile as it is, offers no security.[125] On the other hand, such scholars maintain that the infliction of punishment is too serious a matter for the theory of crime to be allowed to settle on a general scepticism or – which boils down to the same thing – on the functionalist retreat to an 'indifferent' observer perspective.[126]

In the face of these evasive tendencies, reflexive scholars hold fast to the claim of thinking – especially as it pertains to legal philosophy – for universality.[127] The discrepancy between this claim and the knowledge of its unfulfillability is a cause of an insurmountably bad conscience. The 'right' argument is then 'to be reflected upon as a matter of conviction, which one could not of course discard in its entirety, all at once without the loss of one's own identity, but of which one can know that time will one day have rendered it obsolete in its entirety, so that one will later be "ashamed" of one's former "point of view", as Herder put it. One is and is not of a certain conviction, for anticipating a future point of view means one is already aware that the (necessarily presupposed) recent conviction will be overhauled one day.'[128]

Acknowledging the necessarily provisional nature of one's own convictions causes a conflict in the General Theory of Crime that must at any rate *sub specie aeternitatis* be called tragic: with each of their theories, no matter how refined, legal scholars miss their ultimate target, because they always perform less than they should. How to escape from this conflict with decency? The only answer, in my view, is to limit the scope of what can actually be expected in the situation in question. This situation is characterised by a double effect of time. Not only does time exhaust absolute certainties, it also inevitably forces action; in this respect, time is always short. The courts must, therefore, make their decisions and the legal dogmatists their interpretations, without waiting for or even counting on *one* redemptive and definitive answer. The demand for action, however, 'fixates us on what is *now* on our horizon', although we are aware that what at present we

---

125 Flasch (n 71) 36.

126 Jakobs (n 70) 867. Critical of the functionalist approach from this point of view Pawlik (n 60 – *Betrug*) 61 ff.

127 Cf only Flasch (n 71) 274 on the one hand and Spaemann (n 104) 222 on the other.

128 Josef Simon, *Philosophie des Zeichens* (1989) 313.

deem right may disintegrate and drag our present convictions with it.[129] If, however, we are condemned to act in the knowledge of an 'inescapable *indefiniteness* of communication',[130] to have to rely on finite interpretations, we cannot and must not demand of ourselves and others a *sub specie aeternitatis*, but only the *best possible* justification of decisions *at present*, according to our well-considered conviction. A philosophically informed General Theory of Crime is, therefore, simultaneously both humble and self-confident.

129 Simon (n 129) 241.
130 Luhmann (n 7) 141.

# List of Contributors

*Shin Matsuzawa* is Professor, Waseda University, Japan.

*Petter Asp* is Supreme Court Justice, Sweden.

*Thomas Elholm* is Professor, University of Copenhagen, Denmark.

*Kimmo Nuotio* is Professor, University of Helsinki, Finland.

*Jørn Jacobsen* is Professor, University of Bergen, Norway.

*Luís Greco* is Professor, Humboldt-University zu Berlin, Germany.

*Eric Hilgendorf* is Professor, University of Würzburg, Germany.

*Heike Jung* is Professor Emeritus, University of Saarland, Germany.

*Massimiliano Lanzi* is Research Fellow, University of Parma, Italy.

*Liang Genlin* is Professor, Beijing University, People's Republic of China.

*Michael Pawlik* is Professor, University of Freiburg, Germany.